A Country Calendar
and other writings

FLORA THOMPSON

A Country Calendar
and other writings

❧❀❦

Selected and edited by
MARGARET LANE

With line drawings by
CLARE ROBERTS

Oxford   New York
OXFORD UNIVERSITY PRESS
1984

Oxford University Press, Walton Street, Oxford OX2 6DP

London Glasgow New York Toronto
Delhi Bombay Calcutta Madras Karachi
Kuala Lumpur Singapore Hong Kong Tokyo
Nairobi Dar es Salaam Cape Town
Melbourne Auckland

and associated companies in
Beirut Berlin Ibadan Mexico City Nicosia

Oxford is a trade mark of Oxford University Press

First published by Oxford University Press 1979
First issued as an Oxford University Press paperback 1984

British Library Cataloguing in Publication Data

Thompson, Flora, 1877–1947
A country calendar and other writings. (Oxford paperbacks)
1. Country life –England –Hampshire 2. Hampshire –social life and customs
I. Title II. Lane, Margaret, 1907–
942.2'7009'734 S522.G7
ISBN 0-19-281418-4

Library of Congress Cataloging in Publication Data

Thompson, Flora.
A country calendar, and other writings. (Oxford paperbacks)
1. Country life –England –Literary collections.
I. Lane, Margaret, 1907–   . II. Title.
[PR6039. H653C68 1984] 828'.91209 83-22037
ISBN 0-19-281418-4 (pbk.)

Printed in Great Britain by
Richard Clay (The Chaucer Press) Ltd.
Bungay, Suffolk.

Foreword

When Flora Thompson died in 1947 her published work, a series of small country masterpieces, had been known to a limited public for only a few years. Since then, her fame has spread to an extent of which she herself, had it been foretold, would have been incredulous.

I first read *Lark Rise* in the early forties, and when I heard of her death in 1947 felt a self-reproachful regret that I knew so little about her. To discover and record this hidden life now seemed the only response I could make, in gratitude for the pleasure and illumination she had given me; and accordingly, with my friend Joan Hassall, who had originally introduced me to *Lark Rise to Candleford*, set off for Juniper Hill, for Cottisford and Buckingham and Fringford, hoping to recover enough to form the basis of a modest memoir.

My most rewarding journey, however, was to Bath, where Flora Thompson's daughter Winifred had retired and was living with her friend and colleague in nursing, Miss Mollie Money. To both of them I owe much: to Winifred Thompson's vivid and accurate memory, and again, thirty years later, to Miss Money's recollection of details from conversations with her friend.

In this early exploration, too, I was helped by Sir Arthur Bryant and a number of people good enough to lend letters – Mrs H. J. Massingham, Mr and Mrs Arthur Ball, Dr and Mrs Max Tyler, Mr Leonard Clark, Miss Eva Hillsden, the Oxford

University Press among others. The biographical essay was published in *The Cornhill Magazine* in 1947, and later, by Mr John G. Murray's permission, in my volume of literary and biographical essays, *Purely for Pleasure*. It was also republished in 1976, again by John Murray, to celebrate the centenary of Flora Thompson's birth.

Thirty years have now passed since my first tentative exploration of Flora Thompson's life and work, and my interest and admiration, like that of her ever-growing public, has made me wish that more could be added to our knowledge of her life and writings. It seemed a pity, for instance, that there was still an unpublished volume of her reminiscences lying in the archives of Texas University, to which her daughter had consigned it, together with a quite extensive collection of periodical journalism and minor fiction. All these I had looked through in the past with Winifred Thompson, and when Texas University sent me photocopies of this mass of material it was amusing to find, here and there, pencilled notes in my own hand in the margins, written thirty years earlier.

On this second reading it seemed to me that there was much in the random collection that, if published, would be read by many people with interest and pleasure. *Heatherley*, for instance, an account of her life in the village of Grayshott in the years before her marriage to John Thompson, has an interest of its own. Lightly disguised and fictionalized in places, it is a missing chapter in her own experience in the years of the Boer War – 'the turn of the century' in the phrase of the time – and is a period piece with its own flavour.

The years that Flora Thompson spent in the village of Liphook as wife (and wartime assistant) to the postmaster have their own somewhat secretive record in her more or less regular contributions to a small magazine which is still in circulation, *The Catholic Fireside*. These show her remarkable gifts as observer and naturalist, and are delightful reading. Since they were originally written as monthly pieces about the Hampshire countryside it seemed appropriate to make a selection as *A Country Calendar*, for which the editor of *The Catholic Fireside*,

Mr P. Charles Walker, kindly allowed me access to his files.

For illuminating memories of those Liphook years I am grateful to Mrs Clara Hooker, who in the First World War worked with Flora Thompson for the post office there, and whose excellent memory even in her eighties is both delightful and enviable. My kind friends the Rev F.M. and Mrs Hodgess Roper taught me the geography and history of Liphook and Grayshott, so that I came to know my way about that mysteriously unchanged and beautiful country of forest and heath which gave Flora Thompson, in the midst of her busy life, the solitude her spirit needed.

For extending my acquaintance with the Oxfordshire villages which are the scene of *Lark Rise* and its successors I owe much to the Rev John M. Sergeant and Mrs Sergeant, who in the months before his retirement as rector of Newton Purcell hospitably acted as guides to all the places that Flora Thompson lightly disguised as Lark Rise and Candleford. Mrs Sergeant, besides, introduced me to Flora Thompson's niece, Mrs E. O'Sullivan, who lent me letters, photographs, and personal relics, for which I am grateful, as I am, also, to Mrs Edith Plum, of the Old Forge, Fringford, who lent me photographs of the forge and Post Office in 'Miss Lane's' day. I am beholden, too, to Miss Jo Lart, whose local research enabled me to identify Flora Thompson's two homes in Dartmouth and Brixham, and the site of her grave.

Finally, I would like to thank both Miss Ena Sheen and the staff of the Oxford University Press, and Mrs. Anne Mallinson of the Selborne Bookshop for their encouragement in this small but, to me, rewarding task, which has brought me closer to the unknown areas of Flora Thompson's experience than, thirty years ago, I would have thought possible. For the publication, as Introduction, of an extended version of the original memoir Mr John Murray has generously given his permission.

M.L.

Contents

❧❀❧

Illustrations

❧❀❀❦

Grayshott post office, about 1900
Mr J. H. Smith

No. 42 Frederica Road, Winton, Bournemouth,
where Flora lived from 1903 to 1916
Photo by Harry W. Ashley

Clara Louise Woods (later Mrs Hooker),
who worked with Flora at the Liphook post office
during the First World War

Flora in her study and her kitchen at Liphook in 1921,
when she achieved local celebrity as
the 'poetess-postmistress' of *Bog Myrtle and Peat*
Syndication International Ltd.

Flora's grave in Longcross Cemetery, Dartmouth, Devon

Introduction

BY MARGARET LANE

Flora Thompson died in 1947 at the age of seventy, a writer who had produced a minor classic in the last years of her life, and about whom very little else is generally known.

Her work is in a genre of its own not altogether easy to describe, for it falls into no obvious category. Her three books, *Lark Rise, Over to Candleford,* and *Candleford Green,* which first appeared singly and are now published together as a trilogy under the title *Lark Rise to Candleford,* are not really novels, though fiction plays a part in them here and there. Nor are they autobiography pure and simple, for the personal element is evasive and oblique. They are better described, perhaps, as social history; though that, again, is a misleading name to give. They are more intimate, more personal, more alive than social history is usually allowed to be, for Flora Thompson dwells on the humble details which social historians either do not know, or else leave out. They are a simple yet infinitely detailed record of the life of the poor as it was lived in an obscure Oxfordshire

3

hamlet in the eighteen-eighties and nineties, all remembered from a child's experience, all faithfully set down, all true. It is precious as a record of something that has perished, though neither far away nor long ago, as well as for its literary quality, and for the fact that Flora Thompson herself was a cottage child, born in poverty, who wrote with a touch of genius of the life she knew, when 'people were poorer and had not the comforts, amusements or knowledge we have today; but they were happier. . . . They knew the now lost secret of being happy on little.'

It was never her intention to write the story of her own life, and though much can be gathered from her work about her childhood and youth, the rest is obscure and has never been recorded. In its way it is a moving and remarkable story, and should perhaps be set down before all the circumstances are forgotten. It is a story which happily illustrates the unquench-able vigour of those strange gifts which are sometimes bestowed in the most unlikely places, and which in her case developed without education or encouragement and blossomed into fulfilment in old age. Flora Thompson wrote her long masterpiece in the last ten years of her life, between the ages of sixty and seventy; in itself an extraordinary achievement. But when her history is known it will be seen that the whole of her life was a preparation, instinctive at first but eventually perfectly conscious and directed, to this one end.

She was born Flora Jane Timms on 5 December 1876, eldest child in the large family of a stonemason who had settled as a young man in the hamlet of Juniper Hill, near Brackley, during the early seventies – a huddle of 'grey stone boxes with thatched or slated lids of the kind then thought good enough to house a farm labourer's family'. Her father, Albert Timms, was not a local man. He had come to Juniper from Oxford, where his father had been first a master builder, then a publican, and finally, come down in the world through 'drinking, gambling and utter recklessness', a builder's labourer. Albert Timms himself was a man of parts, whose failure in life was due to an unhappy temperament. He had served no apprenticeship to his trade (having grown up, perhaps, during the prosperous public-house period, when the future seemed assured), but he was a skilled craftsman for all that, and in his youth had had ambitions of becoming a sculptor. By the time he settled in Juniper, however, in his middle twenties, he was already soured by lack of opportunity, and made no further effort to escape from the rut in which he found himself. He worked for thirty-five years for a builder in Brackley, travelling the three miles backwards and forwards on foot between work and home and occasionally going farther afield on a building contract. In his youth he was proud of his stone-carving, and liked to remember that he had taken part in the restoration of Bath Abbey. 'They used to haul him to places inaccessible from a ladder or scaffolding', Flora remembered, 'in a cage-like arrangement at the end of a long rope. My mother dreaded to go near the place, lest she should see him dangling like a gigantic spider in space.' He had made his attempts at sculpture, too: a stone lion, a child's head, a carved spray of lilies of the valley had stood about the cottage at Juniper as ornaments in the early days, but as time went on had grown dusty and disregarded, and found their way at last to the rubbish heap, where perhaps they still lie crumbling among the nettles.

If he had been content with his lot, as the inhabitants of Juniper were constantly warned from the pulpit it was their duty to be, his life would have been respectable and his home happy. But he was not content. He was a misfit, brooding in resentment on the unfairness of life and clinging to the belief that he came of a 'good' family. There seems to be some ground for the legend that his forebears had once belonged to a different world, for in childhood Flora could remember faded daguerreotypes of ladies in crinolines, magnificent in heavy lockets and gold bracelets, which her father cherished as proofs of former splendour, and which certainly spoke of a way of life unimaginably out of reach of the hamlet people. Poor Albert Timms was embittered by the contrast. He scorned his neighbours and comforted himself with drink, and was not liked in the village. His drinking kept him poorer than he need have been, and this, and the growing moroseness of his temper, cast a shadow and spoiled the happiness of his home. He was the only man in the hamlet, besides the publican, who was not a farm labourer, and he earned something more than the standard farming wage of ten shillings a week; but it was not much, and to the end of her life Flora remembered that it had been her mother's dearest dream to have 'thirty shillings a week, paid regular and to be depended upon'. 'My father was a terrible spendthrift', Flora Thompson wrote in middle age. 'One week he would bring home the whole of his wages, the next week nothing, and the week he did bring them home he would extort the greater part back in the way of pocket-money. I do not think he meant to be unfair; he never seemed to grasp the fact that he was responsible for our upbringing; he simply wanted the money for this, that, or the other, and had it. He had all of the bad qualities of genius and a few of the good ones.' He died in 1918 at the age of 64, and was buried in the churchyard of Cottisford, 'the mother village'.

Flora's mother, Emma Timms, though she had none of her husband's pretensions, was in her way remarkable. If it was from her father that Flora inherited her uncommon sensibility, she certainly derived qualities no less valuable from her mother – a love of traditional songs and stories, a down-to-earth common sense and dry humour, upheld by a strong old-fashioned sense of duty. She had been a local girl, daughter of a small-holder who followed the trade of 'eggler' round the farms and villages, collecting with a pony and cart and selling his eggs in the nearby market town. Emma Lapper (as she then was) had gone into service at twelve years old, as they all did, and was nursemaid at Fewcott Rectory when she married. She was small, fair, and pretty, and in her years of service had learned standards of speech and manners a little above those of the cottage women. She was a hard worker, a good cook and an excellent contriver, keeping her children clean, well-mannered and reasonably well clad against what today would seem insuperable odds. She was also a great repository of country songs and stories, and would sit by the fire of an evening with her two eldest children beside her on little stools and the latest baby on her knee, singing old ballads and songs and making up fairy tales, until their father's uncertain hand was heard on the latch, when they would be sent up the wooden stairs out of the way.

In later years Flora Thompson described her childhood as 'somewhat harsh and restricted', but she bore no grudge, for the harshness and restriction were a part of poverty, and were common to them all. Nor, for all her sensitiveness, did she resent her mother's rough discipline, or develop emotional complications on account of it, as a more gently nurtured child or one of a later generation might have done. 'Perhaps,' she wrote in *Lark Rise*, remembering the childish disgraces of herself and her brother, 'being of mixed birth with a large proportion of peasant blood in them, they were tougher in fibre than some. When their bottoms were soundly smacked, as they often were, their reaction was to make a mental note not to repeat the offence which had caused the smacking, rather than to lay up for themselves complexes to spoil their later lives.' This practical attitude towards experience, and total absence of affectation, was to be a constant element in Flora Thompson's nature. She was, indeed, a down-to-earth country child, made strange only by the unaccountable poetic streak in her nature, which transmuted every commonplace experience into something precious.

The hamlet, of which she knew every ditch and stone in childhood, is still after more than a century almost unchanged; a nondescript cluster of cottages set down in an open landscape of flat fields, with nothing about it to attract the eye. Time seems to have added nothing and to have taken nothing away. The 'end house', it is true, where Flora lived, is no longer the double cottage thatched with straw which it was in her day; only half of it remains, roofed with slate, and an unsightly lean-to annex has been added. But it still stands, as she described it, 'a little apart, and turning its back on its neighbours as though about to run away into the fields'.

She had been born ('for convenience') in one of the other cottages, belonging to an aunt. 'We lived in three different houses,' she wrote to her younger sister May, 'before settling for so many years in the one you remember.' There was 'the old house where I was born, that house with its end to the road, and the little cottage next door to "The Fox". All those before you were born.' (The Fox Inn is the Wagon and Horses of *Lark Rise*.) All fields have local names, though they are seldom written down, and the big field which in Flora's childhood rippled with corn almost to the cottage door was known as Lark Rise, from the great number of larks which nested in it, and from the fact that it was not quite as flat as the other fields. In making her slight disguises Flora Thompson stayed as near as possible to the truth. Flora becomes Laura, Edwin becomes Edmund, and the hamlet itself hides only behind the name of its biggest field. She allowed herself, here and there, to use the real names of actual places, and the enthusiast who takes the trouble to use a large-scale map can make many identifications; for such minute clues as that the beaded footstool which Mrs Herring offered to Laura's mother, ' "come out of Tusmore House that time the fire was," ' are to be found unobtrusively tucked away in the text, though the classical splendours of Tusmore's façade are no longer as they were in Flora's day. 'In *Lark Rise,*' she wrote in a letter towards the end of her life, 'every one of the characters lived at Juniper and were just as described, with only the names altered'; and as arguments sometimes arise as to the identity of Flora Thompson's villages and country towns, it may be as well to give her own identifications, so far as I have been able to find them, scattered here and there in a few letters. 'The real name of the hamlet is Juniper and the mother village is Cottisford. . . . Candleford is Banbury-Bicester-Buckingham, mostly Buckingham, as that is where we went on that first Sunday outing.' 'Candleford Green . . . is not Fringford, and very few of the characters are Fringford people, though there is a little of Fringford in it, with far more of a village in Surrey.' 'In *Over to Candleford* and *Candleford Green* I wrote more freely than in *Lark Rise*, and do not think I described any house or place exactly as it actually existed, excepting "Miss Lane's" post-office forge, and Shelswell Park, where I used to carry the letters.'

Cottisford (which is Fordlow, the mother village), where Flora and the hamlet children walked to school, is much the same as it was, though perhaps it looks more cheerful. In *Lark Rise* it is described as 'a little, lost, lonely place,' and we are told that 'it was a standing joke in the hamlet that a stranger had once asked the way to Fordlow after he had walked right through it.' The 'little squat church, without spire or tower,' has not changed; it is as small as a chapel-of-ease, and has not lost its solid, whitewashed simplicity. The pew where the Timms children sat (their parents rarely went to church, apart from successive baptisms and occasional funerals) is beneath the modest brass wall-tablet which is Cottisford's 1914–18 war memorial, and Edwin Timms's name, alone beneath the half-dozen other young men from Juniper and Cottisford, is last on the list. The village itself is still much less than a village; the fields come up to the churchyard wall, and beyond the rectory, hidden in trees, the stone-built manor house and the tiny village school at the cross-roads, there is nothing but a scattered handful of cottages. The population is less than half what it was in Flora's childhood, and the school has been converted into a private house. Nowadays the children go to school elsewhere by bus, but Flora Thompson and her brothers and sisters (there were ten of them altogether, but four died young) walked the three miles backwards and forwards from Juniper, from the age of five until they left school at twelve years old. She was remembered as a thin, dark, long-legged child who was never still, a notable skipper, but in no other way remarkable. Indeed, I heard that there was much local incredulity when, more than fifty years later, her books appeared. It stood to reason, people said, they couldn't have been written by Timms the stonemason's girl.

Nevertheless, she did well enough in this primitive little school, where children of all ages sat on benches in the same room and nothing was taught beyond reading, writing, simple sums, and Holy Scripture. The last was the most important; the children were regularly catechized by the fierce rector, and on the Diocesan Inspector's visits the Bible and Prayer Book were the sole subjects of examination. The Inspector's Reports for the seven years when Flora was at the school are still in existence, and give a good idea of the educational programme. 'The children well taught throughout. They answered intelligently in Catechism and Holy Scripture. . . . It would be well if the 1st Class were more taught to write out parables etc. . . . The infants repeated hymns and prayers very nicely', and so on. Flora herself must have done reasonably well, for she was 'commended' twice at the age of ten and the following year awarded the Diocesan Prize. But the chief benefit which she derived from this undemanding system was a lifelong love and knowledge of the Bible, which was to be found in every cottage in Juniper, though rarely read. She and her brother Edwin could recite long passages by heart when the mood took them, and as Flora grew older the prose of the Authorized Version and the miraculous rhythms of the Psalms became a part of her inner listening and imagination.

What made her different from the other children who shared her experiences, but who found nothing in them significant or remarkable, was her marvellously deep focus of observation. The annals of the poor are rarely written; they have no archives. Country churchyards are full of the bones of men and women who have lived her life and found nothing to say about it. To Flora Thompson, even in childhood, every circumstance of the life around her was portentous. 'She sometimes wished she could make the earth and stones speak and tell her about all the dead people who had trodden upon them.' Memory stored what eye and ear drank in, and she was haunted by a desire to fashion something, though it took her a lifetime to know what that something was. 'To be born in poverty,' she wrote when she was nearly seventy, 'is a terrible handicap to a writer. I often say to myself that it has taken one lifetime for me to prepare to make a start. If human life lasted two hundred years I might hope to accomplish something.'

What she did achieve was in a genre of its own, since it is rare to find a creative mind of her quality at work on the bedrock level. She was able to write the annals of the poor because she

10

was one of them, and because one of those strange accidents of genius which can never be explained had given her the equipment she needed. The other chronicler of village life who most readily comes to mind when one seeks for a comparison is Mary Russell Mitford, but Miss Mitford wrote, as nearly all other writers on country matters have done, from the genteel standpoint. Miss Mitford lived in a cottage, it is true, but with a difference. She surveyed her village scene with love, and succeeded in making her readers love it, too; but to do this she presented it as a delicious nosegay, the roots and earth concealed or conveniently forgotten. Flora Thompson's work is as different as the country scenes of Stanley Spencer are from one of George Morland's charming cottage interiors, or the primrose-laden fields of Birkett Foster. In hers there is no sentimentality. It was the true and the real that stirred her imagination. Her integrity was absolute, as Miss Mitford's was not, and it is this deep emotional truth which gives her work, in spite of its rigorous plainness, the bloom of poetry, so that even a pig-killing has a gruesome beauty.

When the pig was fattened – and the fatter the better – the date of execution had to be decided upon. It had to take place some time during the first two quarters of the moon; for if the pig was killed when the moon was waning the bacon would shrink in cooking, and they wanted it to 'plimp up'. The next thing was to engage the travelling pork-butcher, or pig-sticker, and, as he was a thatcher by day, he always had to kill after dark, the scene being lighted with lanterns and the fire of burning straw which at a later stage of the proceedings was to singe the bristles off the victim.

The killing was a noisy, bloody business, in the course of which the animal was hoisted to a rough bench that it might bleed thoroughly and so preserve the quality of the meat. The job was often bungled, the pig sometimes getting away and having to be chased; but country people of that day had little sympathy for the sufferings of animals, and men, women and children would gather round to see the sight.

After the carcass had been singed, the pig-sticker would pull off the detachable, gristly, outer coverings of the toes, known locally as 'the shoes', and fling them among the children, who scrambled for, then

11

sucked and gnawed them, straight from the filth of the sty and
blackened by fire as they were.

The whole scene, with its mud and blood, flaring lights and dark
shadows, was as savage as anything to be seen in an African jungle.
The children at the end house would steal out of bed to the window.
'Look! Look! It's hell, and those are the devils,' Edmund would
whisper, pointing to the men tossing the burning straw with their
pitchforks; but Laura felt sick and would creep back into bed and cry:
she was sorry for the pig.

But, hidden from the children, there was another aspect of the pig-
killing. Months of hard work and self-denial were brought on that
night to a successful conclusion. It was a time to rejoice, and rejoice
they did, with beer flowing freely and the first delicious dish of pig's
fry sizzling in the frying-pan.

That passage comes from the first chapter of *Lark Rise*. In *Over
to Candleford* there is an echo of it, and again the killing of a pig,
so momentous an event in a cottage family, by its depth of
observation and truth carries implications of something beyond
itself.

A little later in her life came the evening after a pig-killing when she
stood alone in the pantry where the dead animal hung suspended from
a hook in the ceiling. Her mother was only a few feet away. . . . Out
there in the wash-house they were busy and cheerful, but in the pantry
where Laura stood was a dead, cold silence.

She had known that pig all its life. Her father had often held her
over the door of its sty to scratch its back and she had pushed lettuce
and cabbage stalks through the bars for it to enjoy. Only that morning
it had routed and grunted and squealed because it had had no
breakfast. Her mother had said its noise got on her nerves and her
father had looked uncomfortable, although he had passed it off by
saying: 'No. No breakfast today, piggy. You're going to have a big
operation by and by and there's no breakfast before operations.'

Now it had had its operation and there it hung, cold and stiff and so
very, very dead. Not funny at all any more, but in some queer way
dignified. The butcher had draped a long, lacy piece of fat from its own
interior over one of its forelegs, in the manner in which ladies of that
day sometimes carried a white lacy shawl, and that last touch seemed to
Laura utterly heartless. She stayed there a long time, patting its hard,
cold side and wondering that a thing so recently full of life and noise

could be so still. Then, hearing her mother call her, she ran out of the door farthest from where she was working lest she should be scolded for crying over a dead pig.

There was fried liver and fat for supper and when Laura said 'No, thank you,' her mother looked at her rather suspiciously, then said, 'Well, perhaps better not, just going to bed and all; but here's a nice bit of sweetbread, I was saving it for Daddy, but you have it. You'll like that.' And Laura ate the sweetbread and dipped her bread in the thick, rich gravy and refused to think any more about the poor pig in the pantry, for, although only five years old, she was learning to live in this world of compromises.

There was no room for sentimentality in the life she was born to; it was too near the bone. Yet in spite of that, and also because of it, it had a value and a saltiness which it would be hard to find in villages today. Life and work were hard, but the work that was done was essential work, and respected, and life was not wasted in a struggle to keep up appearances. In old age Flora Thompson, who like her father was always a bit of a radical (or at least a Liberal, professing 'a mild Liberalism . . . that would be regarded as hide-bound Toryism now, but was daring enough in those days') could see clearly that when poverty was abolished it was not the only thing which had been swept away. 'I fear,' she wrote to H. J. Massingham in 1943, 'that much of the salt of the earth will be lost in the process of transforming the old, sturdy, independent type of farm labourer into the proletariat. The only hope is that the countryman's roots are so strong and so well down in the soil that, after this terrible time is over, the country virtues will spring anew.'

*   *   *

There were relations on her father's side who led a more prosperous life in the market town of Buckingham. One of her aunts had married a cobbler (or 'snob' in the old parlance) with a thriving business next to the White Hart Hotel in Market Square, where apprentices hammered and stitched in the back premises and there was a long garden behind the house, full of roses and apple trees, sloping down to the banks of the river. Here, from the time when Flora was about ten years old, her father would occasionally take the family for a summer visit, borrowing the innkeeper's horse and cart for the day and strapping the children into the back seat with baskets of presentation vegetables. Flora and Edwin were also from time to time left to spend a week's holiday in Buckingham, especially when a new baby was expected, and these occasions were a valuable experience, since their uncle Recab Holland ('Uncle Tom' of *Over to Candleford*) was an intelligent and remarkable man who had stacks of old books in his attic and liked Flora to read *Cranford* or *Villette* aloud to him while he stitched the uppers of his hunting boots and prepared fittings for his lady customers. 'If Laura's Uncle Tom was a snob by trade,' she wrote long afterwards, 'there was nothing else snobbish about him, for he was one of the most liberal-minded men she was ever to know, and one of the wisest.' Exploring the books in his attic and reading aloud to a critical ear (he was helpful in correcting pronunciation) was a small but valuable part of her education. Uncle Tom's shop, house, and garden are today more or less as they were, though no longer occupied by a shoemaker. There are still the old roses and apple-trees in the garden and the solid shop-counter, now covered with electrical goods, has not lost the brass-edged slot in its surface, once used in the stitching and buckling of boot-straps.

*   *   *

When reading *Lark Rise to Candleford*, so rich in detail of sight, sound, and smell that one has the illusion of remembering the very hedgerows for oneself, it is strange to realize that these deep impressions were absorbed by Flora Thompson before she was fourteen, that being the age when she left home to earn her living. It had been supposed that she would go into service at twelve or thirteen, as all the hamlet girls did (some of them, indeed, went out as young as eleven, their mothers frankly declaring, 'I shan't be sorry when our young So-and-so gets her knees under somebody else's table. Five slices for breakfast this mornin', if you please!'); and her mother had planned to get her a place under one of the nurses she knew from her own days in service. But the child's unusual thirst for reading, and the peculiarity of her always wanting scraps of paper to write on, made her mother doubtful of her suitability as a nursemaid, and she decided to place her with another old acquaintance, the postmistress of Fringford, who was willing to take her as junior assistant. So Flora, as she has related in *Candleford Green*, was driven by her father in the innkeeper's cart over the eight miles of country roads to the neighbouring village, and began her adult life as a post-office clerk.

Flora herself has said that Candleford Green is not, strictly speaking, Fringford, but the post office and forge over which Miss Lane presided with so matriarchal an authority can still be seen, though the long, low white cottage has long ceased to fulfil either of its old functions. Miss Lane herself is drawn from a locally celebrated Mrs Whitton, who had inherited the forge from her father and for many years had carried on the business and that of the village post office as well.

I knew Mrs Whitton well [Flora Thompson wrote to an acquaintance many years later]. About the time you were born she was teaching me the rudiments of the post-office business and there is a good deal of her in my Miss Lane. That character as it stands in my books is a mixture of her and of another postmistress I served under in Surrey, but the mental attributes are entirely those of Mrs Whitton, and the blacksmith's business of course was hers. She was a wonderful woman. She had the most observant eye and the keenest brain of anyone I have known, and had she been born later must have left her mark on the world. What a psychologist she would have made! She was very good to me, and as I have said in one of my books, had more influence than anyone in shaping the outward course of my life.

That life, in the early Fringford period, she has recorded fairly closely in *Candleford Green*, which gives an unforgettable account of Miss Lane's household, run on traditional lines which were old-fashioned and benevolently strict even for those days. All meals were eaten in the 'front kitchen', with Miss Lane at the head of the table, Flora and the foreman far apart at the side, the three young smiths crowded together below the salt and the maid-servant at a small side-table of her own. Food was abundant and delicious: it was Miss Lane's one weakness. At tea 'she loaded her scone, already spread with fresh farm butter, with blackcurrant jam and topped it with cream', and majestically indulged herself at other meals, which no doubt accounts for her appearance in the only known photograph of her, standing with her foreman and smiths outside the forge. Here Flora learned the post-office business from the bottom, selling stamps, sorting letters, working the sacred telegraph machine (which was kept under a sort of velvet tea-cosy), and for one long and happy spell acting as letter-carrier, covering miles on foot through fields and lanes with her bag. This experience was important, for it deepened the almost mystical love of solitude and nature which was to grow with the years, until it was the dominant strain in her strong character. The fact that the footmen at 'the great house', Shelswell Park, would ask for a kiss or pull her hair and tease her was an embarrassment, but she knew better than to complain about their behaviour and create a fuss. 'She preferred to endure the teasing, which, after all, occupied but a few minutes during an outing in which there were rich compensations.'

*   *   *

This quiet, orderly, and privately studious life (for she was now more than ever an obsessive reader) continued until Flora was nearly twenty, when she felt an urge to see something more of the world. So, after taking short holiday-relief engagements in various country post offices, she applied for the job of post-office assistant in the Hampshire village of Grayshott, and here, in a world totally different from the one she had known, spent the next three years, until her marriage. She was grown-up now, and independent; it was the period of the Boer War, and life in the village of Grayshott was rapidly changing. What had once been a primitive area of common land, heath and hill thinly populated by squatters in ramshackle cottages and frequented by 'lawless folk', notably the 'Hindhead Gang' who had a reputation for sheep-stealing and highway robbery, was now becoming known as a beauty spot and health resort. Since there was now a railway service between London and Haslemere the area was popular with doctors, writers, and *avant-garde* intellectuals, and the place was becoming civilized. In 1898, the year after Flora arrived in the village, new sanitary by-laws were passed, setting standards for privies and cesspools, and Grayshott acquired its first resident police constable.

In her sixties, after the publication of *Lark Rise* and its two successors, Flora Thompson wrote an account of her three years in Grayshott, which she disguised as *Heatherley*. The book did not altogether please her; the magic of childhood and the old country life were missing, and she decided not to offer it to her publisher. Instead, she went back to the Oxfordshire countryside of her childhood and wove into it a fictional tale, *Still Glides the Stream*, which was published shortly after her death. But *Heatherley*, despite her dissatisfaction, has its value, and now at last reveals much that was hitherto unknown about Flora Thompson's response to life, her creative gift, her sensitive experience.

Having passed through London on her way from Oxfordshire and travelling to Haslemere by train, she arrived in Grayshott on foot, 'dressed in a brown woollen frock with a waist-length cape of the same material and a brown beaver hat decorated with two small ostrich tips, set upright in front, back to back, like a couple of notes of interrogation. . . . The skirt, cut short just to escape contact with the ground, and so needing no holding up except in wet weather, was, her dressmaker had assured her, the latest idea for country wear. The hat she had bought on her way through London that morning. It had cost nine and elevenpence three-farthings of the pound she had saved to meet her expenses until her first month's salary was due in her new post, but she did not regret the extravagance. . . . "A good first impression is half the battle," she had been told as a child.'

She lived first with the postmaster's family, then independently in lodgings. This latter arrangement was the happier of the two, for the postmaster, Walter Chapman, though a skilled craftsman (he was a cabinet-maker by trade) who conscientiously performed his post-office duties, was a psychopath of a very dangerous kind. He quarrelled violently with his wife, often reducing her to a state of weeping terror; he prowled the house at night, sometimes creeping into Flora's bedroom where she would be wakened by creaking floorboards or heavy breathing. His explanation for this frightening behaviour was that he believed an intruder was hiding somewhere in the house – an unlikely theory, since the place was tiny and its three bedrooms all occupied. The following morning, after one of these nightmare alarms, he would be as sober and practical as usual, discussing an order for a new chest of drawers with one of his customers, or carrying out his post-office routine. Fortunately Flora, made uneasy by Chapman's peculiar behaviour and the quarrelsome and unhappy atmosphere in the house, decided to move into lodgings, and there had her first real taste of independence, living in a bare little bed-sitting-room at ten shillings a week. The move was made none too soon, for in that same summer of 1901 the postmaster murdered his wife and child with a carving-knife and was declared insane.

On her own at last, Flora was able now for the first time to read widely, and embarked on the long haphazard self-education which she afterwards described as having been accomplished on borrowed books, free libraries, and the threepenny and sixpenny boxes of second-hand shops. Here, too, she had her first enthralling glimpse of real writers, for the 'Surrey highlands' having been recently discovered by the intelligentsia, and there being no post office at that time in Hindhead, the celebrities who frequented the neighbourhood bought their stamps and sent their telegrams from Grayshott. Conan Doyle, Grant Allen, Richard le Gallienne, and others had taken houses in the neighbourhood, and Bernard Shaw, lately married, had rented a furnished house in Grayshott itself.

I used to listen to the conversation of these [she wrote later], meeting and greeting each other at my counter, myself as unregarded as a piece of furniture, but noting all. Perhaps these 'great examples' encouraged my desire to express myself in writing, but I cannot remember the time when I did not wish and mean to write. My brother and I used to make up verses and write stories and diaries from our earliest years, and I had never left off writing essays for the pleasure of writing. No one saw them; there was no one likely to be interested.

Exploration of the wild and beautiful area of heath, hill, and forest in which she now found herself became a passion. She walked alone, taking her lunch in her pocket on free days and covering distances that to a later generation, brought up on bicycles and motor cars, would have seemed incredible. Eighteen or twenty miles was nothing unusual, and the further she went through heathland and forest, climbing sandy ridges and downs from which she could survey an ancient, primitive, almost unchanged horizon, the more she became aware of the secret life that went on in the heather and bracken. She had, as she now began to realize, the patience and dedication of the born naturalist: the observation which had stored her memory with the details of human life in her childhood was now turned in another, more secretive and difficult direction, and she began, consciously and with delight, serving her naturalist's apprenticeship.

*　　*　　*

When she was twenty-four, however, this independent single life came to an end, for in the course of the penny readings and village soirées which went on in the neighbourhood she met John Thompson, a young post-office clerk from Aldershot, and as soon as he was transferred to the main post office in Bournemouth they were married.

At the time it must have seemed a sensible step, and at first the marriage was happy enough in a humdrum way, but the world of the white-collar working class was alien to Flora and she was dismayed by its narrowness and prejudice. Her love of reading was now condemned as a waste of time, her attempts at writing sneered at. Everything she did, it seemed, was wrong. A book in one's hand or a handful of garden flowers on the supper table was mocked as a ridiculous pretension, yet she found herself looked down on by her new relations for having been born in a cottage. They considered themselves above the labouring class and spared no pains to make this clear to her.

The Thompsons were very poor. The pay of a post-office clerk allowed no luxuries, and the free library, her one resource, had to be reached on foot after the day's work was done, for there was rarely the penny or twopence to spare for the tram.

With a house to run single-handed and with children being born and nursed my literary dreams faded for a time. But I still read a good deal. For the first time in my life I had access to a good public library, and I slipped in like a duck slipping into water and read almost everything. I had no guidance except my own natural taste. But perhaps I was fortunate in this, as I was able to follow my own bent.

A daughter and son, Winifred and Basil, were born during the thirteen Bournemouth years, and when they were no longer babies and she could contrive a little leisure from children and housework Flora began to write again, as secretly as she could because of her husband's disapproval.* Her first attempt was an essay on Jane Austen which she entered for a competition in a women's paper, and which, to her astonishment, was awarded the prize. Encouraged, she sent an article, then a short story to the same paper, and both were accepted. The payment for each was only a few shillings, but the effect of this small success was morally important: if her eccentricities were paid for they would be tolerated. 'I had earned the right to use my scanty leisure as I wished.'

---

*On one of her early experiments in story-writing is scribbled her address – Grayshott Cottage, Winton – which suggests the probability that the young Thompsons had named their first home after the village where they had met. There is still, in Frederica Road, Winton, a little house called 'Grayshott', and one day, perhaps, it will not be surprising to find a plaque on the wall, informing the passer-by that from 1903 to 1916 Flora Thompson lived there.

The discovery that she could earn a pound or two by writing delayed for many years her development as a writer, for she determined to earn a good education for her children, and set herself to the manufacture of 'small, sugared love stories,' which, however artificial she knew them to be, were at least easy to sell. Even for this modest hack-work some hours of freedom and solitude were essential, and to escape from the suburban life that she found uncongenial she would slip away for a few hours into the New Forest – a half-hour journey by local train to Brockenhurst – where she could walk for miles in the forest and heath that she loved best. It is an odd coincidence that in these same years W. H. Hudson, old, gaunt, and frail, was frequently prowling and bird-watching in the same area. They may perhaps have caught sight of one another on, say, the heath between Beaulieu and Boldre, but there is no evidence that they ever met. Flora comforted herself, too, by writing verse, for like many writers of pure and musical prose she believed for many years that her gifts were not for prose at all but for poetry, and her unconfessed ambition was to be a poet. This secret hope was never realized, for her verse never rose above modest magazine level, but her love of poetry did at least bring her the one literary friendship of her life, and this proved to be important. In 1912, after the sinking of the *Titanic*, a Scottish physician and poet called Ronald Campbell Macfie wrote an ode on the disaster which was published in *The Literary Monthly*, and readers were invited, as a competition, to send their criticisms. Flora Thompson's admiring review of the ode won the prize, and so pleased Dr. Macfie that he wrote her a grateful and charming letter, and later made a point of coming to see her.

Dr. Macfie is not often remembered today, but at that time, though never a successful man in the worldly sense, he had published a sufficient number of books, and was well enough known and respected as a writer, to seem to Flora Thompson like a glorious messenger from the inaccessible world she longed to enter. He was a poet who had published a considerable body of verse of a traditional sort, and who was at his best when celebrating some public or national event with a classical ode. He was a prolific writer, besides, on popular medicine, having made a special study of tuberculosis and believing passionately in the importance of public education in hygiene. A man of commanding presence and personality, he was quick-tempered, argumentative, and attractive. His life was divided between irreconcilable interests; between poetry, medicine, travel, and a variety of humanitarian causes; and this scattering of his talents kept him poor. His was a restless temperament, and he had never married. He had, he told Flora Thompson, renounced any idea of domestic life 'in order to get a few months here and there to write the poetry and philosophy in me. Without money (in fact with a heavy burden of debt on my shoulders) I have struggled on and have achieved enough leisure here and there to do a little work, which though almost unrecognized I believe to be immortal.' He was never in the same place for long and they met rarely; but from time to time he would descend for a few hours' visit, and from their first meeting until his death twenty years later their friendship was unbroken. From the beginning it was of great importance to Flora Thompson, for apart from his personal fascination Macfie was the only 'beloved friend' she ever had who shared her interests and gave her strenuous encouragement. 'Forty! What is forty?' he wrote to her in 1918. 'I am fifty-one; but if I could yet have ten years of opportunity to write I should be content. Look forward! Rejoice in your great gift and fight for opportunity, even if it be ten years later; and perhaps I who am still fighting may in a few years be able to find some ways and means for you. Who knows?' It was he who, three years later, encouraged her to send a little collection of her verses to a publisher, and accepted her dedication with pride when the paper-bound volume *Bog Myrtle and Peat* eventually appeared. In spite of kindly reviews it was a failure, and the disappointment convinced her at last that she was not a poet. But the achievement, however modest, had its value, and to the end of her life she was grateful for Macfie's faith in her as a writer. When he died in 1931, she wrote his name and the date on the fly-leaf of a book, and then, cryptically, 'The bright day is done, and we are for the dark.'*

*   *   *

In 1916 John Thompson was promoted to his first sub-postmastership, and they moved to Liphook in Hampshire. It was a sad year, for Edwin, the brother whom Flora so much resembled and loved, had been killed in action, and her one deeply emotional link with her childhood was broken. She was unable to write, for as well as her work for home and children she had undertaken arduous wartime duties at the post office, sorting the mail at four o'clock in the morning and doing the work of the clerk who had been called up. Fortunately there is still one surviving acquaintance of Flora Thompson's who worked with her in Liphook during the war years. This is Mrs Clara Louise Hooker, who as a young girl ('Louie' Woods in those days) joined the staff as postwoman in the same year. Dressed in a smart wartime uniform of dark blue trimmed with red braid and a dark straw 'boater' with a brass G.P.O. badge, it was her duty to bicycle on a round of twenty miles twice a day, with a heavy postbag on her back. When she arrived at a quarter to six in the morning she would find the morning delivery already sorted into piles by Flora Thompson, who had been working since four o'clock.

She remembers Flora as a very quiet and reserved person, particularly nervous and silent in the presence of her husband, who was strict, immaculate, and domineering, a 'sergeant-major type'. The Liphook post office of those days was in the small

*Flora Thompson's long friendship with Ronald Macfie was important in more than a literary sense: to no one else had she been able to write so freely about her life, her work, her hopes. It is sad, therefore, that her letters, many of which he had kept, were destroyed after his death by his literary executor, Lady Margaret Sackville. Macfie was an attractive man, particularly to aspiring literary ladies, and Margaret Sackville, who had collaborated with him in two small volumes of fairy tales, presumably resented this 'warm and grateful friendship', as he described it on the fly-leaf of a book he was presenting to his 'poet-friend Flora Thompson'. There seems to be no other explanation of her destruction of the letters. She 'saw no point', she replied to my enquiry about them many years ago, 'in keeping such rubbish', and had consequently burnt them.

building which is now the Midland Bank; the Thompsons lived in 'Ruskin House' next door, with a passage through from John Thompson's ground-floor office to the post-office area. The mail was heavy, for there were now two army camps in the neighbourhood, English regiments stationed at Bordon Camp nearby and Canadian soldiers at Bramshott, in a conglomeration of tin shacks known locally as 'Tin Town'. (Many of the Canadians were to die, not in the trenches but in Bramshott itself, and now lie under neat rows of gravestones in the little churchyard, victims of the influenza epidemic of 1918.)

It was an exhausting four years, for as well as her long hours in the post office Flora was still the cook and housekeeper of the family. Yet somehow she managed to achieve a little of the solitude and privacy that her spirit needed, and to write her verses in secret, still conscious, as she confessed, of 'feelings of guilt when her pen was idle'. Mrs Hooker remembers a small bare room in the Thompsons' house, furnished only with a desk, a chair, and a waste-paper basket, where she read and wrote whenever possible, and where her husband and even the children were rarely admitted.

Once the war was over she began to write again in earnest; as she wrote of Laura in *Heatherley*, 'the old feeling had revived that in return for the precious opportunity known as life some further effort other than those involved in mere living was required of her'; and on the strength of her small earnings Basil and Winifred were sent to excellent day schools, one to Petersfield Grammar School and the other to Haslemere. The country round Liphook was a renewed pleasure after suburban Bournemouth, and she revived her habit of long brooding walks, feeding her old hunger for solitude and nature. These walks bore fruit of a kind, for she began to write a series of nature essays for a little magazine called *The Catholic Fireside*, and these were so well liked that the series was continued for eight years. No one now remembers how she first came across it, for she had no obvious Catholic connections, but, as we shall see later, she had had her Catholic acquaintances even in the Juniper days, since the original family at Tusmore House had been

24

Catholics from before the Reformation, and had later attracted
Catholic families, Irish farm workers and servants, into the area.
At Grayshott, too, there had been an influential Catholic family,
whose house later became a convent of the Order of Our Lady
of the Cenacle, and from these and perhaps other contacts and
examples Flora had always felt a sympathetic attraction to 'the
old religion'. The work she did for *The Catholic Fireside*, at all
events, was an excellent practice ground for a writer with her
gifts of observation, and this small success encouraged her to try
her hand in a more general field. The *Daily News* and various
women's magazines now printed her occasional essays, and she
felt that at last she had become a professional writer.

She was still, however, a long way from the discovery of the
kind of writing she was best fitted to do, and in the next ten
years incalculable time and energy were wasted in following
false trails. For several years she 'ghosted' for a big-game hunter
who had advertised in the literary press for an amanuensis, and
had the wry satisfaction of seeing her work appear under his
name in *Chambers's Journal, The Scottish Field*, and various
African papers. She also, in 1924, founded a postal association
for literary aspirants, The Peverel Society, and this work, in the
value of which she ardently believed, devoured her leisure and
energy for eighteen years. No one seems to know why the name
Peverel' was chosen. The same title was used for her contributions to the Catholic magazine – *The Peverel Papers* – largely
the record of her naturalist wanderings in the Liphook area,
from which *A Country Calendar* in this volume has been chosen.
The Peverel Society was a modest amateur affair, but it satisfied
her longing for contact with other writers, and since it brought
her a number of distant friends who shared her interests the time
it absorbed was perhaps not altogether wasted. The members
did not meet; each paid a few shillings a year to cover expenses
and contributed something once a month, either prose or verse,
to a portfolio which went the round of the members by post.
Each was invited to criticize and Flora Thompson's criticisms
(the few that survive) are remarkable for their workmanlike
approach. She would have made a good teacher or a good

editor; her advice has nothing amateur about it. Criticizing a
short story or writing a course of instruction for her members
she invariably shows a practical grasp of literary techniques and
difficulties. The pity is that she spent, coaching amateurs, so
many years which might have been given to the development of
her own gifts. There was not time for both, and as the years
went by she began to see that this work, so earnestly
undertaken, was by its very nature doomed to disappointment.
The members fell off or failed to turn into writers, 'saying that
their husband or wife thought writing was a waste of time, or
thought themselves neglected'.

The Peverel Society was begun at Liphook and continued at
Dartmouth, where John Thompson was transferred as postmaster in 1928. The Liphook years had not been unhappy, and
she was sorry to go. A third child, Peter, 'the unexpected late-
comer', had been born at the little post office when she was
forty-one and had thought her days of child-bearing were over,
and though she had not welcomed his birth with any pleasure he
became increasingly dear to both parents and did something to
revive the dwindling comfort of their marriage. It was at
Liphook, too, that she had first achieved a home she really
loved. They had lived for twelve years next door to the post
office and at last had bought a house in the wooded and hilly
country a mile or two beyond the village, but no sooner were
they settled at Woolmer Gate than her husband, in a fit of
restlessness which she found hard to forgive, 'put in for
promotion,' and was transferred almost immediately to Dartmouth. Flora remained behind to sell the house, an operation
quietly prolonged for more than a year; a happy year, spent
alone with her children in the sort of countryside she loved,
endlessly reading and writing without criticism or reproach.

When at last the move to Dartmouth was accomplished,
however, she was pleased with her new surroundings and soon
grew fond of the town and harbour and the steep wooded walks
behind the house. The house itself, 'The Outlook,' was in that
highest part known as Above Town, with a dazzling view over
the whole estuary. Here for the next twelve years she lived a

secluded life, making few friends and seeming to desire none. With only the youngest child at home she had more leisure, and though the Peverel Society still absorbed the greater part of it, she was beginning at last to write to please herself. She spent much time on the beginnings of several novels, but none of them satisfied her. Her only encouragement still came from Dr Macfie, and when in 1931 he suddenly died she was slow to recover from the private misery of his loss. At last, however, she began to feel her way towards the theme which had been waiting unrecognized for so long. She began to write sketches about her childhood.

The first of these was *Old Queenie*, a loving remembrance of the bee-keeper and lace-maker of Juniper, whose cottage had stood (and still stands) at the back of the 'end house' which had been Flora's home. This essay appeared in 1937 in *The Lady*, and is the kernel of a much longer chapter which she presently expanded for *Lark Rise*. This was the beginning; *May Day*, another chapter, was accepted by the *Fortnightly Review*, and with such enthusiasm that she was encouraged to send these and several other pieces of a like nature to the Oxford University Press, where they came into the hands of Sir Humphrey Milford, who instantly recognized their quality and wrote to the unknown author, urging her to expand them into a book. This was the signal she needed; the material was rich and copious, and for the first time, as a writer, she felt at home. She began *Lark Rise* in the autumn of 1937 and worked on it steadily for eleven months. It was published in 1939 and was received with universal praise. The sales were not large at first, but they were encouraging, and her publishers pressed her to write more. *Over to Candleford* was written in the following year and she began to feel the first glow of success; but failing health and personal sorrow were soon to rob her of its satisfactions. In 1940, in the early days of the Second World War, John Thompson had retired from the Post Office and they had left the house at Dartmouth for a cottage at Brixham. Basil, her elder son, had gone some years before to farm in Australia; Winifred, her daughter, was nursing in Bristol, and Peter, the beloved youngest, had left home to join the Merchant Navy. He was killed within a few months, when his convoy ship was torpedoed in mid-Atlantic. Flora Thompson never entirely recovered from this shock. She fell ill, developed pneumonia, and rallied only at the expense of a damaged heart and the loss of much of her sturdy vitality. A year later she forced herself to return to work, and *Candleford Green* was written in the space of nine months, 'under difficulties,' as she wrote to a friend, 'several of the passages to the sound of bombs falling . . . the typescript already looks worn through being taken in and out of the Morrison shelter.' She felt little pleasure in its success, which surprised her by being greater than that of its predecessors. 'I hear that it is the most popular of all my books with the general reader,' she wrote, 'a fact not altogether pleasant to me when I think of *Lark Rise*. I have often thought that I have belittled the latter book by writing these light, gossipy little books around it.' She seems not to have realized that in the three books she had produced a work of art of singular excellence, and even when, in 1945, the three were published together as a trilogy, unequivocally establishing her as a writer, her feeling about it was curiously remote. ('It's got an element of real greatness,' Sir Arthur Bryant had written to H. J. Massingham. 'I put it at least as high as Cranford, and I think higher; for under its quiet artistry and truth there's passion and fire.') 'Most flattering, and astonishing,' she commented, when the reviews began to come in. 'Twenty years ago I should have been beside myself with joy, but I am now too old to care much for the bubble reputation.'

She was nearly seventy. Her small success had come too late, and after too long a struggle, to mean much. Even her husband's surprised pride, now genuinely felt, appealed more to her sense of irony than to anything else.

Words as to the inner emotions do not come readily to me [she wrote to H. J. Massingham, who had written a perceptive introduction to her trilogy], for I have led an isolated life mentally and spiritually. . . . The very few people I know personally . . . are not reading people, and though reviewers have been kind and I have had a few letters of appreciation from readers, no one but you has recognized my aims and intentions in writing of that more excellent way of life of our forefathers.

She had still one piece of work to finish, but it was, as she said, like wearily rolling a heavy stone uphill; she felt that she had said what she wanted to say, and would have been glad to write no more if it had not been for the earnest encouragement of her publishers. *Still Glides the Stream* was finished, with fatigue and difficulty, a few weeks before her heart finally failed. She died suddenly, alone in her room, in May 1947.

*   *   *

It has been stated recently, in more than one magazine or newspaper article, that Flora Thompson entered the Roman Catholic Church before she died. This seems not to have been the case. She was attracted to the Catholic Church, had discussed the question with various Catholic friends, and at her death had a tiny rosary and a missal in her possession; but her daughter Winifred, who had a loving and close relationship with her to the end, had no knowledge of any formal 'conversion'. Flora herself, in a letter to her sister May in 1932, made it clear that in spite of a deep spiritual attraction, there were certain matters that she could not accept. May had married a Catholic and 'gone over to Rome', and Flora, receiving the news after a long period of silence, hoped that her sister would 'find rest of soul and peace of mind in your faith. I myself,' she told her, 'stand just where I did in that respect. I have always had a great love for the Catholic religion from a child, and during the eight years I was writing for *The Catholic Fireside* I found many Catholic friends among my readers, including several nuns. I am fairly well instructed in the faith, as I have read many books on it, and of course have attended many services at different times, but I do not suppose I shall ever take the great step you have taken as there are family and other obstacles.' The 'great step', it seems, was never taken. Flora Thompson was buried in Longcross Cemetery in Dartmouth, after a service conducted by the Anglican vicar of St. Barnabas. The gravestone, appropriately, is in the form of an open book, with her name and that of 'her beloved younger son' on its granite pages.

*　　*　　*

There are very few likenesses of Flora Thompson in existence. All her life she showed a great aversion from being photographed, and even her daughter was able to show me only two faded reproductions – one of a modest studio portrait, with smooth-drawn hair and downcast eyes, the other of a snapshot taken in middle age, when her face had acquired its look of withdrawn stoicism. I am allowed, however, to quote from a letter to Miss Winifred Thompson from Mr Arthur Ball, a Peverel member of the early days who had visited Flora Thompson a few months before her death. They had corresponded for many years, but had never met, and Mr Ball's description gives so excellent an impression of her in old age that it tells us, perhaps, more than any photograph.

When we went to Brixham in 1946 [he wrote], and met your mother, my first impression was quite unlike what I expected. Probably because once, in the Peverel days, members' photographs were circulated, and F. T. seemed dark and willowy, the sort of appearance one would expect from her Christian name, very graceful and feminine. I saw a Flora Thompson who was sturdy, resolute, and, with her features chiselled to an expression of remarkable strength, more like the portraits of Marie Curie than anyone else I can think of. Of course the winning, gentle side was there all right, but she seemed to have attained a remarkable independence in her character, and this struck one immediately. And there was that underlying simplicity which the very best natures usually seem to acquire or have as a matter of birthright. When I think of the terrible time she must have had with her illness I am struck too by her remarkable freedom from absorption in self or self-pity – it was all in the other direction, a vital and eager interest in the people she was talking to.

The few people who remember her dwell on this impression of quiet strength, on a warm and direct simplicity, apparently down-to-earth but not without its humour and quick emotion;

also on a hidden, reclusive element in her which held aloof from human contact and led her into mystical sympathy with nature. She once heavily marked a couplet in her copy of Francis Thompson's *To the Dead Cardinal*, and to the end of her life remembered and often returned to it, as though she found in it the poignancy of personal significance.

> Anchorite, who didst dwell
> With all the world for cell.

All this, and more, is to be found in her best work, which for all her reticence is continuously and profoundly self-revealing. Like W. H. Hudson, whom she admired and whom in some ways she resembled, she was secretive about her own life because it afforded little satisfaction. Like his, her essential experience was within.

A Country Calendar

January

It is seldom a New Year finds the earth so bare and brown as it is this January. The severe frost at the beginning of last month finished the work of the autumn gales, destroying the last of the field and garden flowers, flattening the bracken upon the hills, and stripping the woods to the inmost recesses. Even the oaks, which in ordinary seasons hold their dry leaves to whisper in every wind the winter through, have been cleared this year; and the long line of the woods stands stark against the wintry sky.

Clean-swept and empty as the sky appears, it is impossible to watch for more than a moment or two without seeing some bird or other winging its way across it, not wheeling and darting as in summer, for there are no longer any insects in the air to turn out of its way for, but making straight for some determined point upon some definite errand.

One day, against a mild blue sky with floating clouds, a pale-brown hammer-shaped bird hung like a stationary aeroplane. It had the whole dome of sky, from horizon to horizon, to itself;

no other winged creature was in sight, but from every bush and tuffet of the heath beneath came a subdued twittering – a sound as of warnings and notes exchanged, a calling together of friends and advice to 'lie low'.

At the stillest moment a flock of small birds came flying over the brow of a neighbouring hill, sensed the enemy, and dropped like a shower of dark stones to earth. The kestrel hung for another moment, then darted forward and swooped, scarcely seeming to touch the earth, yet rising and sailing off down the wind with a living ball of feathered flesh between its talons.

The bad moment had passed for all but the victim. The whole heath became alive again; linnets flitted and twittered among the bushes; a bullfinch resumed its tugging at a head of thistledown which had lodged in the gorse, and the chaffinches resumed their interrupted journey – minus one.

That particular tragedy of the air was essentially a winter sight. In summer the kestrel does not trouble to hawk such swift creatures as birds, but lives upon such small ground game as mice, lizards and frogs, which its keen eyes can distinguish from the air. Nothing living seems to come amiss to it, and its appetite is enormous, a case being upon record of the craw of a shot kestrel being found to contain no fewer than 70 caterpillars, 24 beetles, a full-grown field-mouse and a leech!

*   *   *

All round the corner of the field where the sheep-fold is the hollies still stand in their untouched crimson. That is remarkable, because on other trees, in more secluded positions, the berries are fast dwindling. Before November was out the birds had begun upon them; had the crop not been so extraordinarily profuse, every tree upon the downs would have been bare by now.

Why they should have begun upon the berries so early is hard to tell, for the weather was mild and other food stores unexhausted, whereas the berries of the holly are supposed to be the bird's emergency ration, only to be drawn upon as a last recourse in very hard times. Perhaps they were tempted, human-wise, by the unusual beauty and abundance. At any rate, it is one more instance that the only infallible rule in bird life is that 'there is no rule'.

The ivy, even more than the holly, is Winter's own plant; for not only does it fruit, but it flowers also, between Michaelmas and Easter. Last of all native plants to flower, and first in the year to fruit, it provides a feast in a meagre time, first for the moths and bees, then for the birds. Right over Christmas, as long as the mealy pollen dust upon the flowers lasts, you will find upon any mild day a host of winged things of all sizes hovering and sipping at it, hurrying and buzzing and tumbling all the time as though they realized how short the day was and how certain the frost at the end of it.

The enemies of the ivy, woodmen, suburban gardeners and the like, greatly exaggerate its harmful influence upon whatever tree may happen to support it. The ivy, according to them, is a kind of vampire of the woods, taking the noble oak or elm into a deadly stranglehold and gradually crushing the life from it.

There is a tincture of truth in this belief. Upon light-limbed, scanty-foliaged trees, such as the birch or the mountain-ash, the growth of the ivy is always harmful, for it is a plant which loves light, and upon trees which do not give sufficient shade to keep it in check it will flourish only too well, and end by overtopping and destroying its unfortunate host. But upon the forest giant, oak or elm, or, more rarely, the beech, it will do no harm, but stand entwined, like wedded king and queen, a joy to all beholders for centuries.

The only other vivid green in the woods this month is furnished by the mosses. This month and next is the flowering time of many of the species, and upon stump and stone and twined amongst the stems of bush and briar are fairy forests of emerald plumes, some with hairy dark-red flower-cups, quite discernible by the unassisted eye; others dusted with yellow bloom, a buttercup meadow to each square inch, if our human sight were but subtle enough to discern it.

As I stepped very softly and silently over a carpet of it in the depth of the pinewood, I came face to face with a perching mass of yellowy-white feathers, almost on a level with my eyes. It was a barn-owl, and was, I think, asleep when I first came upon it; but even when it opened first one, then the other, of its round wide eyes, it seemed to look through rather than at me, and did not offer to stir.

It looked so quaint, sitting and blinking there close to the tree-trunk, opening and shutting its eyes alternately, swaying and recovering its balance the while, like an elderly lady taking a surreptitious doze in the midst of the family circle, that at first I was amused; but when I saw how wet and draggled its plumage was, and how weakly it swayed backwards and forwards upon its low perch, I knew that misery and exhaustion had made it so tame, and was sorry for it.

The poor bird was probably homeless, for the workmen had been busy close by all the week and had brought down, amongst other trees, an immense hollow oak trunk, which had been the headquarters of its kindred from time immemorial.

I turned aside to look at it. Very melancholy in its fall and decay, it lay across the mossy path, a mere shell of a thing. After its life of a thousand years or more, it must have stood stark and rotting in the earth for centuries, for all round the platform of its pollarded head were little terraced gardens, bird planted, springing with ferns and mosses and honeysuckle and briar festoons, the latter so long established they fell almost to the earth, and draped the naked trunk like a head of hair. The secret chambers where the owls had nested were open to the day; wads of hay and wool and feathers were strewn upon the earth around. Amongst them were more ghastly relics, masses of small bones, pellets of fur, and the almost intact skeleton of some small animal.

Why the particular owl I saw skulking near had not found for itself a new shelter is rather a puzzle. Probably it had been injured in some way, perhaps by a carelessly flung stone, for, sleeping as it would by day, it would almost certainly be at home when the housebreakers arrived. Of its companions in misfortune there was no trace; but, as I took my last look at heath and sky to-night, there seemed to be a strangely human note of trouble and bereavement in the long 'Too-woo-whoot!' which sounded so lingeringly upon the frosty air.

*   *   *

This morning, a forgotten milk-can brought me out of bed early. Afterwards, in spite of the rimey tang in the air, I stood at my cottage gate, and was glad of it.

Nothing out of doors remained quite as it had been. The garden bushes were transformed into snowy crouching animals; trees and hedgerows, with their strange new foliage of frost spicules, were rounded again to the fullness of mid-summer; the heather, blooming miraculously with icy bells, muffled the sharp outlines of the heath to a furry softness.

In the stillness and isolation of dawn every sound was magnified. The birds, whirring from the ivy, brought down a tinkling shower of frost crystals; the feet of the sparrows hopping upon the corrugated iron of the tool-shed roof played a tiny tune. Even the crowing of roosters, far away upon a distant farm, sounded so near and shrill that an old fox, padding stealthily by the garden hedge on his way home to bed, stopped stock still and pricked up his ears to listen.

Later in the morning it was fascinating to walk upon the heath in a small enclosed world a dozen paces in diameter.

In a drift of dead leaves beneath a holly a wren was busily employed grubbing for insects. She paused for a moment, one tiny claw uplifted, to regard me in bright-eyed interrogation; then, evidently concluding she had nothing to fear, she resumed her thorough investigation of the leaves.

Presently another of her family came zigzagging up with that weak-winged flight peculiar to wrens. Perching himself upon a bracken-frond, he uttered two small sweet notes 'Cheep! Cheep!' as though to say: 'I may be half-frozen, but I am not too down-hearted to sing!'

In certain parts of England, I am told, the wren is a very shy and timid bird, and naturalists in those places attribute it to the age-long persecution those birds have been subjected to there. To avenge some legendary sin of a wren, men and boys, until quite recent years, would hunt the poor little birds and bear strings of their tiny bodies around in triumph upon St. Stephen's Day. A strange way of celebrating the feast of a.saint who himself was hunted and persecuted!

In Hampshire the wren has been more fortunate. From remotest times it has shared with the robin the distinction of being regarded as a sacred bird, and such doggerel rhymes as:

'The robins and the wrens
Be the Almighty's special friends.
Who kills them shall thrive never,
But all his luck shall sever,'

or, more tersely:

'Who slays a robin or a wren
Shall never prosper, boys nor men,'

have helped to protect them from the ignorant and to endear them to the more enlightened. In consequence the wren, although a much rarer bird, is almost as trustingly unafraid of man in the south as the robin is; and both are equally beloved.

*　　*　　*

When I reached the summit of the hill this morning there was no sight or sound of any life excepting my own. The air there was clearer and sharper; the crest of the hill seemed to rise like a pine-crowned island from a white and woolly sea. A pigeon cleaving the waves a dozen yards down appeared from above rather to swim than fly. At intervals from the misty sea rose the dark plumes of pine-tops, like other islands, but they were far below and infinitely remote.

Up there, cut off by the white enveloping mist, one seemed to be entirely out of the world. The wind, never absolutely silent where there are pine trees, had sunk to a sigh; the long-drawn wailing of new-born lambs from the valley fold came faintly as from another sphere. To listen intently was to hear the dull roar of silence.

Yet, emptied as the place was of life, there were signs of recent occupancy. The dark, root-threaded earth beneath the trees was strewn all about with freshly-nibbled pine-husks; some time within the last day or two the squirrels had been out and busy.

This in itself was nothing remarkable, for we had fine days during the week-end, and the squirrel is a light sleeper; every time the sun shines for more than an hour together he is out of his winter bed and taking a meal where he can. The puzzle in this case was why this particular squirrel should have taken the trouble to climb several hundred feet of rough sandstone hillside, when there were quite as fine pine-kernels to be had close to the door of his winter quarters in the wood below.

As I stood meditating upon squirrels and their food fads, there was a tremendous beating of wings through the mist, and a large and heavy flyer flapped upwards and sank into a branch above my head. It was a cock pheasant, a bird of magnificent plumage, the crimson and iridescent green of his head shading into the purple shot with gold of his back and wings. Contrary to my expectations, he did not take to the air again at the sight of me, but sat regarding me with round, unwinking eyes and balancing himself upon a branch absurdly slender for his weight in so listless a manner that I concluded he must have been injured in some way.

All day yesterday in the coverts about the heath the guns were popping. A big shoot was on, and the whole male population were in attendance as beaters; so it is quite likely that my friend of the hill-top may have been a slightly wounded survivor. What his feelings were after rising so high and flying so far only to find another of the hated humans in possession can be imagined; but he was too spent to go farther, and sat almost within arm's length, swaying and recovering himself upon his precarious perch, eyeing me with dull resentment, and, no doubt, wishing I would soon depart.

As he had lived through the night and had still the power of flight, it is probable that he would recover. Some survivors of a shoot are not so fortunate, but only manage to fly from the range of the guns to bleed slowly to death in some sequestered copse.

February

When the Romans named this second month of the year they had in mind their own cleansing festival of Februia, but the name is just as applicable to the cleansing and purifying process in nature which is so silently, yet surely, proceeding now.

As a good housewife sets her house in order before a feast, so the earth is cleansed and renovated in readiness for the floral feast of spring. The rains of February wash away corruption and decay; her frosts and keen winds harden and purify. The earth no longer seems asleep; there is a stirring of new life abroad, of promise and anticipation. The air is still cold, the woods leafless, the hillside bleak and bare: but beneath the dark mould a thousand young green plants push upward, and the buds upon the bare boughs burn reddish-purple at the tips and thicken with promise.

Upon St. Valentine's Day this year I found the first primroses. Just a crumpled rosette of soft green and three pale blooms; little enough in themselves, but how precious as a harbinger.

There was magic in them. All around was winter: the tiny plot between the mossed oak-roots where they grew was hard with frost, the dead leaves which sheltered them crisped with rime, and the sky between the bare boughs overhead glinted like steel. Even as I banked them round again a few icy splinters of hail edged in, but beneath the sheltering hedgerow those three pallid flowers had power to create a miniature spring. Immediately to the inward eye sprang a vision of lanes and meadows starred with their fellows, of bluebell copses, June gardens and August poppy fields, of all the sweet pageant of which they were the earliest forerunners.

*　　*　　*

All round the ivied bank of the garden hedge the snowdrops hang their delicate heads, daring the wet and cold in their own miraculous way.

There is a mystic loveliness about the snowdrop, rising as it does from the dark and sodden earth, so pure and frail and spotless. It is everybody's flower, beloved of all in town and country alike, for is it not the first signal of all to tell us the year has begun, that soon the spring will be here and the flowers spring and the song-birds carol again?

It is quite possible that England owes the introduction of the snowdrop to St. Francis, for although botanists have surmised its importation by the Romans, there is no proof of it; and what more natural than that some gardening friar under orders for England should take his last look round the Italian garden he was leaving and add to the selection of vegetable and pot-herb roots a few bulbs of the snowdrop, which, planted in the newly-made garden of the English monastery, would serve as a memento both of the dearly loved founder of his Order and as a symbol of the pure grace and simplicity of that Lady Poverty whose servant he was?

*　　*　　*

One family of birds, and one alone, is both flocking and nesting this month. In the rookery it is spring already. Every day as I pass beneath the tall wind-tossed elms where their home is I see the nests taking form and increasing. The noise and bustle the birds make over it is simply deafening; they seem never to take a twig or put it in place without a consultation of the whole tribe. But, unlike most great talkers, the rooks are good workers too, and their rough bundle of twigs will be in place and young birds within it before the hedgerow birds have put straw to straw.

Last year there were young birds in the rookery by the end of February, and some years they are said to have been earlier still. It may be so from immemorial custom, and Gilbert White may have had this particular settlement in mind when he wrote:

'Sooth'd by the genial warmth, the cawing rook
Anticipates the spring—'

for his own parish of Selborne is only six miles away: and, standing as this group of tall elms does by the roadside, he must often have passed beneath it.

It is easy to imagine him, the very first of English nature writers, with his powdered hair and sober clerical garb, jogging along the road on his fat grey mare, stopping beneath the elms to gaze upwards at the noisy black birds about their business of nest-making, lingering, perhaps, to jot down a date or caress some early spray of blackthorn with his riding-whip; then jogging homeward away over the heath, the most sober and modest, yet happiest, of men.

*   *   *

It is amusing to hear the starlings imitate the cawing of the rooks. These birds are back in possession of the cottage garden and roof again. All the winter they have wheeled about the fields in flocks, sinking at night into the reed-beds or bushes with a hubbub of chattering and surging of wings that only ceased with the withdrawal of the last gleam of daylight. Now they have separated, and the contingent to which this roof belongs are promenading the garden paths, surveying everything with sharp glances, like a human family inspecting their property after wintering abroad.

Like human travellers, too, they have brought the newest and smartest fashion back; the shining black of their plumage is shot with fine metallic lustres of purple and green, each separate feather pointed with a pearl. Only the young birds of last year are still rusty and dingy; their time will come later in the spring.

Travelling has not improved their manners; they do not hesitate to dig up a bulb the moment they see a green spike appear, or tear the crocus buds to see what colour they are going to be. Between one piece of mischief and another they make premature attempts at nest-building. More than a fortnight ago one adventurous couple began to place straws in a junction of the water-spout, and, though the heavy rain soon washed their foundations away, they have been at it spasmodically ever since.

For a few hours in the middle of the day the scolding and chattering cease, and the whole flock fly off in a body to the sheepfold a few fields away. There they spend their time riding sedately upon the broad woolly backs and digging into the deep fleeces for insects. It is comical to see the critical, deeply-learned air with which they perform this operation, black heads poised to one side, cunning eyes gazing abstractedly into the distance, while the sheep, as though unaware of their visitors' ministrations, go stolidly on munching their turnips or tending their lambs.

Other birds as well as the starlings are attracted to the warmth and comfort of the lambing-fold. Wagtails run in and out between the legs of the sheep; sparrows and chaffinches peck briskly in the straw, while the robin, constant companion of man, sings from the hurdles in return for his share of the shepherd's lonely meals.

At a more respectful distance hover the one solitary pair of crows which has grown old in this area. At other times of the year they are seldom seen away from the heath; but at lambing-time they are always to be found round the fold lying in wait for offal, or, failing that, a share of the sweet, juicy turnips which are thrown to the sheep.

Shepherd hates the sight of these 'black gentry', as he calls them, for there is an old superstition that, when crows hang around the fold, there will soon be a dead lamb to feed them.

'Not that I takes any stock of such trash,' he assures me, 'for it stands to reason they can't scent a dead lamb whilst it's still alive. Besides, as long as th' shepherd knows his job and th' weather isn't too hard on him, there won't be many dead lambs about – not if th' sky was black wi' they gentry! But you know how 'tis, an old sayin's an old sayin', and it sort o' works itself into th' brain like, even when all the time you med not believe it at heart. Moreover, them crows be ugly, sooty-looking varmint, and I can't say that I cares for th' look of 'em.'

*   *   *

The hedgerow is so crammed with interest that it would provide studies for more hours than there are in the day. It is one of the old double hedgerows which, thickened with trees and twined about with creepers, used to be a common feature in English scenery. Such hedgerows used to be, and still are where they have been retained, both gardens for every kind of wild-flower and sanctuaries for birds and the lesser animals. Along the banks, between the double hedges, children have made small, well-defined paths, leading, for those small enough to explore them, to many a secret bower entwined with honey-suckle or wild-hop. Between the roots of the hawthorns the earliest violets are always found, and later in the year there are primroses and bluebells, with nuts and blackberries to follow.

Such hedgerows are gradually disappearing, together with the small, irregularly-shaped fields they bounded. The use of the tractor calls for square, open spaces. The modern, scientific farmer does not approve of such waste of space and harbourage for 'vermin'. In highly-farmed districts, the old, untidy, picturesque hedgerow is doomed. In districts such as this, where the soil is poor and the farming casual, they may still be

seen, the hawthorns and hazels which compose them im-
memorably old, the lanes which run beneath sunk six or eight
feet by the traffic of centuries.

The chief glory of these hedgerows in February is the hazel.
Above every lane and along each field-side the catkin tosses,
grey in dull weather, gold in sunshine, turning against the dark
woods to a greenish smoke.

The hazel was formerly regarded as a sacred tree. A hazel rod
was the insignia of Mercury. Armed with it, he was supposed to
walk the earth, and those whom he deigned to touch with it
received the power of putting their thoughts into words. It is
very likely that the veneration with which the ancient Irish
regarded the hazel was founded upon this belief. With them it
was the sacred tree which grew over Connla's Well, and the fruit
which fell from it were the Nuts of Knowledge, giving wisdom
and inspiration.

One instance of the mystical regard in which the hazel was
held survived down to our own day. A few years ago it was a not
uncommon country sight to see the water-diviner, hazel rod in
hand, walking up and down garden or field prospecting for
secret underground springs. The rod was a thin, forked branch,
held horizontally, and, when water was found, it would rise to a
perpendicular position against the bearer's chest. Modern water
finders, I am told, regard the hazel-rod as inessential insignia, or
in other cases replace it with a scientific instrument. But, even
so, the most advanced admit that an inexplicable power exists in
certain favoured people which enables them to tell without
conscious calculation the exact locality of underground water-
stores: so that, even though

> 'The sacred hazel's bloom is shed,
> The Nuts of Knowledge harvested,'

something is yet left to us of mystery and marvel.

March

We have become so accustomed to wishing each other a Happy New Year a week after Christmas that the two festivals have become inseparable in our minds, and it seems strange to us to think that our ancestors kept New Year's Day upon March 25th. This morning Nature kept just such a New Year's Day as our ancestors must have known. Short, sudden showers, with sunshine between, had left the whole outer world clean-washed and glistening.

Seen from the heath above, the valley fields made a chessboard of brown and green – brown for the long-ridged ploughed lands where the rooks were busily promenading, green for the wind-ruffled wheat-fields. At the bottom of the slope a waving line of emerald, like a broad highway across the chequer, marked the course of the stream. Higher up, against the green of a sunny meadow, a number of white dots showed that the lambs with their mothers were out from the fold. In one part of the field the dots had thickened to a crowd, and, although at that height it was impossible to distinguish movement, anyone at all acquainted with the ways of lambs could tell what was going on.

Just at that spot there is a shallow trench, the dry bed of some disused waterway, and every day the lambs gather together there to practise leaping. It is amusing to watch them huddled in

48

a woolly heap upon the bank waiting for one to take the lead. For a long time not one of them will dare it, and they crowd and jostle and dig into each others' fleeces with blunt, black nozzles. In the end, the first to go over is usually precipitated; losing its footing, it jumps, clears the trench, and is followed one by one by the others. Then, after an interval for refreshments, they gather again at the same spot, and the process is repeated.

The strange part of the proceeding is that the lambs of this year are doing exactly the same thing as lambs have done in the same field for countless generations. In other fields and upon other farms it is the same: wherever lambs are turned loose they quickly find a declivity, and the leaping game begins. If the ground in a field is perfectly flat, they practise their leaping upon the level.

The shepherd calls it 'doin' their exercises', and believes it strengthens their legs. No doubt it does; but more learned, although not necessarily wiser, men than he hark back to prehistoric times to account for it. Long ago, they say, the sheep was a wild animal living in rocky and mountainous countries, where, in the course of a day, it had many streams and chasms to clear and precipices to avoid. Under such circumstances the lamb could not be trusted far from its mother's side until it had learned to leap; therefore leaping was its first lesson, and although the sheep has been domesticated for centuries, and smooth pastures have been its home in this country, this primitive need has survived in the form of an instinct.

*   *   *

Above the fringe of celandine in the lane the blackthorn is breaking into bloom. Very chilly and fragile the thin white petals look against the dark and thorny background of the tree. As I stood reaching up for some sprays for my vases today, the earth a few yards from my feet began to heave and billow in a long zig-zag line, as though a small and very local earthquake was in progress. Soon the brown earth showed above the grass for a couple of yards or more. I stood breathless, hoping to catch a glimpse of whatever small creature was burrowing there; but some small involuntary movement must have revealed my presence, for suddenly all was silence.

No doubt the upheaval was caused by a shrew, for in a clump of violet leaves a dozen yards away lay a dead one, its long snout caked with dried blood and its reddish-brown velvety coat muddied and blood-bedabbled. Perhaps it had perished in one of the tremendous battles to the death the male shrew wages during the breeding season, and the tunnelling was the work of the victorious rival prospecting for a home for himself and the disputed lady.

Just beyond our sight such small dramas are played out every day and hour now. A hundred times we pass down the lane without catching so much as a glimpse of even the tip of a tail; then, one day, we stand, perfectly silent, to shelter from the rain, and, after a minute or two of silence, all manner of small noises become audible. The leaves rustle and the grass; there are tiny footfalls upon the earth, hurried scampering around tree-trunks, even a peep of bright eyes, a glimpse of bared white teeth for the very patient, while, all the time, the birds flit past with bright, confident glances, as though to say '*We* are friends. *We* have no need to skulk. We are loved, and we know it!'

Yet, seldom as one sees the shrew, or any of the wild, shy tribe to which it belongs, there are creatures about us far shyer and more alien to man. Upon a stretch of heath about a mile from my door the adder was once so common as to gain the name of 'Viper's Lease' for the spot. The adder is supposed to abound there still; children avoid the place on that account, and the gypsies do not camp there. But, although I cross it almost every day the summer through, only twice in three years have I caught sight of one.

The first time it was but the glimpse of a silvery brown streak darting from before my feet into the heather. I just had time to distinguish the dark diamond markings down the back, and it was gone. The second time I was walking along the top of one of the high turf walls that mark the boundary of the Crown lands here, when, several feet below, on a low bank of turf among the heather, I saw two adders basking together in the sun.

I was so far above, with such a gulf of thickly-growing gorse between, that for the moment I quite forgot my unreasoning dislike of reptiles, and stood still and watched them. As in the case of the shrew, some slight movement betrayed me: they slipped over the side of the bank and away, fortunately for my nerves in the opposite direction to that in which I was standing. Nor, in spite of my knowledge that the adder is far more afraid of man than man is of him, and has never been known to use its poison fang unless attacked at close quarters, or accidentally trodden upon, did I seek that portion of the heath again for the rest of the summer.

*   *   *

New life is everywhere. At every sunny angle of the hedgerows the buds are bursting into a light veil of green; new grass springs in the meadows, fresh rushes beside the stream; things in the garden move so quickly one can almost 'see them grow'. The grass-margin beneath the roadside hedge is a garden set with a thousand tiny, unconsidered wild things, speedwell and wild forget-me-not and the meek, innocent-looking star-of-Bethlehem. Farther down, from the moisture of the ditch, springs the strong lush green of the cuckoo-pint. Soon the children will be searching the long, broad, lily-of-the-valley-shaped leaves for 'lords and ladies', as they call the fleshy pointing finger the plant puts out in spring.

These fleshy, pale red or cream-coloured spikes are not the true flower, but only an insect-attracting device to secure fertilization. The real flower clusters round the base of the spike, a mere dusting of infinitesimal mealy-coloured florets. As soon as the seed is set, spike and leaf alike die down and the whole plant vanishes, to reappear later in the year as a cluster of brilliant orange-scarlet berries at the tip of a single stalk. Not one observer in a hundred connects these bright, evil-looking berries with the cuckoo-pint of spring. In Hampshire they are known simply as 'poison-berries', and no country child will lay so much as a finger upon them.

They *are* highly poisonous; but then, so are the leaf and spike as well. So it would be interesting, if it were possible, to trace back to its source this superstitious shrinking from the berries only. Perhaps some bold experimenter, some Ancient Briton or man of the Stone Age, partook of the tempting-looking fruit and perished, and through the centuries his fate had faded from memory to tradition, and from tradition to instinctive repulsion.

* * *

Very soon we shall all be listening for the cuckoo; but this year I am before the times, for I have already seen one. Seen, but not heard, for the one I saw six weeks ago when the snow still lay upon the ground was a caged one. I had called at a cottage to buy eggs, and the woman of the house showed it to me with great pride. She had heard, she said, that I was interested in such things, that I hung out cocoanuts for the tits, and bribed small boys to refrain from poking hedgehogs; but this was a sight she was sure I had never seen.

I had not, and was glad of it. True, I had once seen a seagull cooped far inland, in a rabbit hutch; but that, in spite of clipped wings, preserved a smouldering spark of its own wild nature, and appeared a jocund creature compared to the puffed-up, shivering ball of misery in the cage by the window.

What an outrage it seemed! A cuckoo in a cage! Such a small cage, too, intended for a skylark, or, at most, a thrush. The long spread-out rudder of a tail protruded through the wires. Its eyes were glazed dully, it leaned sideways as it stood.

Its mistress was hurt and a little offended at my protestations. No mortal bird upon this earth, she said, was ever better treated. The children 'thought gold' of it, and fed it before feeding themselves at meal times; when it would peck at anything, that was, for lately it had been in the sulks, and they had had to cram it like cramming a turkey. But they meant to keep it alive somehow, for the schoolmaster had promised them half a crown each if they still had it when the wild ones came. There was a saying that a caged cuckoo could not live the winter through, and, if this one did, he was going to write to the papers about it. Somebody at Birdwood had kept one till November once, but none had ever lived right over Christmas before in these parts.

She was surprised to find I didn't like the idea of it: several people had been up from the village specially to see it. 'Quite a curiosity,' the curate had called it, and he knew what he was talking about, without a doubt!

Think it minded? She was sure it didn't. Why, it sat there day after day as contented as a lamb. It had fluttered and beaten itself a bit at first, but that was the 'urge' inside it; all overseas birds had that when it came to flitting time and they were kept back!

For one wild moment I thought of outbidding the schoolmaster, but recollected in time that to do so would only be for it to exchange one prison for another, for to have freed it at such a season would have meant certain death. The only other thing I could think of was to present it with a roomier cage; but, while I was deciding whether it should be one of the circular wicker ones, known here as 'magpie cages', or something really substantial in wood and wire, news came that neither was any longer needed. A neighbour's cat had solved the problem by toppling its present one and destroying the inmate.

*   *   *

The swallows have not returned yet. Every morning I expect to see them preening themselves upon the roof and darting hither and thither for wet mud to mend their nests with, but still they delay. In the meantime their place in the evening sky is taken by that quaint and eerie understudy of theirs, the bat. Every year at about this time the three or four which have haunted the heath upon mild nights since the frost broke up are increased to a score or more.

Where they come from is a mystery, for there is no old barn or church tower at all near, but there they are, swooping and tumbling against the darkening sky, only their queer, flittering wing movement and shrill mousey squeak distinguishing them from the graceful birds they contrive to caricature in the half-light.

As soon as the swallows arrive the bats will decrease in numbers; so perhaps it is a case of supply and demand – the insects are hatched out by the sun, and the bats suddenly spring from nowhere to enjoy a supper of them; then the swallows come, assert their superior right, and the bats retire.

No animal is more social in its hibernating habits than the bat. Not only do they sleep in companies, but they actually cling together in their sleep. The sexton of an old Sussex church once told me that a few years ago, when his tower was under repair, a large and interlocked mass of the sleeping creatures was discovered by a workman beneath the leads. They were hanging by their claws, heads downward, and the man detached them and sent them down in the wooden cage used to haul his tools up and down. And there, as my friend related, they lay upon a grave in the sun, 'for all the world like a girt bundle o' rusty old leather'.

The workmen wanted to destroy them, but the sexton objected, for what, as he said, is a belfry without a few bats about it? So, one by one they came to life in the warmth, and flapped off around the tower and away, looking, as he repeated, 'most darn'd unnater'l in the daylight!'

*   *   *

The pools here are no longer small mirrors for blue sky and white cloud, for the frog-spawn has appeared upon the surface and tinted even the water with the prevailing green. If this spreading jelly-like substance is examined it will be found to consist of long ropes of eggs matted together into a glutinous mass. In the centre of each egg the black pinspot which represents the embryo frog is already visible, and in a month's time the brown water will teem with thousands of wriggling tadpoles. The immense number of these eggs, even upon the surface of one small pool, is so amazing that it might well be supposed that a new plague of frogs was threatened; but not one in a hundred of the five to ten thousand eggs each female frog has been estimated to lay yearly will survive beyond the tadpole stage; probably not half that number will advance so far, for every carnivorous creature in and about the water is ready to prey upon the immature frog at every stage of its development.

The frog, for his part, has no right to complain, for he, too, loves an animal diet, and preys upon such things as caterpillars, worms, and grubs. If these substantial delicacies fail he does not disdain smaller fare, and spends many an hour lurking unseen in some crevice and thrusting out his long tongue to catch gnats or other small flies. From a small winged insect's point of view, this long tongue of the frog is a fearsome weapon: for not only is it long and lissom, with the power of darting far, but it is covered with a sticky secretion which acts like the treacle on a fly-paper. If his appetite demands more substantial fare he hunts it in the usual way, then, seizing worm or caterpillar with his jaws, thrusts it down his throat with his forelegs.

The clothing question does not trouble the frog at all: as soon as he outgrows one skin he peels it off and finds a new one beneath. At such times the old skin splits down the back and the animal wriggles out of it, drawing it over his forelegs and head as a child does a rather tight jersey. That done, he makes a neat bundle of the discarded skin and swallows it!

*   *   *

I have never seen a kingfisher's nest; never even met anyone who had a friend who had a friend who had seen one, so I cannot describe it from first, second, or even third-hand experience. In former times the nesting of the kingfisher, or the halcyon, as it was called then, was supposed to be one of the romances of nature. About Christmas time the hen was believed to put out to sea on her nest, as on a raft, and during the time of her incubating such a tranquillizing spell was exercised that the very wind and waters were stilled.

Modern naturalists, following Truth even more assiduously than Beauty, and often finding them one at the end of the pursuit, have tracked the kingfisher to its real home, and given us facts instead of poetry. They tell us the bird makes its home underground, usually in the banks of the stream which forms its fishing-ground. A neat oval opening leads into a tunnel two or more feet long, and that, in turn, leads into a circular nesting-chamber, where the pure white eggs repose on a bed of disgorged fish-bones.

It is not difficult to account for this secret underground home, for the brilliant colours of the hen brooding on a nest in the open would expose her and her young to all sorts of dangers; but, none the less, it is a striking thought that the flash of gem-like light we call a kingfisher should be bred in darkness.

April

To no part of England does spring come with more enchanting loveliness than to these secluded valleys beneath the southern hills.

In the woods it is primrose time, and primrose time upon the Hampshire and Sussex borders is a pale yellow floodtide. Every copse is a primrose copse, and every lane a primrose path.

The scent of the primrose is the very breath of April. It is less a perfume than a fragrance, a sweet, fresh, wholesome scent, instinct with honesty and goodness, yet at the same time full of delicate suggestions.

It is strange how closely the sense of smell is associated with the memory. A whiff from a passing haycart in a city street; the scent of a flower in the hand of a passer-by; the leather of old bookbindings – even such odours as those of bread from the oven, mackintosh, home-spun tweed, or cigar smoke may be potent to unlock the memory and transport the mind a hundred miles or a score of years.

For me the scent or sight of a primrose holds this magic. I never see, smell, or think of them but I am carried back at once to a day in the last April before the war. It was a day of warm sun and sunshine showers, and I stood alone upon one of the low wooded hills of the Isle of Wight. All around and as far as I could see were primroses – primroses springing from the turf at my feet, breaking into foam at the edge of the clearing, and yellowing the land right down to the little grassy fields which fringed the cliffs.

A light shower had just fallen, and the scent of the flowers was indescribably fresh and sweet. As the sun reappeared a cuckoo began to call from a tree close by, and, as I straightened my back from my flower-picking to listen, I saw a rainbow spanning the steeples of Ryde in a perfect arch.

It was one of those rare moments which live in the memory for ever.

*   *   *

Lovely as the wild-flowers are, and pleasant as it is to pick and carry them, the chief interest now upon a country walk is the bird-life. After each shower, a perfect chorus of song arises; a thousand blended notes ringing from every copse and hedge-row, until the whole world of wet green appears to be bubbling over with joy.

Some of our birds sing right on through the rain, the blackbird is one and the thrush another. To shelter beneath a tree and listen to their clear, strong voices, while the rain patters down and the whole outside world turns misty, is one of the greatest joys of an April walk. But both the blackbird's and the thrush's are old and familiar voices. The thrush began singing this year before our mild January was out, and the blackbird joined in a week or two later; they dominate the chorus still, but there are other and new voices to fill in the pauses – voices which have been silent for six or eight months.

During the last fortnight, many of our overseas migrants have returned. The first fortnight in April brings the first rush of returning life to our shores; and, strange to say, the very earliest to dare our inclement climate are the smallest and weakest of the wanderers. First of all to appear are the different members of the warbler family, light, slender, delicately built birds with sweet, tender little voices and the shyest of manners. How such atoms of feather and bone accomplish the thousands of miles they journey twice a year over sea and land is a mystery.

For over a week now, the chiff-chaff has been back, flitting from bush to bush with sweet musical repetitions of its own name. 'Chiff, chaff! Chiff, chaff!' it goes, as though to say: 'I know I am no great singer, as the thrush is, but I have a sweet, tiny voice of my own, and can use it to fill in the pauses for your delight.'

Its song is the plainest and simplest of any bird's that can be called a singer at all. Just the two syllables of its own name, varied by the tremulous rise and fall of its voice. All day long it flits, a tiny brown and yellow ghost of a bird, through the wet green of the woodlands, its note rather a musical exclamation than a song. So it will go on, uttering its sweet, tremulous repetition of its own name, long after the summer heat has silenced most of the other birds.

The nest of the chiff-chaff is built with a tiny dome-shaped roof, and is a wonder of feather-lined warmth and softness. Often it is placed sideways amongst the stumps or roots of bushes; and, perhaps on account of that position and the tiny lid-like door, is called a 'wood oven' by the country children.

The other warblers which return from overseas about the same time as the chiff-chaff are the closely related wood-wren and the willow-wren. The three birds bear a strong resemblance to each other; each of them has the same slender build, the dark, brownish back and wings with a creamy-yellow underside; their haunts are the same, too, and they have all the same shy, fugitive manner of flitting rather than flying. There is a slight difference in the plumage if the observer can manage to get close enough to detect it, for the wood-wren, alone of the three, has yellow markings in the brown of its wings and tail feathers, while the back of the willow-warbler is a soft chestnut in colour, instead of the greenish-brown of the chiff-chaff and wood-wren; but the shy, secret flittings of the birds makes such observation difficult, and the only reliable means of distinction is the song of each bird.

The willow-warbler, or willow-wren as it is oftener called, is the most accomplished singer of the three. Pausing in its search in the tree-bark for insects, this tiny, quiet-tinted songster will poise itself upon some topmost bough, and, head thrown back and throat quivering, pour out a strain which is tender, silvery clear, and very lovely within its limits.

Very different is the song of its cousin, the wood-wren. There is no finished perfection there, even on the smallest scale; far from recognizing its own limitations and keeping within them, as the willow-warbler does, it always appears to be striving to capture something just beyond its range. Its strain is, indeed, rather a sweet, tremulous quaver than a song. First come a few hurried notes, then a long, shivering trill, ending in a break, as though the singer gave up the attempt in despair. The sight of it as it sings gives the beholder the impression of almost painful effort, for not only its throat and wings, but its whole body seems straining to put into sound feelings which will not be expressed. But in spite of the frustrated desire in it, the song of the little wood-wren is one of the sweetest of April's voices; it is one with the tender and delicate things of the season – eggs warm and blue in the nest, purple-veined wood-sorrel and violets hidden in their own deep leaves.

*   *   *

This morning amongst the finely-cut leaves and rose-flushed petals moved an incongruous mound of rusty prickles. It was a late riser of the hedgehog family, who had waited until the earth was well warmed and aired before venturing from its winter 'cubby-hole' beneath the upturned roots of a fallen pine: It moved slowly and stiffly, a few dead leaves still impaled upon its quills, regarding me out of small 'piggish' eyes, without the least attempt to quicken its pace.

Had my dog been with me he would have sprung upon it with a yell, only to encounter a tightly rolled ball of prickly spines. As it was, the creature knew instinctively it had nothing to fear, and plodded on towards the banks of the pool, intent, no doubt, upon a nourishing diet of slugs and snails to repair the ravages of fasting.

In the country there is a prejudice against this harmless animal. Otherwise kind-hearted boys will stone them to death, or use them as footballs without compunction. Gamekeepers dislike them, too; and I once saw a whole hecatomb of five lying dead together. Even the gipsies, although they do not share the prejudice, pursue them just as eagerly, for in their menu the hedgehog figures as a choice dish, and country people say they are able to locate them by the smell.

The method of cooking is primitive and curious. The dead hedgehog, with prickly coat still on, is encased in clay and roasted in the hot embers of a wood fire. When the joint is done, clay, prickles and skin all shell off together, leaving the meat inside clean, juicy, and done to a turn. Those who have tasted it say that the flesh of the hedgehog is superior to almost any other meat or game, somewhat resembling chicken, but more luscious.

Other people prefer it alive, and the hedgehog as a pet is said to be most affectionate and amenable. It is quite easy to tame, and, if kept in a garden or greenhouse, will well earn its saucer of milk by keeping down slugs and other pests. I once saw one which responded quite readily to a whistled call, creeping out from the bushes and lying flat while its quills were stroked backwards by its mistress's foot.

Amongst the bushes where I sheltered from a shower I found a nest with two tiny sky-blue, breast-warm eggs in it. The gentle warmth of them took me back in a moment to just such a day in my childhood when, playing truant, I came upon a pheasant's nest. In it were thirteen eggs near to hatching. In the shells were tiny pinprick holes and I heard – or was it imagination? – little voices within crying 'Cheep! Cheep!' I felt so sorry for them, pent up on such a day, that I sat down forthwith amongst the moss and ferns and hatched out the whole lot by peeling the shells from them! Afterwards I was horribly afraid lest I should be found out and sent to prison as a poacher; but the next morning they were alive and well and following their mother through the bushes in fine style.

*   *   *

As yet the elms are without a vestige of leaf, and will be at least for the next month; but they have stolen a march upon other trees, apparently more forward, by getting the business of flowering and fruiting over by the middle of March. The winged seed-cases, consisting of two flat yellowish-green discs pressed together with the seed between, are formed to float upon the air. The wind carries them great distances, and if one in ten so distributed struck root and grew the whole country would soon become a vast elm-forest. Probably not one in ten thousand will come to maturity. Birds will eat them, water rot them; they will be choked as seedlings or uprooted as weeds; but, by scattering elm-seed as lavishly as though only that one form of vegetable life mattered, Nature has done her part.

Fluttering upon the air with the elm-seed this morning was one white butterfly – the first of the season. It flew weakly – for its wings were still damp and crumpled – poising first upon one leaf or flower, then another, until it gathered strength to rise to the height of the garden hedge, and soar off upon the short adventure of life.

61

It had chosen its birth county well. In these parts we look upon the first butterfly with delight as the harbinger of spring; in some localities it is regarded as a bringer of bad luck, and must be pursued and killed if misfortune is to be averted.

Once, in the Midlands, I remember seeing just such an early visitant as mine of today causing quite a mild commotion in a village street. It was Friday morning, and the old people of the place were intent upon drawing their old-age pensions while the sunny weather lasted. As the butterfly fluttered past, first one, then another old man or woman would set down basket and umbrella to grab at the insect as it floated above them. One or two of the more active even attempted a chase, but the butterfly had easily the best of it, and dipped suddenly over a high wall, leaving a group of flushed and panting old folks to laugh together over their temporary loss of dignity.

May

On May Day, as I gathered branches to decorate my kitchen for the 'Mayers', I came upon an unsuspected thrush's nest in the garden hedge. The mother-bird was sitting, and did not stir at the sight of me as I parted the boughs. I was, in fact, far more embarrassed than she was, for her bright, wise, patient eyes were so human I felt as though I had stumbled into a lady's chamber, and felt an impulse to apologize as I hurriedly drew her green curtain again.

May

The old May Day customs are fading here from men's memory. Twenty years ago, when I was a child, there were great doings. Every child in the village school rose early on that day and donned its simple finery and, garland in hand, went in procession from house to house singing May songs.

Then a famous artist came to live there. Our crude rejoicings did not satisfy his fastidious taste; he found our customs staled and debased from the handing down of many generations, and attempted a revival of Merrie England. Henceforth, there was a maypole and dancing on the green. I myself queened it for a day, in a most uncomfortable daisy crown, the effect of which was greatly lessened by an elastic under the chin! Then the great artist died. No one else was clever enough to design the dresses, or rich enough to provide the tea; the maypole was blown down in a storm; the children ceased to walk in procession; the whole thing collapsed. Only a few free-lance stragglers took garland in hand and begged frankly for pennies.

This year I was beginning to fear that even those would fail me. I was sorry. I had made some scones. I had put out jam and milk for them in the flower-decorated kitchen. Just before noon, two girls and a tiny boy came bashfully up the path. The girls were hot, dusty and giggling; they carried a money-box which rattled hollowly as they walked. The little boy was tired and cross; he trailed his garland in the dust behind him.

I made them eat and drink, then seated myself in state at the window, while they went outside again and sang. Two little, weak piping voices – for the small boy was busy sweeping the doorstep with his garland, and did not count – where once had been a well-trained band of thirty or more. But, if they were survivals, was not I the same? One solitary woman listening alone and dreaming of the bevy of bright heads that once, on long ago May mornings, pressed with hers against the pane: of those left in Flanders, and of those others, getting and spending a whole world's breadth away.

Then their song arrested my wandering attention. I had not heard it before; they said their granny taught it them. She said they called it a carol, and always sang it on May mornings. Here

63

it is as well as I could make it out from their childish gabble, all the words running into one:

> All on a bright May morning,
>   When buds were glistering new,
> The Mother took her pretty Babe,
>   To lave in morning dew.
>   O, carol, sweetly carol,
>   To welcome in the Spring:
>   That Mother was the Queen of Heaven,
>   That Babe our Lord and King.
>
> All in the dewy May-time,
>   Beneath the greensward tree,
> The lambkins frolicked at His feet,
>   The birds sang blissfully.
>   O, carol, sweetly carol,
>   To welcome in the May,
>   For Jesus Christ, our Saviour,
>   Was once a child at play!

*   *   *

May comes sweet and complete in every detail. Along every lane and hedgerow bank spring a thousand small and seldom considered things – Nature's embroidery, to finish off her festal robe to perfection. Within a few feet, massed closely together, may be seen the blue eyes of the speedwell, silvery stitchwort stars, cowslip, coltsfoot and violet, with dog's mercury powdering them all with the gold-dust of its pollen, and dead-nettle with honeyed coronets of rich cream.

Such hedgerows in May are everybody's garden; no one who walks the country roads at all can fail to be cheered by these small, familiar blooms. Even the housewife on her way to church or market will stoop to pluck a few blossoms to smell, and children on their way to school make fragile nosegays to pin on their frock fronts. That, perhaps, is why these small hedgerow flowers have always been favourites, with pet names and legendary stories, while rarer and more showy plants are seldom known to ordinary country people.

And how appropriate these popular names are! The 'little speedwell's darling blue', for instance, is 'angels' eyes' or 'birds' eyes' to the country child. The name fits it well. Take a spray up and examine it, and a dozen expressive bright blue eyes return the gaze. Upon close examination this eye-like appearance is seen to be due to a number of faint purple lines which radiate upon the blue petals. Scientists tell us these lines are honey-guides to point out the way to the nectar to bees; but most of us prefer to forget such utilitarian purposes and to think of the little flower as a small blue eye of earth.

In those districts where the speedwell is known as the 'bird's-eye' children are taught not to pluck it, for, if they do, says the old superstition, birds will come and peck at the eye of the despoiler. The evanescent beauty of the flower scarcely needs such a safeguard, for it fades so quickly that even young children soon learn that it cannot be carried in small hot hands even for a dozen yards. So the speedwell is left alone, and paints the roadside banks with a rare blue, pale and yet bright, a blue that is only seen besides in rain-washed spring skies, or, once in a generation, in human eyes.

The stitchwort, inseparable companion of the speedwell as it is, has a very different story. Stitchwort, or stitch plant – the plant good for the stitch, or pain in the side – once figured largely in homely medicine. Apothecary and housewife alike would go out on dewy May mornings to gather a store; for a decoction of the silvery stars of the flower in white wine was esteemed as a sovereign remedy for any kind of internal pain.

*　　*　　*

A pair of blue-tits have built between the double wooden walls of the tool-shed here, and I am able to watch them through a knot-hole in the wood from within, myself unseen. In one hour each of the parents paid over fifty visits to the nest, coming each time laden with sufficient food to divide into five portions, so that every one of the open mouths was satisfied. When they themselves find time to eat is a mystery. Perhaps they are like the lovelorn cook-maid in the story, who, during the whole time of her affliction, was never known to eat at table, but subsisted entirely upon the morsels she was compelled to swallow in 'tasting' the different dishes she prepared.

But the blue-tits are not the only young family in which I am interested. Down by the pool, on a tussock of grass surrounded by water, a hen dabchick has made her nest. Yesterday her patience was rewarded; she brought off her six little 'dabchicklets', and within half an hour of the first 'Cheep! cheep!' was careering proudly round and round upon the water with a small flotilla of black downy balls of living fluff in her wake.

Farther out, in the midst of a reed bed, sits a swan; the snowy grace of her brooding curves suggests a 'Patience' carved in alabaster. It is not wise, however, to presume upon her apparent immobility; come but a little nearer, and she becomes a hissing and spitting fury.

This is the first time I have known the swans to nest here, but they come at all seasons as visitors, for there is a chain of ponds at distances of a mile or two all along the valley, and they fly from one to the other as the fancy takes them. Sometimes the pool here is deserted by them for weeks; then one morning I find a pair or more in possession, sailing round the banks on a tour of inspection and examining everything that comes in their way with the calm hauteur of a noble family visiting one of their lesser country seats.

*   *   *

A fortnight ago, a family of travelling people set up their tents and caravans upon the heath. When first I saw their smoke go up and heard the shouts of children, the barking of dogs and the clucking of fowls let loose, I was a little dismayed. I need not have been; they have proved themselves the most exemplary of neighbours, and I shall be quite sorry now when they go.

That will not be for another week at least, for the men of the tribe, who are horse-dealers, have gone by road to a fair in Norfolk and left the women and children here to await their return. They were all thither-bound, had worked their way up from Devonshire so far, but an old grannie of the tribe fell ill here, and they halted to get medical advice for her.

The doctor suggested the infirmary, but, at the very mention of the place, the old crone fell to weeping and wailing like a banshee. She'd not be 'put away' between four walls, she cried; if they didn't want her, let them leave her beneath the nearest 'fuz-bush'. In the open she was born, and in the open she meant to die, with her cup of tea and her old black cutty-pipe beside her, and 'not none of them there 'ospital messes!'

It was not long before the chidren discovered that I, too, raised my smoke nearby; and not a day has passed since we first became acquainted but one or other of them has knocked at my door. Usually they bring some small offering, a rare orchis from the bog, or a chipped flint which they think may be a stone arrow-head, such as they know I search for and cherish. Or they will plait me a tiny rush basket, and fill it with a fern to hang in my window; they are as ingenious as so many lovers in inventing occasions for what they call a 'jaw' with me.

One of the elder girls, Fanny, or 'Feena', in her own language, has undertaken to give me lessons in the Romany, but at present we have got no farther than: 'Rinketty rawny, Romany tawny!' And although I gather that I am the former, she the latter, I am not at all clear as to the precise meaning of either.

She has made far more progress in my tongue than I have in hers. In her broken schooldays, interrupted by constant travelling, she never quite mastered the art of reading; so, the first day I met her, I proposed that this enforced halt should be taken advantage of to finish her education. At first she had to spell out all but words of one syllable, but now, a fortnight later, she can read quite nicely. She is a strange girl, not so vivid, perhaps, as some of the others, but interesting in quite another way.

'Feena,' I said to her today, 'what would you like to do with your life, if you could choose?'

She hesitated, gazing through me, her amber eyes ages and

continents away. I expected something quite picturesque and glowing in the way of wishes, for, a moment before, she had been telling me tales of the past grandeurs of her people; of the great-grandfather who, six feet five in his moleskin cap and scarlet waistcoat, was known as 'King Stanley of Brockenhurst', and dealt out laws to the whole of the New Forest tribes. But Feena hesitated, twisting the coral rope at her small brown throat reflectively. Then, with an air of having considered every possibility imaginable –

'I'd like to live in a house – a house with a front room.'

'But, Feena, what would you do there?'

'Wear velvet dresses, and sit on the sofa and sew all day,' declared the degenerate child.

'But, Feena,' I remonstrated, 'just think what that means! No more paddling in the pools upon the heath, or catching the horses by the mane for a ride!'

It was no use; she still persisted that her heart's desire was to be married to a house-dweller, as her cousin Maria was, and to have a shop, with grapes and oranges in the window, and a parlour opening out of it, like hers in Portsmouth.

It is quite likely that she will attain her desire, for her father has many business connections, one of whom she may meet and marry. But I doubt, if she does, that she will live 'happy ever after', for I have heard Cousin Maria's story, and it is sadder than that of a caged skylark. Still she may be happy, and then, perhaps, a century or so hence, some remote descendant of hers will be wondering why he or she can never 'settle down', but is impelled by some mysterious inner power to throw chance after chance in life away, just to gratify that urgent craving, which he cannot understand, for the open road and the wind on the heath.

June

Those who go to the country in search of quiet should not go in June. It is the noisiest month of all the year there.

In this green cup of a valley, between the North and the South Downs, where hills rise all around, and the village is like a lump of sugar at the bottom of a cup, not only the days but the nights also are full of sound. Every night for the last six weeks a nightingale has sung in the garden fruit-trees. Sometimes it begins before sunset; at others so late that, thinking I have been overlooked for once, I am on the point of locking up and going to bed. Then suddenly the 'Jug, jug, tireau!' bubbles up in the soft, warm dusk, like a fountain of golden rain.

But not even the lightest sleeper who ever came out of a city would complain of the song of the nightingale. Indeed, there is a legend here that a certain hotel in the neighbourhood charges it as an extra and is paid for it! There are other and less romantic sounds abroad in these short June nights.

The domestic cock is the worst offender. Round about midsummer he appears to sleep with one eye open, and the least alarm sends him shrilling out in the darkness, and all his family clucking and flapping. Soon his challenge is taken up and answered from farmstead after farmstead; then a fox, far away on the downs, barks his regret that he cannot make the personal acquaintance of each individual rooster, until a whole chain of barks and cries seems to echo around the whole neighbourhood.

Later in the night that same fox, perhaps, will be responsible for the sudden commotion by the pool, when a quacking and flapping and splashing will be followed by the beating of heavy wings in retreat, then, for a little while, by silence.

There are other winged things besides nightingales and bats abroad these summer nights. Moths, so silent and ghostly they can scarce be distinguished from the petals of white flowers, float here and there about the garden beds. All day they have each of them slept in some tiny crevice, under stone or leaf, or between the furrows of some rough-barked tree. At night they awake and seek nutriment for themselves, performing at the same time their allotted task in the scheme of things by fertilizing night-blooming plants.

The moth is a creature little considered except by collectors. Butterflies are known to all; yet there are many more species of moths than of butterflies in this country, and the study of their dim, mysterious lives is most fascinating.

A common sight at this time of year is the Ghost Moth, which hovers above the fields and hedges at dusk – at one moment a pale, floating shape flitting across our path, then suddenly vanishing. It is usually still within reach of our hand, although invisible, for it has only to alight and fold its wings to disappear in the half-light. The upper side of its wings is mealy-white and glimmering; the lower side, coming into view when poised, a most perfect disguise of brownish grey.

Some of the day-flying moths are so royally marked and richly coloured as to pass with the casual observer for butterflies. The difference can readily be distinguished by the shape of the body. The butterfly has a waist like a wasp, the moth has none.

June in the New Forest is a green month. To-day was a rest day, and I wandered all the morning in the woods alone. I had a book with me, but, although it rained a little and I sheltered for an hour beneath the hollies, I did not even open it.

I never greatly care for out-of-door reading. The words of

70

man, even the words of the greatest, always seem pale and inadequate before the vivid, spontaneous joy of Nature; yet, if I take no book at all with me, I am sure to be overtaken by that sudden, urgent need of one known to all book-lovers. So I keep a small selection which I carry abroad with me but seldom read. Not the books I love best indoors – they would be quite out of place – but old, quiet, soothing things – 'The Excursion', 'The Faery Queen', and an old battered, dog-eared book of sonnets, of which the chief merit is that it exactly fits the pocket of my knitted coat.

Some day, when I have time, I mean to compile an anthology for out-of-door reading, with some exquisitely lovely thing to chime with one's every mood. All the poems about birds will be in it: Shelley's 'Skylark' and the less known but equally beautiful 'Skylark' of Frederick Tennyson; Hardy's 'February Thrush'; the 'Nightingale' of Keats, and that other 'Nightingale' by a great living poet – I wonder if you know it? This is how it goes:

> 'Hidden 'mong the forest trees,
> Chaunt thy liquid melodies,
> Passionate nightingale!
> Sing in tender tremolo
> Soft and low,
> Sad and slow!'

Then, there will be poems about the woods and the hills and the sea; about clouds and rain and rainbows; of boys swimming and climbing trees; of babes and lambs at play; of bees and dragonflies and flowers; and all bound in a serviceable, weatherproof cover at the modest price of a shilling, for I am sure by the time I have finished it the paper shortage will be a thing of the past.

Today, as I had no anthology, I sat and dug idly with my hands amongst the warm pine-needles, revealing all kinds of curious, unsuspected creatures – wood-pigs, which curled up into hard, steely balls at a touch; a battalion of ants carrying pine-needle lances; centipedes; one solitary beetle with bright green mail and shining wings.

The withered leaves in the bushes stirred and a hedgehog

71

crept out, stretched his prickles, and scurried away. He did not see me, but the woodpecker, tap, tapping on a tree-trunk, caught my watchful eye and flew screaming down the glade.

Presently a fox came slinking. So near was he I could have touched the red-brown brush he was swinging so proudly. I must have been to leeward of him, for he passed on without sensing me.

As I rose to go, a mother squirrel, very sedate of step, as became one just about to undertake the cares of a nursery, looked down upon me from the fork of a beech, but, in spite of the frantic tail signals of her mate, did not trouble to move. Indeed, her bright, critical, beady black eyes were scornful, as one who should say:

'My dear, do be more dignified! You never were any judge of character! That small human below, with her brown dress and hair and eyes, is just as much a creature of the woodlands as ourselves. Besides, she could not aim straight to save her life. It is those small, forked humans who climb trees and rob the poor birds we have to fear. You trust to my intuition!'

* * *

The hare is often confused by town-dwellers with the much commoner rabbit; but it is not only a larger, but a wilder and more beautiful animal. Seen at close quarters against a background of green, its sandy coat, unmixed with grey, is almost golden. Its long sensitive ears, dark, pleading eyes, and figure, the very incarnation of swift grace, make it one of the most beautiful, as well as the wildest and shyest, of English wild animals.

It is well for the young leveret that it does not come into the world naked and helpless, as the young of the rabbit does: for the hare has no safe, warm burrow under ground to deposit its young in, but makes its nursery upon the bare earth with only a tuffet of grass or a clump of bracken to shelter it. From this 'form', as it is called, the young leverets are taught to scatter at the approach of danger. Sometimes, if the danger is sudden and close at hand, they will trust, as their parents do, to their protective colouring, and crouch motionless against the sandy earth until the intruder has passed on.

In such cases a hare will allow a human being to come within a few feet of it, or even to walk round it. By averting the eyes and walking very leisurely and unconcernedly, it is quite easy to persuade any wild creature that it is unnoticed, but the hare is more than ordinarily confident. As a child, I once witnessed the taking of one through this trait. My brother and I were playing 'lighthouses' upon the top of a hayrick in the corner of a small ploughed field. By a footpath across the same field a number of farm labourers were going home from their work, smoking and chatting as they went, with the low, dazzling sun in their eyes. As they shambled on, the foremost of them started a large hare from the grassy pathway. A cry of 'Tally-ho!' was soon raised, and one of the men, a little more active than his fellows, started in pursuit.

'Better keep y'r breath to blow y'r taters,' his mates called after him derisively: but he was away and across the field, soon outdistanced, of course, by his quarry.

His chase must have been inspired by some primitive sporting instinct; for, had the rick not come in the way, he might just as well have followed the wind. The hare fled one way round the rick; the man, hoping to cut it off, took the opposite direction, but when he had circled it and came out on the sunny side again the hare had completely disappeared. The hunter stood, his hand shading his eyes, scanning the furrows for a clue, while his mates, with many a jeer at his folly, passed on towards home. He lingered, pretending to light his pipe, until the last of them crossed the stile into the next field; then, taking off his coat and spreading it upon his arm, he proceeded leisurely over the ploughing in the opposite direction to that in which the path lay.

Partly buried in the hay, we children had escaped notice, and were about to resume our game when we saw the man suddenly throw himself sideways to the earth, his coat outspread. The poor hare had trusted too well to its protective colouring;

experienced eyes had detected it, squatting earth-coloured upon the sandy earth, for all the dazzling brilliancy of the sunset light.

A great scuffling and struggling ensued, from which the man emerged with a dead hare wrapped in his coat, to be buried in the hay for removal after dark. The whole scene had only taken a few minutes, and he was off across the field, whistling as though nothing had happened, and calling to his mates not to be in 'such a deuce of an 'urry,' before the thin wailing cries of the hare, so strangely human, had ceased to echo in our horrified ears.

Very sad, of course, that a seemingly respectable workman should be a secret poacher! But, with wages at twelve shillings a week, and six or eight mouths to feed, I think that, after this lapse of time, we may hope that, although out of season, the hare made a savoury stew.

*   *   *

Of human life upon the heath there is scarcely any. I walk there for days together and meet nobody; but I do not think this area was always so sparsely populated. To the discerning eye there are many traces of the occupation of man, from the arrow-heads of the Stone Age to the half-filled trenches of Kitchener's Army.

There are paths and cart-tracks, too, without number; some of them still in occasional use, but most of them overgrown and deserted. Some have been so long disused that pine trees have sprung and come to full stature between the still clearly-defined cart ruts.

Sometimes I follow these deserted paths, winding in and out to skirt the hills and the marshes, just as they were first trodden by the naked feet of primitive man. Sometimes they end in the tawny, bramble-grown cliff-face of a deserted gravel or sand pit. This is a happy hunting ground for the lover of wild life. At one's approach rabbits scutter; just a glimpse of a white tail, and that is all of them. Lizards dart behind sand-heaps; sometimes a hen pheasant whirrs up and takes wing, leaving her dozen or more light brown eggs to their fate. But at one I came upon yesterday there were no such sights or sounds of sudden flight.

The reason was soon apparent. Rounding the cliff suddenly, without sound, I came upon a happy family party. Basking full length in the sun lay a mother-fox, her warm reddish-brown coat a shade or two darker and deeper than the sand hill behind her. Around and above her, in playful pursuit, tugging her ears and brush, and romping over her just as though she had been a feather bed, sported her two bright-eyed, prick-eared little cubs. The father of the family sat upon his haunches some yards apart; such childish games were, apparently, not for him. His back was towards me, but I did not think it advisable to reprove him for his lack of manners. Instead, I turned discreetly, and retreated as silently as I had come.

July

July is Nature's breathing space, her pause between flower-time and fruit-time. Of the year's leaves, every one of the millions is unfurled; the fruit is formed upon the tree; the grain stands green upon the stalk. Soon the leaves will be tinted and fall; the corn harvested, and the fruit ripened and gathered. But first comes this pause of perfection, when Nature stands still to survey her work, and even the birds' songs are hushed, and only a faint rustle of leaves tells of earth's motion.

There are more butterflies than birds to be seen. Sitting or lying upon the turf, one sees the cabbage whites and the sulphurs drift in twos and threes upon every current of air against the overhead blue. They are so numerous and float so silently that they seem a part of the July atmosphere, scarcely more noticeable than the tiny yellow clouds or the scent of pollen-dust.

The larger coloured butterflies do certainly raise a thrill of interest, and there are few wayfarers who will not pursue one of them a few yards, hoping it will settle, and so allow its species to be discerned. Usually it turns out to be either a peacock or a tortoiseshell.

The peacock butterfly no one can mistake, for it bears its signature upon each of its four wings in the form of four perfect peacock's feathers imprinted in natural colours upon the velvety brown. The tortoiseshell is not so easily distinguished, for its marking is less pronounced and its colouring apt to vary, but that, too, bears a characteristic mark, for upon the tortoiseshell wings, reddish-orange with black mottlings, it wears a tiny row of blue dots, like a border of turquoises.

Another very handsome butterfly is the red admiral, a gorgeous creature with deep scarlet bands upon its dark brown wings, the scarlet of the hinder pair picked out with black dots and the edges scalloped to a lace-like delicacy. This butterfly is very fond of old gardens and may often be seen when the dahlias are in bloom, poising itself upon the broad platform of one of those flowers and opening and shutting its wings as though asking to be admired.

At the same time of year comes the painted lady with a broken design of white, red, and orange; both that and the red admiral linger on into the autumn and may at that time be found fixed to a curtain or wall indoors, where they have crept to avoid the first breath of cold.

These are the beauties of the insect world that even the least observant cannot fail to notice, but they are only a few of the more conspicuous of our sixty native butterflies. One particularly beautiful in a quieter way is the little common blue.

This little insect is found all over the British Isles, and, being fond of open places, may be seen in great numbers upon the moors. The blue of its wings is a soft mauvey tint, akin to that of the harebell, but lighter, and it has a way of settling in bevies down a long blade or bent, each butterfly forming a living petal of a strange blue flower unknown to botany.

The female of the common blue is often brown, which modest and inconspicuous colour is almost a livery with the heath-flying butterflies of later summer, when the meadow brown, the skipper, the different families of fritillaries, and a host of others are abroad, many of them to be distinguished only by the slenderness of their bodies from moths.

It is, indeed, often difficult to distinguish between butterflies and moths. The general rule is, of course, that butterflies are brighter in colour than moths, and fly by day, while the majority of moths fly by night. But to this rule there are many exceptions, some butterflies being drabbish, while some moths are brilliantly marked; there are also many day-flying moths, though no English butterfly flies by night. Further distinctions between the two are that a butterfly, when at rest, folds its wings in a vertical position, while a moth holds them horizontally; also that the antennæ of the butterflies are always clubbed, or blunted at the end, while those of the moths are pointed.

Some of the larger day-flying moths are almost as beautiful as the butterflies they are so often taken for. Chief among these is the tiger moth, a fine fat fellow with tiger stripings of brown on a cream velvet ground upon its front wings, and the hinder ones of rich red spotted with black. The caterpillar of this moth is familiar to us all, for who in childhood has not shrunk from the hairy crawliness of the woolly-bear, and watched its snakelike wriggling upon the garden paths with fascinated horror?

Still more fascinating, though less common, is the fearsome death's-head moth, which bears upon its thorax the imprint of a human skull. This heavy brown and buff insect is the largest of all our native moths, the span of its wings being about four and a half inches. When irritated it is said to utter a small shrill shriek, something like the cry of the bat; and this, together with its gruesome marking, has caused it to be regarded as a death warning by the superstitious.

The eggs of the different butterflies and moths are among the lesser marvels of creation. Clustering in soft white masses upon the under-side of a leaf, they appear to the naked eye to be smoothly rounded and more or less oval in shape; but, placed under the microscope, they are revealed as infinitely varied, some resembling a fir-cone, others an ear of maize, while yet others are like a flower with the petals moulded in bold relief. Infinitesimal, scarcely visible things, yet each one so patiently and lovingly wrought, they seem, like Tennyson's flower in the crannied wall, to hold the secret of all things.

*　　*　　*

Between the cornfield and the water-meadow the hedge is clotted with the soft, cream-coloured masses of the elder-flower. The scent of it, strong and peculiar but not unpleasant, mingles well with that of the water-mint and the cattle-trampled grass.

It is pleasant upon a hot afternoon to sit beneath one of the tall bushes with the cool green light flickering upon one's face, and watch the delicate tracery of the pale, lacy flowers outlined against a blue sky.

The elder is a tree of many virtues: of many superstitions, too. The gipsies regard it with traditionary awe. It is an unlucky tree to camp under; better no shelter at all than the shelter of an elder tree. Yet when the thunder crashes it is the safest refuge, for the elder is the one tree of all the wood that the lightning never strikes. At night, when the camp fire is lit, no matter how late the hour or scarce the fuel, every elder twig must be rejected.

'You burn y'r luck if you burn elderwood,' say the younger generation.

They do not know why; 'some yarn o' th' old 'uns.' The old grandmother, if she is in a communicative mood, and 'likes your face', may condescend to tell you that there is a curse upon the elder tree, root and branch, for of that same wood wicked men made the Cross.

'It wer' a tall, fine tree in them days: but since, it's been but a low, scrubby thing. Other folks forget, but we gipsies never forgets, my dear, and we'd scorn to touch it!'

In other parts of the country the cottagers say that the elder was the tree upon which Judas hung himself, or that witches had the power of turning themselves into elders, and sometimes were unable to turn back again. Therefore, if you cut an elder and it bleeds, it is a witches' tree.

Old tales, and idle ones! But they tell how closely natural objects were once associated with human life. The repeating of such legends may not have been more edifying than cinema-going or backing winners, but they had a wild beauty.

The elder had practical uses, too. It furnished a whole pharmacopœia to the housewife in the days before the large multiple chemists had a branch shop in every market town. Blossom, berry, and stem each had its uses; of them were compounded ointment and lotion, pickle and preserve, and at least two kinds of wine.

In those days every woman who valued her complexion gave it the benefit of a two weeks' treatment with elderflower water once a year. One old friend of my childhood, who at seventy had a face like a soft crumpled rose-leaf, used to enlist my help in handing down the blossom to her. These she would steep, fresh from the tree, in boiling water, and, after straining and lacing with Eau de Cologne, she had a face-wash fit for a queen.

Such a lotion might well be used still to replace for a week or two once a year the more costly cosmetics so dear to many of us. If the elderflower-water were not, as indeed it is, extremely beneficial in itself, it would still do good by giving the complexion a rest from artificial concoctions.

The same old lady used to make a wine from the flowers. This was called 'ladies' elder wine', the 'gentlemen's' being the strong, heady beverage, much like port, which was brewed from the berries in autumn. The wine made from the flowers was a sparkling drink, very light and harmless, which was brought out and handed with a sponge finger to lady and children callers, that they might sip genteelly and not find the time long while their hostess hunted up the requisite number of eggs from the nest, or weighed the honey or clotted-cream they had come to purchase.

The elderberry wine was reserved for winter evenings. About Christmas time, when the hours of darkness were long, and the whole family gathered about the blazing logs, the elder wine was brought out, mulled with spices, and handed round as an innocent accompaniment to work and chat.

'The world went very well in those days,' we are inclined to say, and to compare them with these, to the disadvantage of the latter. But we must remember that to every farm kitchen or shop parlour, with good mahogany and sparkling brass, there were at least a score of labourers' hovels with little warmth and comfort.

I came upon the ruin of such a place a few days ago, a cottage recently condemned and left derelict, even in these days of house shortage. I was at first attracted by its charming exterior. Roses and honeysuckle draped the low moss-grown roof and russet walls. The windows were small and diamond-paned; the thatch jutted over the door like a penthouse.

Open to the day, but still dim, although the windows were broken and the door gone from its hinges, were two small rooms, neither of them much larger than a ship's cabin. At the back was a windowless hole, which had probably served as a larder. That was all. Within that compass families of ten or twelve had been brought up; babes had been born; bodies had awaited burial. For over a hundred years some family or other had been glad to call it home.

And what of the dwellers in such homes?

Within living memory there was a time when the labourer's wage in this part of the country seldom exceeded the sum of ten shillings weekly. Out of that one poor half-sovereign ten or twelve mouths had often to be fed; for clothing they depended upon charity. Herded like animals for lack of space; insufficiently nourished; the elders crippled with rheumatism; the young stricken down with consumption – for what availed the keen moorland air without when the diamond-paned windows were not made to open, and the room within was close and fetid – the world did not go so well for those in the cottage as it did for those whose comforts their labour helped to support.

A little thought given to this aspect of 'the good old times' should help to reconcile us to the red-brick boxes of dwellings which at other times seem a blot upon the countryside. They have, at least, weatherproof roofs and serviceable sash-windows. The ugliness, let us hope, is but a passing phase. As people read more and think more, taste must follow. Future generations will demand beauty as well as usefulness. This is but a time of transition.

*   *   *

Except in the vicinity of the pool, where the tinkling of water is ceaseless, the woods this month are almost oppressively silent. The birds left weeks ago for open country, preferring the last small, sweet gleanings of the strawberry fields, or the first toll of the ripening orchards, to all this closed-in leafiness.

The only feathered creature left behind is the woodpecker. He taps away at his mossed tree-trunk like an industrious little craftsman left at home to finish some piece of work while all the rest of the world makes holiday. His 'tap! tap!' sounds faintly through the shade. That and the teasing humming of the gnats are the only sounds.

Sometimes, if the passer-by is silent enough, he will appear close at hand, a quaint little fellow, with his green and yellow plumage and crimson cap. But he is very suspicious, glancing continually over his shoulder as he zigzags up the tree-trunk, tapping with his bill as he goes to test its soundness. Even when he has discovered a spot where the sound signifies that grubs are beneath the bark, and dinner is ready, the least sound will send him dipping across the glade, uttering his harsh scream of sardonic laughter as he goes.

It is this outrageous laughter which has won for the green woodpecker the name of 'Yaffle.' The word, with each letter prolonged, comes very near to the sound; but only the

woodpecker itself can give the exact note of derision. The ladies
of the Middle Ages who kept the popinjay,* as they called him
then, as a pet must sometimes have found him a disconcerting
inmate. It must have been vexing to hear that sardonic laugh
ring out just as a false stitch was discovered in the tapestry, and a
week of unpicking was found necessary; or Sir Hugh was
sighted crossing the drawbridge with four strange knights, and
nothing in the buttery but cold venison!

*　　*　　*

The sea had been calling for days. There was a salty tang on the
wind in the early morning. I could not rest in my sequestered
garden at noon but a gull must come flapping across the blue
field of my vision. Then yesterday I saw a trail of wet, sword-
shaped seaweed glistering across the handlebar of a passing
cycle. It was enough. This morning I packed the luncheon
basket and locked my cottage door for the day.

I had intended to walk the whole of the way, but, just as I
struck the highway at Piper's End, a fast-trotting pony with a
gipsy-cart overtook me and the driver pulled up to ask if I
would do him the honour of accepting a lift. The honour was
mine, for he who invited me was of royal blood, a descendant of
the house of Lee, the old kings of the Romany tribe.

As his gaily-painted little cart ate the miles of white ribbon of
the road, we had much to talk of, for I had not seen him since he
came back from his soldiering, and he was an old friend of my
childhood, sworn blood-brother to my brothers, and ringleader
in many a truant escapade. So we recalled the old times, the day
we took the wild-bee's nest and I dripped the honey all down my
new red coat; the day Edmund, having climbed the big cedar for
the wood-pigeon's egg, slipped and hung for one terrible
moment suspended by his clothes to a bough; of the other time
when I lost a shoe in Hatley Bog, and, finding it inconvenient to

---

*The 'popinjay' of the Middle Ages was not the woodpecker, but the parrot [ML].

walk home in one, took off the other and, smearing my legs with peat, pretended I was *his* sister, while Edmund walked aloof in outraged dignity.

I scrambled down by a disused, overgrown lane, to the solitary beach of a tiny bay. There was no cliff, the summer bounty of the land had overflowed and trailed in festoons of wild rose and honeysuckle amongst the pebbles of the shingle. The sea was a steely mirror, just blurred by a Titan's breath of mist. The air was very cool and still, the soft lap, lap, of the waves so faint I could hear the stir of the wind in the barley field which sloped down to the shore behind me.

I unlocked the warped, sun-blistered door of the old bathing-shed; it is no longer mine, but the owner is abroad, and I have the key. I swam far out and floated for a long time. The sun had burst from the clouds and was hot upon me; it was as much a sun-bath as a sea-bath, invigorating, life-giving.

Afterwards, my hair hanging seaweed-fashion to dry in the sun, I dug idly with my fingers in the hot sand. My hand struck something cool and hard, and I brought up a flint. No common flint, such as lay around me in thousands. This one was shaped and wrought, triangular, flaked to a point, a stone arrow-head.

It is not uncommon in this part of Hampshire to unearth these relics of the Stone Age. I myself have dug up a spearhead in my potato patch, have found a rude hammer-like weapon amongst the earth around the upturned roots of a fallen tree; but this one, embedded in the sand of the seashore, set me wondering.

Did some human once sit there as I sat now, all unwitting of the lurking danger? Did the arrow lie for years amongst his mouldering dust? Or did it miss, and sink harmlessly into the sand, to be dug up, ages after, by the sunburnt hand of an idle woman and carried away in the same basket as a Thermos flask?

The flask was empty. So, in obedience to an inward prompting, I turned inland. In a rustic cottage beside the highway they had opened a new tea-shop. The name, 'The Orchid', painted upon the newest of new-art signboards, made a grand splash of colour at the gate. The window curtains were violet, the walls pale mauve. The ladies-in-waiting – I cannot insult them by calling them waitresses – were dressed in purple. The fine linen was there, too, edged with crochet, upon the dainty tables.

I was charmed until they placed my tea before me. Such stale bread, such sophisticated butter, such rocky rock-cakes! I thought of the good cheer at the 'Staff of Life', and wished I had had the energy to travel on the other mile. Decayed gentle-women who elect to run tea-shops should be compelled to serve an apprenticeship to a common landlady.

* * *

The other day I had an experience which reminded me of the amenities of the old coaching days and the honours of the box seat. The inside of my 'bus happened to be full, and the driver kindly offered me a place by himself behind the steering-wheel. Having done so, he shouldered the responsibility of his act, and proceeded to do the honours of the country we passed through. He should, by rights, have had a whip in his hand with which to point out places of interest, but, as it was, being busied most of the time with his steering-gear, a nod of the head or a hurried wave of the hand had to suffice.

We passed through the heart of the Gilbert White country, and within a mile of his own village of Selborne. The narrow lanes, with honeysuckle which brushed the 'bus windows, must often have seen that father of English nature-lovers jogging along on his sedate and steady-going grey mare. Now our driver manœuvred his heavy vehicle through them, skilful, alert and attentive, as he had need to be when the road was so narrow and the windings of it such as to make every encounter with another car a trial to even his well-inured nerves. How he had managed to observe the countryside as he had was a mystery. His eyes seemed all the time to be fixed upon the stretch of narrow road just in front of him, yet not a tree, a clump of fern, a cottage or signpost out of the ordinary had escaped his notice. He knew just the point where the wedge of chalky soil cut through the sand for a mile or two, and was ready to point out the effect of the change — harebells and succory instead of heather, and traveller's joy wreathing the hedge in place of the honeysuckle.

Then the sight of a dead hedgehog, squashed flat upon the road, brought up the perennial problem as to whether they milk the cows at night or not. I had an open mind upon the subject, having often been told that they did, without ever having met an actual eye-witness. The driver was a convinced believer — for the best of all possible reasons. One morning a few weeks before, he said, while stamping and stretching himself outside a wayside inn where they halt for five minutes, the landlord shouted to him from a field gateway close by to 'Come and look at a sight he'd likely not see again.' He ran to the gate of the pasture, and there, couched upon the grass inside, chewing placidly, legs outspread, apparently well content, was a fine Jersey cow with a hedgehog clinging to her udder like a big brown burr.

I might have heard more about the hedgehog, but just then came a halt beside the railway bridge beneath which two pairs of jackdaws had built in the spring, and he broke off to point out one of the families, the parents very black and sleek, the children more slatey-grey and downy, promenading upon the turf of the embankment above our heads. One of the young birds my driver had captured as a fledgling, had brought it up at home by hand, and was now teaching it to talk. His family, it appeared, had always had a fancy for the jackdaw as a pet, and he had many amusing stories to tell of their ways.

One was that when he was a boy his mother brought out an old bridal veil, much cherished in the family, and proceeded to bleach it in preparation for the wedding of an elder sister of his. Wetting and drying it alternately, she spread it upon some grass by the cottage door. Presently, however, an old rag-and-bone dealer appeared upon the scene, and in bringing out and selling the contents of her ragbag she forgot it for a time. When she remembered and went out to wet it again it had gone.

She searched the garden and the borders of the common outside, hoping some stray breeze had only carried it off a few yards, but there was no trace of it. Gradually a horrible suspicion arose in her mind that she had accidentally gathered it up with the rags and pressed it with her own hands into the dealer's sack. Perhaps the dealer had himself been dishonest and stolen it. It really was a magnificent veil; all embroidered by hand, and fifty years old at the least, it might well be a temptation to anybody! The more she thought of it the more precious it became to her; every moment it went up in value, until the loss of it became a calamity.

She ran to the village constable, and set him scouring the country lanes for the rag-and-bone man. She went to every cottage around and enquired if he had called there. No one had seen him; he had knocked at no other door than her own, nor had he even visited the inn for liquid refreshment. But for the empty ragbag lying upon the seat in the porch, and the fact that the veil was missing, she might have dreamed the whole incident.

Nor was he ever seen or heard of after, and she could only conclude that he had turned aside from the main road to visit her house, which happened to be the first in the village; then, unexpectedly making such a rich capture – for the veil by that time had become of fabulous value – had mounted his donkey-cart in haste, and had made off for some large town.

The wedding-day came, and a length of ordinary tulle had to serve the bride as a veil; but the next autumn, when the cottage roof was under repair, the thatcher plunged his arm into a hole by the chimney-stack and brought out a long strip of lacey material which had once been white.

The hole where the veil was hidden was a favourite resort of the family jackdaw, a place for him to retire to sulk when punished, or to carry any special delicacy to enjoy in peace. Sometimes, for days together, he would play at building a nest there for a non-existent mate. In one of these moods, they concluded, he must have carried off the veil with which to soften the chimney bricks for his imaginary family. How he gathered up the soft folds of the net and conveyed the veil to the roof without being seen remained a mystery.

It is a staid and sober earth we live upon this month. The glory of the year's flowering-time is past; such blossoms as bloom now are in isolated tufts, and so mixed with foliage as to make little effect in a world of darkening green.

All the more striking to eyes accustomed to this cool monotone was the sheet of vivid colour I discovered in the woods today. Wandering a little farther from home than usual, I came suddenly upon an open space sloping down to the railway line where the whole clearing was painted blue with the viper's bugloss in flower.

I was not the first discoverer. Drawn up beside an almost overgrown cart-track was a gipsy caravan. A gaunt white horse, all hoof and rib, munched the thistle-like bugloss stems with keen enjoyment. There was no other sign of life; the van door was fast closed, and from the open window, with its floating curtain, came no sound. All was so sunny and quiet that it seemed like a fairy scene; human life and its turmoil seemed incredibly remote.

Suddenly, with mechanical swiftness, the small, green-painted door opened, and a district nurse, bag in hand, ran down the steps and made for the path which skirted the railway. Had she come out of a tree-trunk her appearance could not have been more unexpected; and, to cover my confusion at being found stock-still and gazing apparently at nothing, I ventured some remark about the flower.

'The viper's bugloss,' she echoed abstractedly. 'So that's what you call it? I should never have noticed it, but, then, I was called here at five o'clock this morning, and have been shut up in that hole ever since. A beautiful child, though, with eyes as blue as that flower there; not what you'd expect from a gipsy at all. And it *is* a nice day, now you mention it, and somebody's got to look after the poor little thing, gipsies or no gipsies!' And Nurse went on her way with a dawning expression which said that, after all, things weren't so bad but a good tub and a cup of tea would make her herself again.

Inside the cramped space of the van, then, was a weary mother and a babe born to no pleasant or easy life. Also, most probably, an ancient crone who had received the nurse with sweeping curtseys and obsequious words, only to wet the child's hair with gin and spit upon it 'for luck' as soon as her back was turned.

A poet, perhaps, would have waxed lyrical over the child with blue eyes born amongst the bugloss on such a morning as that, but to the more practical mind other aspects presented themselves. These half-caste gipsies, hawkers, clothes-peg makers, beggars and petty pilferers as they are, lead but a wretched life, and one fears that it will be but *viper's* bugloss for the poor babe.

* * *

We find, when we come to study a small stretch of country at all intensively, that every field and lane, every tree and clod, has a history. I wonder that no educationist has suggested that the school children of a parish should be appointed its historians. What a multitude of little regarded facts, likely to be intensely interesting to future generations, those small, sharp eyes would note.

In this parish, for instance, the shell of a hollow tree was recently felled to make way for the builder. Up to just before the war there was still a floating legend that this tree, two miles distant from the present forest bounds, had once marked the verge of the Royal Forest of Woolmer. It was swept away unnoted. Not even a paragraph in the local paper recorded the going of it.

If the school history had been in being, the disappearance of so ancient a landmark would certainly have been chronicled, with a description of the exact spot where it stood, and perhaps a snapshot to show to what a mere hollow tooth of a tree it had dwindled.

Supposing the school history had been in being before Queen Anne put the pinnacle upon her renown by dying, upon the day the old tree fell we should have turned back the pages for the description by an eye-witness of the procession of that Queen and her courtiers beneath the green and spreading boughs of that same tree in its prime. That she did pass beneath it as she went to review her drove of red deer in Woolmer we know; but, having no child-historian to appeal to, only the bare fact of her passing that way is thrown to us incidentally.*

And not less interesting would it be centuries hence to those for whom the great war would be but 'an old, unhappy, far-off thing, a battle long ago', to learn from the school history that the soldiers in those old romantic times camped upon such a heath, or drilled in such a field.

Then our history, linking all the country together in a network of parishes, would be a natural history, too. Records would be kept of climatic conditions, of rare bird visitors, of the making or draining of ponds, of the planting and felling of woods, and so on.

The connection of any famous, or likely to become famous, name with the place would be found there, too. The well-known poet who stayed at the hotel, and spent hours gazing upon a certain view; the farmer's son, a native born, who became an engineer and patented a world-shaking invention – such facts as could be obtained without impertinence relating to such ones would be there, ready to the hand of future biographers.

It would make interesting reading for the people of the year 2,000, this 'New Domesday Book; or Every Parish its Own History'.

---

*Gilbert White, in *The Natural History of Selborne*, wrote in the 1780s: 'There is an old keeper, now alive, named Adams, whose great-grandfather . . . grandfather, father and self enjoyed the head-keepership of Wolmer Forest in succession for more than a hundred years. This person assures me, that his father has often told him, that Queen Anne, as she was journeying on the Portsmouth road, did not think the forest of Wolmer beneath her royal regard. For she came out of the great road at Lippock, which is just by, and reposing herself on a bank smoothed for that purpose, lying about half a mile to the east of Wolmer-pond, and still called Queen's-bank, saw with great complacency and satisfaction the whole herd of red deer brought by the keepers along the vale before her, consisting then of about five hundred head. A sight this, worthy of the attention of the greatest sovereign!' [ML]

August

It is strange how the counties personify themselves to the mind's eye.

Dorset is a dairy-maid, all curds and cream and roses. Wiltshire, a princess of the Stone Age, fugitive, aloof. You may tread her vast open spaces and breathe her pollen-scented air for a month, and never once catch a glimpse of her; although the most ancient of counties, she still awaits her poet to interpret her, or perhaps she crowned him such ages ago that his very language has faded from man's memory.

Then Sussex, with her springy thyme-turf, the pearly white of her Downs and the dim, distant blue of her wealdlands. But ask the Sussex people about *her!* Every man of them who can hold a pen has written at least one book about his own particular town or village; they teach their babes in school to sing her praises, and draw the very place-names out into a song!

But Hampshire, dear, warm, tender Hampshire! Very few have praised her. Yet she is most worthy; a dark Madonna, with heather-purple robe and deep pine-tresses, sitting in the sun with a blessing for all who seek her.

A good many do seek her this month. The highroad at the end of my lane is alive with traffic – motor-cars, motor-cycles, coaches and charabancs powdering the trees and ferns, and deadening the grasses as they pass and repass in a cloud of gritty white dust.

Some of the lowlier sort of charabancers put up at the village inn here, make a bee-line for the beechwoods, picnic in the glades, strewing the turf with luncheon papers, tear up fern and foxglove by the root, and with their jollity scare the forest creatures – all, that is, excepting the ponies; these have a sense of humour of their own, and delight in doing the scaring, grouping themselves in twos and threes on a narrow path, refusing to move one way or the other, and making the charabancers pick their way round through the bushes, tearing their silk stockings and wetting their patent-leather shoes in the process.

One party even brought a gramophone, which was, as it truthfully declaimed, 'For Ever Blowing Bubbles' of execrable din.

They take their pleasure. I take mine. And mine, this month, lies quite in an opposite direction. I never, if I can avoid it, set foot upon the highway, but, as soon as my work is done, drop over the orchard wall, cross my neighbour's valley farm, climb the opposite hill, and there, upon the upland heath, I have all the solitude heart could desire.

What a bounteous, piled-up and running-over season the coming one will be! My garden, in rich reward for very slight pains, is a feast of colour – all the deep glowing tints of autumn, golds and purples and crimsons, with, here and there, the clear-cut freshness of a white single dahlia against its dark background of leaves.

The honey-bees hurry from flower to flower, as though they knew that the season sped and the time for completing their winter store was limited. I counted five of them, all mealy-winged and thighed, upon the disc of one huge sunflower by the gate today. Really, they had no business there; they should have been upon the moor outside, collecting the heather-honey for which this district is noted. But although myriads of them drone away in the heath-bells until the sound of them seems to be the living music of the moors, myriads more seem to make a rendezvous of my cottage garden.

The heather honey they make is not to everyone's taste;

town-dwellers usually reject it with scorn, for the colour is dark and the flavour stronger than that of the honey of commerce, but to those who have a taste for it it is ambrosia. Every time I taste it I resolve to buy a swarm and set up bee-keeping; a rash resolve, for, alone of all living creatures, bees have a marked antipathy to my person, stinging me upon the least provocation, and even going out of their way to attack me, an enmity which caused me much distress as a child, for the country people used to say that 'it is only the black at heart that the bees dislike'!

Our forefathers had many customs and superstitions regarding these insects. One of the most widely diffused was the idea that the bees shared in the joys and sorrows of the household to which they belonged, and must be formally told of each joyous or tragic happening, or they would pine away at the lack of confidence, and die. Marriages and deaths they were supposed to take a special interest in:

'Bees, Bees, there's joy in the house,
For a maid has promised to wed!'

was the formula upon a marriage eve.

The telling of a death I myself as a child once overheard. I had stolen away from my elders one hot Sunday afternoon to enjoy a not too Sabbatical book in the tangled wilderness of long grass and tree stems one always finds, a kind of No Man's Land, at the extreme end of old-fashioned country gardens. Just beyond this outpost of the household of grownups I was visiting was the end of another garden, where, half buried in a thicket of flowering thyme, stood a row of straw-plaited, red-pan roofed beehives.

To these, presently, came a tall young country giant, the village blacksmith, as I recognized, for I had often lingered to watch his sparks flying. His father had died that morning only, but he was already from head to foot in shiny black. Tapping the roof of the nearest hive, he said softly: 'Bees, Bees, your master's dead, so now you must work for your missus', laid upon the hive a shred of black crape and weighted it down with a pebble. Then he passed on down the row of hives, repeating the proceeding at each.

This custom of 'telling the bees' has died out now, even in the most remote country places. Probably my blacksmith was a survival, for his parents were aged and old-fashioned, and my elders, when I told them, were much shocked at what they considered his 'ignorance'. The modern world has no time or taste for such fancies. Yet it is a curious fact that, in spite of scientifically constructed hives and patent winter foods, the honey bee no longer thrives in this country as it did in the days when it was regarded as not only a purveyor of honey, but as a confidential friend of the family as well.

*   *   *

'Go to the ant,' said the wise man long ago; 'study her ways, and be wise.' Countless generations of men and insects have flourished and passed away since he said it, but the good example of the ant is just as well worth following today as it was then. The ant was probably the first co-operator. 'Each for all and all for each' has always been its motto. It forms communities in which all the inhabitants work cheerfully for the common weal; each individual has its definite place in the scheme of things, and its appointed task to perform. Amongst those I saw today, two upon the outskirts of the mound were hauling a pine-twig between them; almost beyond their strength it seemed, for it was in bulk equal to at least ten of its bearers, but they pushed and pulled at it, stopping every few seconds to rest, until they were within a few inches of their goal. Then a surprising thing happened. From the citadel came a relief party. Four found easy the task which had overtaxed two. The rest of the journey was made without a halt, and the twig was soon in its appointed place.

But, although the ant is such a hard worker, it has its playtime too. The microscope will show them skipping about upon their hind legs and embracing each other with their antennæ in a kind of dance. They have their domestic animals, too. The green aphids one finds upon rose-trees are kept and

A Country Calendar

milked by them, just as man keeps cows.

In one respect they lag behind civilized man, for one at least of our native species are slave-owners. The next time you come across an ant-heap examine it, and if you find it tenanted by two different species together, be sure that the larger insect is the master, the smaller the slave. These small jet-black slave-ants are carried off from their home nest in the pupa stage and trained to perform the manual work of the large red-headed, red-thighed ant, their captor.

One very touching incident in ant-life takes place when the female, back from her marriage flight, prepares to make a home for the coming generation. The first thing she does is to nip off her own wings lest she should be tempted to disport herself in the sunshine, to the detriment of her maternal duties. There is something very human about this action, as many of my readers who are mothers will understand. I wonder no modern novelist has taken it for a text.

*   *   *

Long after the swallows have left the sunset sky to the moth and bat, the nightjar 'Chur-r-r-rs!' on through the twilight. Now the sound will come from one side of the heath, now from the other, as though two of these strange solitary wild creatures were conversing, with acres between them.

Every summer night that harsh, long-drawn-out note, something between a rattle and a saw, may be heard near here: but until a week or two ago I had never caught a glimpse of the bird which utters it. Then, returning after sunset from the village, one started up from before my feet upon the heath. With its pointed, light-brown speckled wings and spreading tail-feathers, it was at first a puzzling stranger, but it soon enlightened me as to its identity by 'Churring!' as it flew, a special act of consideration for my benefit, for authorities say that it is seldom or never known to utter its cry upon the wing.

Another creature of the moors I met recently was a fox. That, too, was between sunset and twilight. I was walking very quietly down a narrow, mossy path in the woods when we came face to face a few yards apart. Like the nightjar, the fox, too, refused to act according to text-book. By every rule he should have fled like the wind before his natural enemy, man. Instead, he stood stock-still for a moment, sniffed a little contemptuously in my direction, then turned and took a side road, departing with leisurely calm.

September

According to the newspaper reports, the swallow families have been scarcer than usual about the country this year. This probably applies to the midlands and the north. I, when staying in Northamptonshire last month, scarcely caught sight of one for days together. There was something strangely brooding and desolate in the wide stretches of yellow harvest field and open sky with no martins or swallows on the wing, and what other birds there were, were so small and so few as to be almost lost in the vastness.

When I returned home the air seemed alive with them. House-martins, sand-martins, the true swallow, and the last lingerers of the swift family, the main body of which had already departed, flitted above the heath and threaded the valley and winged through the graceful figures of their set dance against the sunset sky. Every day since they have increased in numbers, for not only are our regular summer visitants with us just now, but other contingents arrive daily to await a favouring wind for their long flight overseas. Some of them have already gone, no doubt; but other arrivals have taken their places, and they are not missed. So it will go on until, upon some grey morning in late October, the last lingerers will be missing, and the sky will seem very desolate and clean-swept without them.

That time is not yet. This month is swallow-time. All along the roadsides and across the heath, wherever the telephone lines go, they thread themselves upon the wires, like living notes of music. At morning or evening, when the sun is low in the sky, their small, pinky-white breasts glow opalescent as pearls; at midday, when the light strikes down upon their steely upper portions, they are as jet.

The sweet, low, twittering note of their tiny song is one of the most soothing sounds in nature; it tells of the calm of harvested fields, of garnered fruit, and the golden haze of hot, still September afternoons.

Other years I have seen but the swift and martin tribes: but this year a company of the true swallows took up their abode with me. A pair of them built beneath the tiles inside a disused loft in my garden, and all the summer it has been a common sight as I sat at my desk to see them dart in and out of the open door to their nest amongst the cobwebs. I could not investigate their domestic affairs as I had no ladder, and there was no access to the loft from within; but, judging from their actions, they must have brought off brood after brood. I first noticed them at the end of March, and from then until the second week in August they seemed to be continually feeding young, skimming in and out a hundred times a day.

These large, strong fliers do not build beneath the eaves, as their cousins the house-martins do, but choose some secluded spot within a chimney, or beneath the inner roof of an outhouse, for their nest. Formerly, when the wide, old-fashioned chimneys, large as a small room, were in use, they were known as 'chimney-swallows', and it was a common sight to be able to peer up from the chimney corner through a veil of soot to their nest against the square of sky at the chimney top. Often they may now be found, adapting themselves to modern conditions, beneath the steel girders of a railway bridge or under the high roof of a motor garage.

The departure of the swallow tribes is the great break in the year. Other seasons merge imperceptibly into each other. Spring steals upon winter by slow degrees, and burgeons silently into summer; but the day the last of the swallows disappear we turn indoors to look for other joys: the season is over.

*   *   *

The finest blackberries I have ever seen grow upon a heath about two miles from here. A much-frequented main road from London to the sea cuts through it, and motorists, halting for a picnic lunch, marvel at the exceptional size of the blackberries there. It is no wonder, really, for those particular brambles have had a costly pruning: it took a European war to bring them to their present perfection.

For five years this heath was the site of a camp. Where from time immemorial had been nothing but briar and bracken, row upon row of wooden huts, churches, shops, and theatres sprang up in a week or two. Where only the lapwing had cried or the skylark sung, the drill-sergeant's word of command rang out. The whole place became a populous town.

Tens of thousands of Canadian soldiers sojourned there. One contingent after another arrived, the men often soaked with rain or moiled with heat, and always cramped from the close quarters of wartime transport. There they had a breathing space, saw a little of the 'old country', and learned to love it. They were drilled upon those open spaces so flattened by their feet that even now the heather has scarcely begun to grow again. Then each battalion in its turn passed singing along that same main road to its fate.

In the course of these operations such flower and bramble roots as were left were cut back to earth and received a dressing of all kinds of camp residue. When auction sales and motor lorries had removed the last vestiges of the buildings, and a small army of workmen had laboured for months removing rubbish and filling in holes, Nature set to work to heal the scars; and almost the first growth was the long green shoots of the blackberry brambles. The fruit, when it followed, was of the finest – cultivated fruit indeed, and cultivated at what tremendous cost!

Now the bushes are of full size again, bracken has grown up and filled the rents made by bomb-practice. The heather has returned in waves, a purple sea. Very soon all will be as it had been for countless ages before war broke out, and only the avenue of maple trees the Canadians planted will mark any difference between that heath and a score of others by that same roadside.

*   *   *

This morning I harvested the lavender and sewed it into little grey muslin sacks garnished with purple ribbons for the friends in town. It was a grey day; the day of my lavender harvest usually is, for I love to see it upon the stalk, so I postpone the gathering until the last possible moment, then snatch it in the face of a coming storm.

But today, although the rain threatened, it came to nothing. All morning the swallows wheeled and tumbled and darted beneath a dome of livid, purplish grey. Then at midday the sun broke through, and they subsided, like the little false prophets they were, and strung themselves, preening and twittering, along the telegraph wires at the end of the lane. These wires run, a whole sheaf of them, from London to Southampton, and are a constant delight to me, for I do not share other people's dislike of them.

The lavender has done well this year; the hot, dry weather has suited it. The flowers are fewer, but finer than I remember for years. When mine was rubbed out I had nearly a pound of it, and stalks enough to make a fire when I feel in a Sybaritish mood enough. For the present I have bound the stalks into little sheaves with scraps of the ribbon, and hung them with bunches of mint and thyme in the kitchen window to dry.

The lavender is but a small part of my harvest. Already my store-cupboard shelves are crowded with jars of jam and jelly and bottled fruit; in corners are roots and seeds, and jars of runner-beans shredded down in brine. Upon the bacon-rack on the kitchen ceiling repose vegetable-marrows enough to feed a garrison. They have been so plentiful here, it was useless trying to give them away. Perhaps, about Christmas time, when vegetables are scarce, some neighbour will deign to accept one. Meanwhile they are a pleasure to look at, glowing mildly yellow through the oaken spars, as comforting as a bowl of daffodils, or a wood fire upon a chilly evening.

The apples have yet to be gathered, but they do not need to go begging. They have their own special place of honour, a little loft up under one of the gables called the 'apple room'. Some of my neighbours have done badly this year, but my crop is quite up to the average – golden pippins, red and yellow streaked, and the leather-coat russet by the orchard gate.

The orchard is a favourite haunt this month. I love to run out there before breakfast to collect the windfalls. After the heat-parched weeks that have gone, the crisp morning air, with the new, keen edge of autumn upon it, is deliciously invigorating. It is good to stand, one's drenched feet in the long, dew-sparkling, gossamer-threaded grass, and draw in new life and energy with every breath.

The corner of the orchard is given over to the golden rod. It has been cast out of the garden at some distant date, and has taken root and flourished where it was carelessly thrown. Now there is a golden sea of it, much beloved of the autumn butterflies who flutter above it, poise themselves delicately, and seem to slumber for hours. Perhaps the new keen edge on the air, which fills me with new energy, makes them drowse.

Next week I shall be busy with my small boy assistant picking and sorting the apples. A few of them I shall give away, a few keep for my own use, but the main crop will have to go to the grocer to be transmuted into candles and biscuits and China tea to comfort me in the dark, cold days of winter.

*   *   *

In the dim green underworld beneath the bracken fronds are vivid splashes of red and yellow and tawny, the weird and elfin harvest of the different kinds of fungi. Some are rounds of bright scarlet with greyish spots, like the toadstools in modern fairy pictures; others waxen yellow, honeycombed beneath, or pearly white, shaped like umbrellas turned inside out by the wind. Out upon the open stretches of turf puff-balls are scattered like showers of giant pearls. They have a clean, wholesome look, which does not belie their nature, for, when gathered young and fresh, and sliced and fried, they make a dish fit for a fairy queen.

There is a prejudice against fungi as a food – a very useful and reasonable one considering the many cases of poisoning from indiscriminate indulgence – but for those able to distinguish the edible kinds an autumn banquet may be had any day for the mere picking. The mere names of such species as the champignon, the ivory cap, or the cream bolet are almost a guarantee of their wholesomeness. The difficulty lies in finding, or rather distinguishing them.

In the lean months following the armistice I feasted royally many a time upon such dishes; but a friend, when she came, regarded what she considered such a suicidal menu with so much horror that, to calm her fears, I was obliged to promise to abstain for ever after from such doubtful dainties.

My pledge-keeping was strengthened soon after by an interview I enjoyed with the author of a standard and learned tome upon English fungi, when I learned from his own lips that since the publication of the book he, the specialist and authority, had experimented one time too many, and suffered in consequence such agonizing pains and humiliations that he vowed

100

he would never look at even so much as a common mushroom again in a cooked state! So perhaps upon the whole it is well to regard the quaint and brilliant morsels as a feast for the eye alone.

*   *   *

Upon the thistles a number of small birds are busy – two tiny blue-tits in one place pulling and tugging at the down; in another a bullfinch, having eaten his meal, poises lightly upon a prickly stem to pipe his thanksgiving.

There is an abundance of that food to last them for months, for upon our light loose soil the thistle flourishes. Of the fourteen native kinds, four grow plentifully on and about the heath, while many of the less common ones can be found for the searching.

A delicate contrast to these strong coarse-growing things is the honeysuckle, which has come to its second blooming, and shows fresh waxen clusters of sweetness among its orange and scarlet fruit. There is no other wild flower so deliciously scented. 'Virgin lamps of scent and dew' Rossetti called the honeysuckle flowers; and, as is so often the case, the poet's words embody a scientific fact, for the pale flowers are actually lamps, in the sense that they glimmer through the dusk to attract the night-flying insects.

Not that the honeysuckle has no day visitors: the humble-bee booms perpetually over it, but the nectar lies so far down in the deep trumpet that after the first few sips even his long tongue will not reach it, and most of the work of fertilization is left to the moths, especially the hawk-moths. After a floret has been visited by an insect the colour changes from creamy red-streaked white to a pure, pale yellow, then, later, to a faded orange, all three shades being seen upon one cluster at the same time, marking the age of each individual floret.

*   *   *

From the summit of a hill a week ago the distant cornfields

101

showed like lakes of sober gold between the dark shores of copse and hedgerow. During the last few days small black specks have appeared, and move hither and thither like bobbing buoys upon each golden surface. There are sails, too; the long, red revolving sails of the mechanical reaper. Harvest has begun.

A few days more and there will be slow, heavily-moving, highly-piled waggons there. Then the dull booming of the threshing machine will fill the warm drowsy September air. After that, the dim, mealy sweetness of the mill for the corn and for the fields the silence of the long winter sleep.

Looking down upon him from the hill-top, I could almost envy the harvester. His calling is so sure, his toil so immediately beneficial that no doubts of his use in life can ever assail him. The sower goes laden with faith and hope, as well as seed corn. The harvester scarce has need of either; he feels the weight of the corn tangible to his touch, and knows himself for God's almoner. No scoffer can pass him by with a shrugged: 'What's the good?' He moves, for all his speed, with the dignity of one who knows himself indispensable.

It is only the uplands which are so deserted. Upon the lower slopes, as I climbed today, I had plenty of company. A lapwing, apparently resentful of my presence, circled round and round above my head following or preceding me for a mile or more. I do not know why its cry should have been so plaintively protesting, or why it should have feigned a broken wing, unless it had an unusually late brood to protect. Perhaps it had, for the eggs are much in demand here, both to be sold to provide plovers' eggs for hotel breakfasts and to make a relish for cottage teas at home, and the nests are rifled again and again. So wholesale is the robbery that I have heard of a labourer making a meal of the spoil, fifteen eggs in an omelet! Poor birds! It is very discouraging, but like Bruce's spider they persevere, and a run of bad luck right through the season may account for the seemingly maternal anxiety of the one today.

A direct contrast in bird life was a glimpse I caught today of three goldfinches poised upon a thistle. How they pecked and pulled and tugged at the silken down, then, at the sound of my approach, listened with heads thrown back, a dainty silhouette in colour.

Resting beneath a solitary pine for shade, I suddenly felt a sharp shower of pine husks rattle down upon my hat. Looking upward, I beheld a squirrel sitting upon its haunches, tail erect, pine-cone held daintily in forepaws, sharp, prick-eared little head turned questioningly aside from its meal as some sudden stir upon my part revealed my presence below.

For a perceptible moment it sat at gaze, then dropped its dinner and vanished among the upper boughs. The little creature must have possessed an adventurous spirit, for the tree in which he was dining stands quite alone, fully a quarter of a mile from the nearest clump, and the blazing desert of heath he had to traverse must have seemed a Sahara to one of his size. But no doubt the pine-kernels tasted all the better for it; they would have done to me!

His little rattling shower of husks reminded me of a far rarer sight I saw a week ago. I was sitting very quietly in the depth of the wood near a pine clump when, flitting to and fro against the dark boughs, I beheld a bevy of exotic-looking strangers. Deceived by their hooked beaks and red and blue and orange plumage, I thought, for one wild moment, that a family of parrots had escaped from an aviary; but, creeping cautiously nearer, I recognized them as crossbills, birds one seldom sees in downland, but which I remember seeing occasionally in the New Forest.

I need not have been so cautious in my approach. They took not the slightest notice of me, but flitted from bough to bough, their bright colours glinting, making sudden, swift little pecks at the cones, or at their nearest neighbour's head or wing, whichever came nearest: or making a kind of gymnasium of the tree, hanging by their claws from the twigs, head downward, for all the world like a party of gaily dressed trippers out to enjoy Bank Holiday.

According to the naturalists the crossed beak, which at close quarters gives this bird the appearance of having suffered some accidental injury, is a provision of nature for its special needs, a perfect tool-chest in little, for, at one single operation, it enables its possessor to secure, split open, and devour the cone or seed it desires.

Upon the day I saw the crossbills, I was not looking for such rarities. Had I been, no doubt I should have missed them, for such much-coveted sights always flash before one unexpectedly. My errand that day was to attempt to trace an old pack-horse road which I had discovered from an eighteenth-century map.

I found it without much difficulty; had, in fact, crossed its briar-choked course by another path many times without suspecting that the ditch-like channel was, long ago, a well-worn and notable artery of traffic; that between its deep banks, up hill and down dale, had wended packman with his pack, knight with his lance, holy palmer, telling his beads as he walked barefoot, rosy farmer's wife with her market-baskets, and little hooded, long-skirted maid upon her pony.

Only just here is the old pathway so overgrown; farther on, over the Sussex border, it becomes a well-defined track again, sometimes a green lane between honeysuckle hedges, sometimes a straight, narrow, sandy cart-road across the heath, or through a wood. In one place it masquerades as a tar-sprayed, granite-paved road for motors; but only for a mile or two. At the first curve it parts company and leads through a sloshy farmyard to the hills again.

Stopping only to eat my sandwiches or consult my map, I followed it for miles, quite forgetting that I had to retrace my steps some time or other, and only by a lucky chance as it approached nightfall found a shilling in my pocket and a railway station at hand to bring me back to the twentieth century.

Although the pack-horse way as a whole no longer leads to any place in particular, it was not so deserted as one would have expected. Once I came upon a tinker sprawling beside his barrow in the sun; in another place a gipsy caravan had drawn up for washing day. There were traces of earlier camp fires, too: so many of them that I could not help wondering if some tradition of the road preserved the knowledge that there was a public right of way there.

The wayfarer whom I ventured to question about it confounded me by a hastily doffed cap and discarded cigarette. He had been told about the place by a pal, he said, somebody he had 'dossed' with a day or two before. The words sounded oddly spoken with so unmistakably a public-school accent that for a moment I thought his dusty, untidy tweeds and half-soled basket of oranges were a disguise. Alas! the stiff mechanical leg he stretched so rigidly before him as he sank back beside the basket upon the turf again was only too real.

The man at the doss-house had told him that this road, a green, tree-shaded lane at that particular point, was a public way, and that by some immemorial law every wayfarer was entitled to halt there for two nights and a day without risk of police interference. He had come out of his way – 'If I can be said to have a way!' he added whimsically – to take a day's rest and save lodging-house fees. Orange-selling as a profession did not run to the Ritz: in fact it barely kept him in shoe leather. But he had pension enough to keep him in bread, if he had to 'wangle' his cheese; and to carry a basket gave one a kind of standing in the doss-house at night.

I suppose he had already said more than he intended, for, at the first hint of sympathy in my tone, he withdrew within himself like a tender-horned snail to its shell, and there was nothing to be done but to pay for my oranges, wish him well, and pass on. But I wonder what his story is?

In harvest time a wet day is a serious setback, for not only does heavy rain beat down the corn and make the labour of cutting it double, but ears bowed to earth never see the sun, and so cannot ripen. Even where the corn is in sheaves when rain comes on, contact with the wet soil causes the grain to swell, and ruins it; so twelve hours a day of bright sunshine is the farmer's most urgent need just now.

The labourer shares his employer's anxiety. Days spent sheltering in outhouses with one eye upon the weather means short pay. So at the first gleam of daylight now anxious faces scan the sky from upper windows, and the smoke of wood-fires and the savour of frizzling bacon exhale their homely odours upon the pure, cold air of dawn.

At such times neither toilet nor breakfast are elaborate matters, and the first rays of the rising sun strike red upon gleaming scythes and the revolving arms of the mechanical reaper. These long, sail-like arms of the older-pattern machines are already becoming picturesque with antiquity. A few years ago they represented the most daring advance in agricultural mechanism; but now a more up-to-date reaper, a thing of steel cogs and knives forging round the field by its own power, is gaining in favour, and soon the older type, with its gracefully revolving sails, will be as obsolete as the sickle and the singing army of reapers.

There is a holiday air afloat in the harvest-field. All the trades union and Board of Arbitration ideas of the present day have not entirely succeeded in making the labourer look upon the soil he cultivates as so much productive material. The earth to him is still the earth, not merely 'master's land', or somebody else's; and at the sight of a good crop well carried he cannot but be glad, even though his pride in it is tempered with the rueful remark: 'It's a pity it doesn't benefit them as sweats over it!'

Still, even in that respect, things are a little better than they were; the thirty shillings a week of today, with extra pay for harvest and overtime, are an improvement upon the twelve-and-six to fifteen shillings of pre-war days. In those times, it is true, under some masters there were advantages – a can of skim milk for the asking; turnips and swedes for the pot in winter, or a rabbit for each man after a big shoot – but these benefits were given as favours; there was a flavour of charity about them, and the present arrangement of so much per hour in hard cash is far more satisfactory.

As in all reforms, so in this one of agriculture, many picturesque customs have gone; the harvest-home, or harvest supper, is a thing of the past. No longer do master and man, mistress and maid, sit down to feast together that one night in the year. Now the farmer entertains his friends to dinner or luncheon, and the labourer spends a portion of his extra pay in taking his wife to the 'pictures' in the nearest town. Master and man, when work is over, go their separate ways; the old personal relation has perished.

To those who feel the fascination of the past this may appear sad; but it is not so really, for, even while it existed, this surface good will was often but an empty show. Only too often the farmer who had drained his men of their strength to harvest his grain, paying them all the year round wages so low as to keep them underfed, placed before them at the harvest feast such plenty as to tempt them to gorge, and, even as they did so, made a secret butt of them. The men, on their side, cheered and toasted the hated tyrant on the strength of that one meal, and all the rest of the year criticized, if they did not curse him. Now there is seldom bad feeling between them; the labourer, like any other workman, is out to get a fair wage for his work, and the farmer of the new school is in sympathy with him, and willing, in spite of his own difficulties, to do what he can to meet him.

Yet those old harvest-home feasts created a pleasant warmth for a day. Once, as a child in the Midlands, I had the good fortune to be in for the fun of one. Such a bustling in the farm kitchen for days beforehand – such boiling of hams and roasting of sirloins – such stacks of plum-puddings, made according to the Christmas recipe, piled up in the dairy for heating up on the day – such casks of ale and long plum loaves would astonish any child of this generation.

Then, when the morning of the great day came, what anxious eyes scanned the skies for the weather signals, for the long tables were laid out of doors in the shade of a barn already stuffed to bursting with the corn already threshed. What would have happened if the day had been wet nobody knew, for as the children of the house declared: 'Father always has it fine for *his* harvest-home!'

Dinner was at one, and every man, woman and child in the hamlet was invited, the poor to feast and the sprinkling of better-off to help with the different tables. The only refusals were from the bed-ridden and their attendants, and to them, the day after, portions, carefully graded as to quality according to the social position of the recipient, were carried by the children from the remains of the feast. The only person who could have come, but did not, was an old bee-wife called 'Queenie', who was under the delusion that her bees would not work unless she sat in the sun by the hives all day and hummed to them.

At one o'clock, then, the cottagers sat down to the feast. Outwardly it must have appeared an idyll materialized. The tables spread with abundance of good things – the guests in their Sunday best – the master with his carving-knife – the mistress with her tea-urn – the children in their white frocks running hither and thither to see that everyone had what they required. As a background the rickyard, with its yellow stacks, and over all the mellow sunlight of a September afternoon. Passers-by stopped their dog-carts to wave greetings and shout congratulations upon the weather. If a tramp looked wistfully in, he was placed upon the straw beneath a rick, with a plate upon his lap. It was a picture of peace and plenty.

But it did not do to look too closely. People who live upon the brink of semi-starvation do not study table manners. Upon the actual feasting I will draw a veil; suffice it to say that it was a recognized custom in the parish for people to fast, and make their children fast, for a meal in advance, that their appetites might do justice to the food provided. Amongst the farmer's well-to-do friends half-concealed nods and winks went round as waistcoats were unbuttoned and sashes loosened; and the white-haired old vicar, whose own rosy face was a testimony to his love of good cheer, went about exclaiming: 'God bless my soul, it does one good to see them eat!'

He was sincere enough, no doubt; but a child often sees farther than a wise man, and to one child there it seemed the saddest of sights to see people too used to being hungry to behave well when, for once, they had enough.

The games, again, after the feast was over, seemed planned as much for an entertainment for the hosts as an amusement for the guests. Climbing a greased pole to bring down a leg of mutton, or dipping into a tub of water to retrieve sixpences with the teeth, when undertaken in such deadly earnest, were games less calculated to bring out the dignity of those taking part in them than to amuse the lookers-on. Yet it was all well meant, and when the farmer paused in his carving at the supper-table indoors to listen to the distant cheers for himself of the last home-going group, and ejaculated: 'A good lot of chaps! A good lot of chaps!' both master and men, as far as they understood, were perfectly sincere.

Now, with the glamour of the past upon them, we are inclined to look back upon such old-world holidays with regret, and to consider the present-day dances in village halls, with their travesty of evening dress and town manners, a poor substitute for the old country dances upon the green. From an artistic point of view they may be; but in individual freedom and independence of spirit they mark a stage upward, and with that for the present we must be content.

*   *   *

The corn harvest being stacked, man has now turned to other activities. There is still much to be done in the way of gathering and garnering. From apple orchards comes the sound of laughter, mingled with the soft, leafy swishing of boughs released. On the richer and lower lands the potato fields are studded with rows of new sacks, some filled and some in the process of filling, and the air is blue with the smoke of the smouldering haulm.

Out of sight, but only a few miles away, the whole countryside is transformed to one huge picnic. Hop-picking has begun. A week ago our local contingent started from the village square: mostly women and children, with one or two otherwise unemployed men and lads. The most exhilarating excitement prevailed, for the 'hopping' is the one holiday of the year to most of them. The quantity of baggage taken was surprising, the bags and bundles occupying as much room in the waggons as the passengers; even the smallest of the children clutched some small property or toy they could not bear to be separated from. Even then everyone appeared to have forgotten something, which they had to run back home for, and many were the false starts made. No sooner did one of the drivers give the starting word to his horses than his arm was seized from behind and the whisper went round that somebody was missing.

At last, in despair, one of the carters brought forth his luncheon of bread and cheese, and commenced carving it with his pocket knife. That was the signal for the whole party; baskets were opened and food distributed, although it still wanted two hours till the usual dinner-time. At length the last straggler was hoisted into the waggons, and, with much shouting of farewells and waving of handkerchiefs, they all jogged off happily enough between the berried hedgerows.

These hop-pickers from our own and the neighbouring villages are ordinary cottagers, respectable workmen's families, not the extreme poor. They go hop-picking every year as much for pleasure as for profit. Mothers who have a sickly or ailing child made a special point of going, for the scent of the hops has a great reputation as a cure for all ills. This faith in the hop cure is as well founded as that of their so-called betters in more costly foreign 'cures', for, although it cannot, of course, cure mortal sickness, it is a certain fact that, after an epidemic of measles, whooping-cough, or such-like complaints, after a month of the open-air picnic life children who have gone away pale and drooping come back strong and sunburnt.

* * *

Arranged in a neat row upon the top bar of a field gate were three young robins, so immature that their breasts were barely flushed with red, and their wee tails mere tufts of down. They sat, strung upon their rail, regarding me with bright-eyed attention as I filled my basket with red and yellow streaked crab-apples. As long as I pretended not to notice them they were unafraid; but the moment I turned and looked fully at them they tumbled, rather than flew, from their perch and disappeared in the blackberry bushes.

As I parted the brambles for another look at them, a monster toad shuffled with ungainly haste from the wet ditch into the stubble. Poor creature! The mere sight of a human being made it palpitate with fright, and the warty, leathery brown of its back melted into the other browns of the stubble in a moment.

It is no wonder the toad is timid, for it comes of a persecuted race. For countless centuries it was killed at sight as a noxious creature, much as the snake has always been and is still. Until our own grandfathers' time, indeed, the taking of sticks and stones to the toad was considered a public duty; for not only was it supposed to be so charged with venom that the very touch of its skin was poisonous, but it was actually credited with the power to eject poison, or even to spit fire!

The toad is known now to be the most harmless of creatures; modern science has discredited the poison, and modern common sense the fire-spitting. It is known to be as shy as it is innocent, its only apparent desire being to keep as far as possible from man. Yet there are still many people who regard the toad with loathing, and say there is something in the squat, bloated form and the cold dampness of its skin which makes their 'flesh creep'.

Others confuse it with the frog, thinking that the two names stand for one species. This is a mistake; the toad has a general resemblance to the frog, but they belong to two distinct families. A very little observation is sufficient to distinguish them. The toad is larger and more puffed-up-looking than the frog; its legs are shorter and weaker-looking, and it is unable to leap as the frog does, but drags itself laboriously at ordinary times, breaking into a kind of shuffling amble when disturbed. Its coat, too, is darker and more warty than that of the frog, the latter having shades of yellow and green in its skin, while the toad is usually a dull earth-colour.

Although, like the frog, the toad frequents and breeds in wet places, the tadpoles of the one being almost indistinguishable from those of the other, the adult toad may often be met with upon high and dry land. They are especially fond of cultivated fields, but may also be seen in meadows and upon heaths, or even at times upon the pavement in a suburban road.

If one can be captured and induced to remain in a garden, it makes a useful as well as an interesting pet, for it feeds upon just those grubs and insects which the gardener detests, and its appetite is tremendous. Such a tame toad may be seen upon a sunny morning, its hindquarters tucked back into some nook in a wall or hedge, its mouth wide open and tongue protruding, ready to dart at and devour every insect which comes its way.

A few years ago several discoveries were made in different parts of the world of living toads embedded in blocks of stone. At first sight there appeared no outlet to these prisons, and it was concluded that the animals had become entombed there in some great upheaval of the earth and, dispensing with food and air, lain dormant for countless ages. Fabulous tales grew up as to the age and size of the captives, and even scientists were puzzled; but at length it was proved that in every case some slight aperture existed between the cavity and the outer air, and through this the toad had not only been able to receive insect food, but had probably entered itself when small.

October

In October the forest heaths vie with the woods in richness of colouring. Gold is the predominating note: gold in the mellow, autumnal atmosphere; gold on the distant background of the beechwoods; tawny russet gold on the bracken at one's feet. Nor are other colours lacking. The heather still holds its purple, slightly blanched by sun and rain, it is true, but purple still. The crimson of the whortleberry leaf carpet is repeated in berry and leaf and briar.

Down the sandy, deep-rutted lane rumbles the cart of the bracken-harvester, piled high with its load of lightness. The man who walks beside the rusty little forest-pony in the shafts is tawny, too; the sun has scorched his face to the same colour as his beard, and his weather-stained corduroys are the exact shade of his load. The sight of him and his surroundings brings that despairing, baffled, impotent envy of the painter's medium that the mere artist in words must always feel in the face of colour.

But let poet and artist rave of colour, the New Forest commoner, for the moment, prefers black and white. He looks to his title-deeds, and considers if his forest rights of 'turbary' and 'estovers' can, by any chance, be stretched a little farther than last year. Almost every house of any antiquity whatever carries these rights of digging turf and gathering fallen boughs, and, with a good peat stack and wood pile at one's threshold, coal strikes and the rumour of them are but exotic, far-away misfortunes, moving one to a vague pity for those few millions unfortunate enough to exist beyond the forest bounds, but affecting oneself scarce at all.

There are other rights current in October. Most valuable among them is 'pannage', or the right to turn so many pigs out to fatten upon acorns and beechmast. In these days the beauty-worshipper, walking with hushed tread in the inmost sanctuaries of the forest, may, if he is not careful, stumble over a small boy in charge of a squealing mob of porkers. Such a bored child, too, as a rule; so glad to be told the time, or to accept an apple to munch, or even, in extreme cases, to be told a tale. The day must seem very long to them in the depths of the great, silent woods with only the animals for company. Their parents do not encourage the joining of forces; the pigs might not fare so well if they had to compete for their food. Besides, we have a proverb here: 'Two boys are half a boy, and three boys are no boy at all!' They might, in the excitement of their games, forget their charges altogether and let them stray off into some forbidden enclosure.

Just outside the village today I watched the water-finder at work. This year, for the first time within living memory, the well upon the green ran dry, and people had to travel far and to beg a pailful where they could. So now new wells are to be sunk, one for every separate group of cottages, and every housewife is anxious to have one as near to her own threshold as possible.

The water-finder was a stranger, a quite young man, whose Harris tweeds and easy graceful bearing seemed to forbid the idea that he had been engaged by the estate agent at so much an hour. Whoever he was, he did not disdain tradition, for, before his breast, he bore the forked hazel-rod which modern scientists have discarded as mere insignia. He paced up and down, and round and round, until he must have touched every separate lavender bush and cabbage stem in the cottage garden.

One of his following of villagers and builder's men drew up and informed me that he 'had been on the job this hour or more, an' nothin' doin'.' The spectators were getting bored, some of the women drifted away to prepare dinner; the men whispered to each other of the exact spot where, in their opinion, he ought to seek, and the children munched apples in wide-eyed patience.

Suddenly he stopped. He dug his heel into the soft mould between the gooseberry bushes. 'Just there,' he announced, 'at the depth of seven feet, you will find!'

A babel of voices arose, and I passed on; but tonight the postman told me that, at the exact depth he had predicted, they came upon a spring. What a strange and mysterious gift! Surely those so endowed must be nearer to Nature's heart than the rest of her children!

This afternoon I cut myself a rod and experimented, but, although I walked deliberately over the old, bricked-up well at the bottom of the orchard three times, there was not a quiver.

To soothe my wounded vanity, I concluded it was still empty from the drought. I must try again in the spring.

*   *   *

Since the breaking up of the hot weather, it has been safe to walk anywhere on the heath without any particular care where the next footstep should be placed. There need be no strict keeping to the paths for another six months at least, for the adders, as well as the more innocent grass-snakes, slowworms, and lizards, have tucked themselves away in peaty bank, sand quarry, or loosely built wall, for their winter's sleep.

Other hibernating creatures, more akin to ourselves in their tastes, are enjoying this last spell of sunshine before they retire. The squirrels are particularly lively, and it is a common thing when walking in the woods to feel a sharp little shower of nutshells rattling down about one's head. They have grown so fat and tame the last few weeks that they seem to have lost all fear, and will sit and crack their nuts unconcernedly a few feet overhead, eyeing the passer-by meanwhile in the sauciest manner.

Unlike the squirrel, which is liable to wake up and require food during any mild spell in winter, the hedgehog makes no provision for its long nap, but, rolled in a prickly ball, snout and tail touching earth, he sleeps unbrokenly from October to March. When he leaves his couch, above ground level amongst the dead leaves in a dry ditch, or in the thick carpet of furze-needles beneath bushes, he will find plenty of food to hand, for by that time the slugs, grubs and snails which form his staple diet will abound, not to mention the birds' eggs which he sometimes takes as a strengthening luxury.

The dormouse is another sleeper which hibernates above ground level. Just at present it is busy constructing its winter sleeping nest of moss and dead leaves, usually in or near a bush wreathed with honeysuckle, which plant, for some mysterious reason, has a great attraction for it. At the first approach of the next cold snap it will retire to its nest, curl up in it and sleep till the spring.

A dormouse will sometimes save itself the trouble of making a winter nest by taking possession of a bird's nest in good repair. The winter before last I was out in the woods one day with a schoolboy friend when we came upon a thrush's nest we had watched the preceding April. Scrambling up the bank to the low stump in which it was placed, the boy thrust his hand into the nest, and called to me to come, as there were young birds in it. Before I could reach him he had decided that the young birds were mice, or perhaps a squirrel, and finally we found that a dormouse had taken up his winter quarters there. Curled into a perfect round to fit the accommodation, head to middle, hind legs and tail neatly encircling the whole, it lay so stiff and cold to the touch that it might have been supposed to be dead. As gently as possible, we replaced the dead leaves which had covered it and left it to have its sleep out.

It is natural to us to speak of this hibernating state of the animals as sleep, but it is in fact rather a halfway house between sleep and death. All natural functions are suspended; the creature does not hear, or see, or require food; its breathing is imperceptible, its body rigid and cold. Nature has turned down its tiny spark of life to the faintest glimmer.

Other still smaller and shyer creatures than the dormouse steal away for the winter. The shrew-mouse burrows into the soft leaf-mould of the ditches; the mole sleeps in his own citadel; and their winged relative, the bat, hangs himself up by the feet, head downward, to the rafters of some old barn or church tower.

At one time it was believed that the swallow hibernated in the same way as the bat is known to do. The idea arose, no doubt, through the habit these birds have of congregating in large flocks a few miles inland from the Channel coast in autumn and disappearing and re-appearing at intervals of a few days for several weeks. The patient observations of bird-lovers during the last hundred and twenty years have established the knowledge that these congregations are composed of different birds, one flock departing overseas and another from farther north taking its place; but a century ago this disappearance and re-appearance had not been accounted for, and it was thought that in bad weather the swallows retired to some winter retreat close at hand, to be coaxed out again by every spell of fine weather until the winter finally closed down. Then, as they were so often to be seen skimming the surface of the water at that time, it followed that they should be supposed to hibernate either in the crevices of the banks of ponds and streams, or to plunge, fishlike, into the warm mud at the bottom.

That most famous of our early bird-lovers, Gilbert White of Selborne, played with this idea all his life. Although he was convinced that the majority of the swallow families migrated, he thought it just possible that the weaker birds of the late broods might remain in this country, and, in order to settle the question, he offered a handsome reward to anyone who could produce a hibernating swallow for his inspection. Naturally enough, although there were country people who were ready to swear they had seen the birds hanging from the rafters like bats, or had helped to fish them in masses from the bottom of ponds, not a single specimen was forthcoming.

*   *   *

This place has been unusually populous today; not only the

bracken harvesters have passed my door, but schoolboys have been nutting in the wood, and the sound of their trampling and laughter has turned an ordinary day into a holiday. For all the enjoyment they seemed to get out of it the actual 'bags' must have been meagre; for this has·been a poor year for nuts, and I doubt if the whole yield of the wood would more than fill one of their knapsacks.

But although the crop is small the squirrels have had a picking, and there are more empty shells upon the moss beneath the trees than full shells upon the branches. The hazel nuts are a kind of dessert to the woodland creatures. They eat them when they can, and enjoy them, but do not look for anything so delicious as a matter of course; the beech mast and pine kernels are their serious food.

A schoolboy friend told me the other day that he had seen two kingfishers in the hazel thicket, 'running up and down the trunk of an elm like mad, upside down or right side up, more like flies than birds!' The birds he saw were really nuthatches; but the mistake was a natural one, for the nuthatch, although a much smaller bird, is a kind of understudy in colour and form of the kingfisher.

In the nuthatch the iridescent green and azure of the kingfisher is toned down to a slatey blue; its breast is a delicate rose instead of rusty scarlet. But these subdued echoes of colour, combined with the similarity of the large head and stumpy tail, certainly make up as good a resemblance as may sometimes be seen in so-called 'doubles' in human life.

The habits of the two birds are entirely different. The kingfisher frequents pond and river banks; he lives largely upon fish, and is seldom seen far from water. The nuthatch is a bird of the deep and quiet woods. In spring and summer he is seldom seen at all. Just once or twice in the year a glimpse may be caught of him, running up and down a tree-trunk, tapping for insects, as his cousin the woodpecker does. In autumn he becomes more bold; his passion for nuts is so great that he will risk the publicity of a hedgerow or orchard in quest of them.

The treasure found, he wrenches one from a cluster of green

husks with his bill and flies with it to a rough-barked tree. Here he forces it into a crevice and, throwing his whole weight upon it, hacks and hews at it with his beak until the kernel is exposed. The tree selected is usually an oak or an elm, and if the rough bark of such trees is examined an empty shell still fixed in the trunk will often show that the nuthatch has banqueted there.

*   *   *

Of all the trees of the wood the oak alone is untouched by the finger of autumn. 'Laggard to come and laggard to go' is true of it in a seasonal sense as well as a lifelong. Not until really severe frost comes will the leaves blanch from their sober summer green, and even then they will hang and rustle upon the tree till the turn of the year comes and the sap rises.

The life-span of the oak is probably longer than that of any other living thing, animal or vegetable: 'Three hundred years to come and grow. Three hundred to stand and stay. Three hundred to dwine and go', is the foresters' old adage about it. Even this may fall short; there are oaks still standing which are mentioned in the Doomsday Book, and they must have been well grown even then, or they would not have been selected for landmarks.

The fall of one of these giants of the woods is a moving sight. In the New Forest one day I happened to pass at the final crash of one. Woodmen stood around mopping their brows and congratulating each other upon the neat job they had made, guiding its fall scientifically to an inch to avoid injuring the branches of other trees.

'There it is, down in a day!' said one of them. 'Down in a day! And not the wisest man in all the world could set it up again!'

But, noble as the New Forest oaks are, I have never, there or elsewhere, seen such a giant in girth as one I saw hauled through the streets of Oxford last month. Before it appeared the colleges, with their carved and crumbling antiquity, had seemed immemorial compared to the little span of man's mortality. Then through the narrow passage between them came the King of the Forest, its progress full of unpremeditated dignity, for its bulk was so great and the way so narrow that motor-buses, cars, cycles, and foot passengers had all to draw aside and wait while the traction-engine which drew it negotiated the turning.

Its length exceeded that of the timber-carriage upon which it was lashed, and it was supported at the end by a temporary extension. Its great grey girth, rough barked and fledged with lichens, brought the top of it on a level with balconies and upper windows. Its progress through the narrow streets had the slow stateliness of a procession.

To earn that pomp it had weathered who knows how many centuries? Standing, perhaps, upon some height above the city, it had looked down upon the Oxford of its saplinghood, a castle tower with a cluster of mud huts around; had watched spires and domes arise where before had been green meadows and glinting waterways, and seen those same spires and domes turn from snowy white to grey antiquity.

Of its thousand leafages some at least must have fluttered at the feet of men, then living in the flesh, whose names have also weathered the centuries. Shakespeare may have halted in its shade as he rode from Stratford to London, for it is a tradition that he always turned aside to sleep at the Davenants' hostelry. Shelley may have leaned against its trunk upon one of his country walks. Newman may have paced beneath, torn by inward questionings. Who can tell?

Now, after all the patient years, it had come down to the city, and bustling and impatient man stood aside to give it right of way. Perhaps one or two of those who stood at the crossing paid silent homage to its antiquity. All I heard was an American tourist complain to his daughter of the waste of time and protest against the way the traffic was controlled. A schoolboy brought forth his camera and snapped it. Motor-bus drivers chaffed the driver of the traction-engine: 'Come along, old tortoise! Think we can wait all day for you to bring that old stump along?' and the old oak was coaxed round the corner, and the waiting crowd surged on.

*   *   *

Today has been the harvest-home of the heath. All day they have been carting bracken, snatching in the tawny heaps hurriedly, because yesterday was the first drying day for a week, and, as one of my neighbours said, 'It mid be now or never!'

A queer assortment of vehicles was pressed into the service, from a newly-painted farm-waggon, resplendent in ultramarine and yellow, to a superannuated station fly with the top taken off. These two, with donkey-carts, hand-barrows, and perambulators, have wound down the sandy lane past my house all day, filling the usually silent spaces with gaiety.

When they get the bracken home they will spread it again to finish drying, then build it into quaint, circular little ricks for winter litter.

Now, one side of the heath is left bare and stubbly, while the other, divided by the faint trace of what was once a turf wall, still waves untouched. Low and half obliterated as the wall is, no commoner would take so much as a frond from the other side, for the laws of common rights are strictly laid down, as becomes laws framed by the Norman Kings, and the land upon the other side of that age-long boundary is the property of the Crown.

Crown land and common land is all the same to me. The War Department, since the end of the war, have made little use of their share, and I wander where I will and eat my sandwiches or botanize in the shelter of decaying notice-boards inscribed with terrifying warnings of bomb practice and gun-fire.

There was one havoc-working day a couple of winters back, when they tested a new make of tank upon the downs, and huge reptilian monsters waddled over hills and through woods, flattening the gorse and bearing young trees like straws before them. Once again, in summer, one of the smaller hills was snow-capped for a fortnight with the tents of an Officers' Training Corps, and pink-cheeked, drab-haired boys, all of a pattern, ranged the heath and swam in the pool, and caused their elders to exclaim in thankfulness that the war *they* waged, thank God, was only a mimic one.

To the common land I have a more tangible right. The tenancy of my cottage carries certain common-rights, and I might, if I so desired, amass wood for my fire, as much as I could gather 'by hook or by crook' – in other words, dead branches that could be reached down or picked up without chopping. However great my need or my energy, I must not 'take axe or billock to lop stick or stock' under the most blood-curdling penalties.

* * *

The rook in Hampshire has a great reputation for wisdom, usurping the place of the owl in that respect, for the latter bird, considered elsewhere the very emblem of wisdom, is here looked upon as 'a poor silly thing', and anyone looking particularly distraught is said to be 'as balmy-looking as an owl in daylight'!

Whether the rook is as wise as he is supposed to be is an open question, but he certainly shows great discrimination at times. A few years ago some birds in a neighbouring rookery suddenly, for no apparent reason, deserted a favourite elm in which they and their ancestors had nested from time immemorial. Not only was the one central tree avoided, but several others grouped around it; outside the proscribed circle they built their nests (if building it can be called to cross a few twigs roughly into a platform) and brought up their broods as usual.

In March that year came a terrific gale which felled the central tree and brought down huge limbs of the neighbouring ones, all nestless! An expert in forestry tells me that he has known the same thing to happen before, and that always in such cases the topmost twigs of the fallen tree are found to be dead, and from such a slight sign the birds must be clever enough to deduce some central unsoundness which may send the whole tree toppling in the first gale.

The farmers are more tolerant of the rook than they used to be; they are learning at last that the rook at certain seasons is the farmer's friend. In spring, for instance, it feeds upon the larvæ of certain insects which, if left to come to maturity, would ruin the root crops. Just now, when winter wheat is being sown, it is a different matter, for Master Rook is capable of clearing whole rows of seed corn almost as methodically as the tractor drills it in.

At one time little boys of eight or ten used to be employed at twopence a day to scare the rooks from the corn with a wooden clapper. Poor little fellows, it was a dismal task! Sent out into the heavy ploughed fields before daylight, with a hunk of bread and a shred or two of fat bacon to last them the day, with no human creature to speak to from morning to night and no means of telling the time but the often invisible sun, the day must have seemed endless.

I remember when I myself was a child one such boy running the whole length of a ploughed field to enquire the time of my brother and me. His face fell blankly when he heard it was still an hour before noon, for he had already consumed both dinner and tea under the impression that a day which seemed so long to him must be nearing twilight. To bribe us to keep him company for a time he carved for us a wonderful death-head out of a turnip, which, with a lighted candle inside and a commandeered table-cloth draped round, was set at night upon the gatepost at home and scared not only the uninitiated but the two per-petrators as well!

The carving of turnips is a lost art. That is a pity; but upon the other hand, poorly paid as the farm-worker still is, little boys of ten are no longer sent to languish all day alone in the sodden winter fields to add a mere shilling to the family income.

*   *   *

In company with the traveller's joy there are still a few straggling trumpets of late honeysuckle, and to these and to the ivy blossoms, still in their prime, a few bees and other insects come daily. One day last week, upon a pale green ivy corymb, a queen wasp had alighted. The other insects had dispersed at her coming, and she was burying her jaws in the honeyed recesses of the flower, her whole frame quivering with enjoyment.

That would probably be her last meal for this year, for it was already late in the season for her to be about. By now, she has crept into some warm crevice of tree-bark or fencing, where she will sleep the winter away. Then, upon a warm, sunny day next spring, she will emerge to found a miniature nation.

For the first few days she will flutter feebly about, gaining strength of wing, and seeking at the same time some sunny bank to make her kingdom in. The ideal site discovered, she will commence the work unaided, boring into the earth with her jaws, and dragging forth any small stone or twig which lies in her way, until she has tunnelled a passage leading to a small cave.

From the roof of this cave she will then hang clusters of cells made of a papery substance, in each of which, when completed, she will lay an egg. From each of these eggs will emerge in due time a worker, or neuter female grub, and each of these the queen will feed with her own royal jaws until she has a small army of fullgrown handmaidens round her. Then the work will proceed apace. Under the queen's directions the whole palace will be enlarged and improved, and every one of the underground chambers hung from roof to floor with tier after tier of the papery cells.

At that stage the queen will leave all menial work to her attendants and devote herself to maternal duties. In each cell she will lay an egg – both male and female this time, for the queen wasp shares with the queen bee the power to discriminate and regulate the sex of her offspring. Very soon she will be at the head of a populous nation, and by the end of the summer may be surrounded by as many as twenty thousand of her own descendants, all fated to be regarded by man as enemies and destroyed at sight – but how marvellously produced and organized!

One more public-spirited than I have any pretension to be would have nipped her career in the bud, and might, like Sampson, have boasted of having destroyed thousands. But public-spirit is as far removed from my powers as the queen wasp's skill and industry; besides, there was a deep and muddy ditch between her Majesty and the path where I stood.

November

Upon the fourth of November, three swallows appeared in a sky deserted for more than a fortnight by the last of their kind. It was a dull morning of east wind and cutting showers, and the shrill cries of the three birds may have been due to cold. Just as probably, they were hunger cries, for a keen wind clears the air of insects even more completely than frost, and the swallow depends entirely for its living upon hawking for insects upon the wing.

Other birds have endless resources; they snap their prey here and there where they can. They know exactly where to find such insects as may be expected to be abroad – the banqueters above the ivy bloom, the hoverers for warmth above the midden – either will do equally well; winter appetites cannot afford to be fastidious. When winged things fail, there are still grubs to be dragged from tree-bark or from wooden fences, or the farmer's plough will provide wire-worms in the newly-turned clods. But the swallow has not been bred to such frugal ways. All the summer its food has come to it as freely as the air it has breathed; it has never known what it was to search or scratch for a living; and, when food fails in the upper air, it must seek other climes where the sun still shines and insects dance in its beams, or, if forced to remain, it must hunger.

That is why only the most pressing circumstances will keep these birds behind at migration time. If two or three of them are seen after October is out, there is always a story to account for it, and the end of that tale is often tragedy. Of these three, perhaps, two were parent birds, the third a nestling of a late brood. At the time when the family should have migrated, the little one was probably a weak, pathetic, unfledged thing, the last, perhaps, of a brood of which the others had flown. Then love would war with instinct in the hearts of the parent birds, and love would win. They would see the skies swept clear of their own kind; the nights would grow chill, the mornings seem long in coming; for the first time in their lives, perhaps, they would know hunger and cold. For the whole of one day and part of the next they hovered above the heath, uttering their mournful cries, as though keening the departed summer; then, in a sudden burst of sunshine, they disappeared over the rim of the seaward hills.

*   *   *

From November until March this valley is a fairy garden of flowering mosses. Upon the banks of the boggy stream, creeping up the slopes and about the tree-roots, the soft spreading cushions of green are powdered with fawn and rust and yellow. The prevailing shade is a soft rusty red, and from this I have named it 'Red Moss Valley'.

In the small pools in the bog, where encircling rushes have held the sphagnum at bay, sudden splashes and bubblings tell of shy denizens of the place, disappearing before the sound of a human footstep. Now and again a water-rat may be seen, or a newt, slipping down into the water, its orange under-surface upmost.

The innocent newt has a bad name in these parts, and schoolboys hunt and destroy it unmercifully. They quite believe that the bite of one, or even its mere contact with the human skin, would be poisonous. The newt never gives them a chance of verifying this belief. Unless surprised too far from the water, it is gone like a streak of lightning; if taken at a disadvantage, its only desire is to hide beneath the nearest stone. All the newt asks of man is to be left alone, and, as neither its haunts nor interests clash with his, nor is it armed for warfare with him, by poison glands or otherwise, it seems but fair that this wish should be respected. It takes no toll of his food, as the birds do, nor does it burrow in his fields like the rabbit. It makes its home beneath a wet stone beside a stream, or in the midst of a marsh; the stream and the stone are its whole world, and man, when he appears, is a huge and fearsome apparition to be avoided.

These small fellow-creatures, so far removed from ourselves, have a quaint beauty which should appeal to modern taste, with its love for the odd and bizarre. Even the common newt, to be found in every pool, is most *uncommonly* interesting. Shaped something like the lizard, his colouring is far more attractive. His back and sides are a greyish-brown, his under-side orange, splashed with brown. Like the larger and more showy great water newt, the male grows a crest in spring; and a crested newt in a clump of kingcups is as wonderful in a smaller way as a tiger in a tropical forest.

The newt has sprung straight from the soil, or rather from the peaty water. He takes care to be seen seldom, but, when seen, his presence raises no wonder. Far different is the case of another, and not seemingly very different creature which may sometimes be seen there. A few days ago, as I bent over the water in search of the newt, I saw the dark form of an eel swaying out from the bank. That eel was certainly not born in any stream round here, but far away, among swaying weed beds in the Atlantic Ocean, and, if no accident, such as being cooked and eaten, for instance, overtakes it, it will go back there to die; for the eels, although they spend much of their lives in fresh water far inland, are natives to, and fulfil their destinies in the boundless sea.

This, when they are found in rivers, may appear no miracle; they make their way down to the estuary and out to sea much as the salmon do. But, when they are seen in a heath-encompassed pool, with no water outlet whatever, and acres of prickly gorse and heath between that and the next pool, the thought of their journey, hither and hence, is astounding.

How and when do they go? There is, as far as I know, no record of one being seen travelling overland, but it is established beyond dispute that, after three or four years in these inland waters, the eel, waxing fat and strong, puts on its bridal suit of yellow and sets out upon its great adventure. It never returns. After once bringing forth inestimable numbers of young in one breeding season, both male and female parents perish; but the young return, led by what we call 'instinct', to whatever place is good for them and that they were intended for.

*   *   *

One day last week, as I passed on my way to the village, I stopped to watch the hedger-and-ditcher at work. Upon one side of him the thorn boughs lay prone in the puddles; upon the other, the old hedgerow still stood brown and shaggy and berried, just as it *has* stood untouched for a generation or more. I could not help admiring his dexterity as he stripped the shoots which his billhook had spared, drew them down and laid them horizontally, interlacing them to form a long, low fence, about the height and thickness of a hurdle.

'Takes some doin', that does!' he remarked in answer to my unspoken thought.

He was a stranger, a tall old man, apple-cheeked and direct of eye, one who knew his own worth, probably, and demanded his due, always taking care to give good value for it. The very way he handled his billhook proclaimed him highly skilled, as indeed he must have been, or he would not have been imported to do that especial job while many younger men went workless.

*   *   *

Yesterday I came upon the first living mole I had ever seen, although I had often come upon a dead one lying by the roadside. Had I not been on the watch for it I do not suppose I should have noticed it then, for its greyish-brown velvety coat matches well with the colouring of the winter earth, and its swift, gliding movement, much like that of a clockwork mouse across a carpet, helps to make it practically invisible.

The house of the mole is a tiny subterranean castle consisting of an elaborate central chamber, with long burrowing runs radiating from it in all directions. Here, in a nest lined with moss and leaves, it lives and brings up its family. This little home is usually made at the base of a large molehill, but we must not on that account conclude that every molehill we see conceals a dwelling; most of them are simply heaps of sifted earth thrown up in the search for roots or earthworms.

At one time the mole was thought to be blind, but now it is known that the eyes, though feeble, are at least sensitive to light and darkness. Its character, too, has been somewhat rehabilitated of late years, for the farmer is realizing that the mole, although destructive to pastureland turf, is a valuable ally to man in the destruction of slugs and snails, not to mention the more unmitigated pests, such as wire-worm and leather-jacket.

But in spite of the growing toleration of the agriculturist the life of the mole is still a precarious one; for, to supply the ruthless demands of fashion, thousands of these little creatures are slaughtered yearly for their fur.

It is scarcely to be wondered at. What other pelt, excepting perhaps the rare and costly sealskin, can make a wrap so luxuriously supple and silky, or so universally becoming? Yet, if women could only be made to realize the terrific price exacted – fifty warm, palpitating living things trapped and tortured and ultimately slain to make a muff or a stole – who, indeed, would be found to take pleasure in such a garment?

The so-called 'mole-coney' is a different matter. That fur, a miracle of the furrier's art, and in the better qualities scarcely distinguishable from the genuine moleskin, is furnished by the homely rabbit, a creature which, if crops are to flourish at all, must be kept down in numbers. There is no more cruelty in wearing such fur than there is in eating rabbit-pie for dinner; so it becomes just a matter of taste, and for those fastidious ones who consider the wearing of any slain animal's pelt 'barbaric' there is still the fleece of the living sheep, with the rainbow hues to choose from.

*   *   *

There is something very attractive about the first winter evening: it is a landmark, just as the first note of the cuckoo is a landmark in the year. 'The Little Festival of the Toasting-fork', as we, as children, used to call the first tea of the season by lamplight, has its own intimate appeal to the heart.

* * *

The forest is hushed. The more homely singers, robin and thrush, have attached themselves for the winter to the haunts of man. Other birds have gone overseas, have sought the berried hedgerows, or the last scanty gleanings of the stubble. The blackbird, it is true, still skulks, scratching for food among the dead leaves beneath the hollies; but, at sound of an intruding footstep, he utters one sharp complaining note and takes short, swift flight to the next group of bushes; otherwise, his beak is sealed.

But the stillness and silence are only apparent. Stand still a moment, and the *tap*, *tap* of a woodpecker comes faintly from a distant tree; a jay flashes screaming from one thicket to another; tiny feet patter upon the pine-needles, each small creature about its own business.

The squirrel's granary is full, and he has eaten so well of the surplus that he has become fat and lazy and bold – 'saucy' as the country people say. I saw one today, lying flat upon a tree-limb, tail and paws outspread, sunning himself and drowsing, the very picture of luxurious ease. Nor did he trouble to move when I swished the fallen leaves up at him, but regarded me with bright, black, beady eyes, as though to say: 'Well, the summer is over. And what a summer! Still, good things cannot last for ever, and I, for one, am quite ready to tuck myself up for my winter nap.'

His fellow-sleeper, the hedgehog, is still busy. One scuttered so quickly across my path today I mistook him for a rabbit.

Trippers and hotel visitors alike have gone; one may walk the forest all day now and meet no one more exotic than an acorn gatherer, a gardener collecting leaf-mould, or a gipsy woman rooting ferns for suburban conservatories. The two former are almost as inarticulate as the tree-trunks beneath which they labour, but the latter is always ready to break off and beg, or to promise one all the good luck in the world for a sixpence.

The one I met today was not that kind, though. She did not beg. From her appearance, she had no need to, though that is the last reason in the world to a forest gipsy why she should not! She told me she was eighty-nine, and I could believe it, for although her black, glossy plaits had scarce a grey hair, and her eyes were small penetrating black flames, her face was more seamed and wrinkled than any I have ever seen. She was gorgeously and uniquely clad in a man's crimson quilted dressing-gown, finished with hob-nailed, steel-tipped boots that would certainly last her as long as she needed any.

She was looking for wood-sage, she said: one of her grandchildren was out of sorts, and she thought a good, stiff dose of wood-sage tea would set her right. I turned out of my way a little to show her a nearer patch of the herb than the one she knew of, and to thank me she promised me all the delightful happenings she could lay tongue to.

No, not quite all; there was no dark or fair stranger. Neither did she promise me riches; she passed such things over disdainfully, as stock properties kept for the commonalty who crossed her hand with a shilling. She even confided that she did not go by the hand at all, that it was only a formality to secure the shilling.

'It's the face,' she said, 'not the hand. It's all writ in the face what a person is. And, if I know what you are, I can tell pretty well how things'll go with you!'

She was certainly able to read the secret desire, for she promised me love and praise and friendship!

'You are goin' to be loved,' she said, 'loved by a lot o' folks – strangers shall become friends – people all over –' and she waved her bundle of wood-sage to include the entire horizon.

Nonsense, of course. Yet, after I parted from her, I trod more lightly, and strange to say, when I reached home I found a letter awaiting me from a complete stranger praising some trifle I had written.

All about the downs the large holly trees grow in clumps, usually in a ring, with a well-roofed-in space as large as a small room in the middle. Often there are pine trees mixed with the hollies, and a layer of soft dry pine-needles, a foot or more thick, forms a luxurious carpet as a finishing touch to one of the snuggest out-of-door retreats imaginable.

These thick covers of holly and pine must often have served primitive man as a dwelling. Occasionally they are still used for that purpose, both by the poor and homeless and by camping parties from town. A permanent home of the kind survived here until a few weeks ago. In the shelter of a circle of hollies, old trees, almost as tall and bushy as oaks, a tinker and his wife had made their home for forty years. Inside the circle of the trees was a space as large as a cottage, thick foliage formed the roof and walls, and the floor was the natural earth, hardened by forty years' use.

The little home was neatly arranged; there was room for the sleeping tent, for the kitchen part, with its brick fireplace and pots and pans, and even a corner fenced off with hurdles and lined with straw for the donkey. Honeysuckle draped the door opening, and before it stretched Nature's garden, miles wide, of heather, bracken and gorse. Every day the occupants went out with their knife-grinding apparatus and china-riveting outfit and earned enough to supply their needs – earned more, indeed, as it proved in the end, than was good for them.

Poor and ignorant in some things as these people were, they were no common people. They were both of them, the man especially, true nature-lovers, knowing and loving every bird that visited the heath, and pointing out anything out of the ordinary in tree, bush, or flower with a proprietary pride akin to that of an estate owner taking a visitor over the Home Farm. Scores of times I have stopped to listen to the involved tale of the efforts of certain local authorities to eject them, a tale which the old man always concluded, waving his pipe for emphasis:

'But they found they couldn't do it. No! Not even the King of England 'isself c'd turn us out arter forty years. Squatters' Rights, we've got, Squatters' Rights! 't 'ud take more nor a

Lord of th' Manor to shift such as we!'

Alas! What the law could not do, the one secret flaw within accomplished in a single night. Both husband and wife had one weakness, being possessed of such an inordinate thirst that the hardy little donkey which drew their cart would stop of his own accord at sight of an inn sign. Every day poor Neddy stood for hours outside the Good Intent, or the Staff of Life, as familiar a fixture to the passer-by as the signboard. One night last June, the little party went home, the donkey the only sensible being among them, or, at any rate, the only one of them who was never suspected of dropping the match which set fire to the place and left the holly roof and walls a ring of charred skeletons and the beds, tents and household goods within a heap of smouldering ruins.

Poor old things! Their fate is a humble illustration of Meredith's line –

'We are betrayed by what is false within.'

December

December and January are the bare months. Our grandmothers, when they compiled their floral calendar, could not find a flower for December at all and took the holly-berry instead. Their choice is understandable. Christmas and holly, holly and Christmas. Who could think of one without the other? But December has its own flower, the ivy, which they overlooked.

This year it is flowering as never before. Every wreathing garland in the woods and upon the hedgerow tree-trunks is thick with the pale, mealy-yellow corymbs. There is a glamour about the ivy bloom. It is one of those flowers one is not taught to love, but left to discover for oneself. In childhood, it simply does not exist for most of us; we pass it year after year, unseeing. Then, one season, our attention is drawn to it by accident, and we look closer, and see how exquisitely fashioned the florets are, how beautifully the greenish-yellow clusters harmonize with the dark leaves; and every winter after it meets our eye wherever we go and makes a mild sunlight upon gloomy days. Some of this ivy-magic may be due to Shelley's vision of the poet:

> 'He will watch from dawn to gloom
> The lake-reflected sun illume
> The yellow bees in the ivy bloom . . .
> And from these create he can
> Forms more real than living man.'

Who, with these lines in mind, could call December barren?

The snails alone would make a winter walk in the most commonplace scenery interesting, for it is surprising to find the number of varieties existing side by side in any lane or hedgerow. The spotted or garden snail is a common sight everywhere, although few notice it, except children and gardeners. Between the snail and the latter there is a deadly feud (deadly to the snail, at least), for its taste in vegetables is too human to make it a welcome guest in any garden. The youngest of green peas, the crispest of lettuce, the fattest asparagus stems, the peach ripening upon the wall – the taste for such things is fitting in man, but out of place in a snail.

Children and boys are the only friends of the garden snail; the former love to hold it by the shell and chant the immemorial charm:

> 'Snail, snail, put out your horn,
> And then I'll give you a barleycorn,'

just for the pleasure of seeing the sensitive horns, in which, most probably, the snail's senses of sight, touch, and hearing are concentrated, slowly and cautiously put out, as though newly growing.

These largest of our land snails were a favourite dish with the Romans in Britain, and are said to be eaten in certain districts in the West of England to this day. If so, the cooks in those parts deserve credit, for once during the war, inspired by a newspaper article, I experimented upon a dish of them. After an elaborate and prolonged preparation my dish was set upon the table, in appearance much like stewed oysters in melted butter. Alas for appearances! The should-have-been savoury tit-bits tasted exactly like morsels of stewed rubber; and, although I brought both the appetite and the obstinacy of the pioneer to the dish, I could not away with even one of its contents.

In spite of this personal failure, it is quite probable that no one need starve while there are slugs and snails to be found and a fire is forthcoming to cook them by. In a certain village in the Midlands there used to be a tradition dating from the old sheep-stealing days that once a poor widow with a large family was suspected of receiving and hiding stolen mutton, because, having no means except the starvation allowance of the relieving officer, her children were yet the plumpest and rosiest in the parish. One day the authorities searched her cottage and found a barrel of meaty morsels salted down in her larder. This at first was taken for finely minced mutton, but, upon examination, proved to be slugs which she gathered in wet weather to provide all the meat her children were likely to taste.

* * *

I often wonder what the ploughman thinks of as he cuts his furrow hour after hour in solitude. A poet or philosopher should flourish upon such a life. A weak man might brood and turn sullen; but my ploughman, judging from what I know of him, meditates only upon sane and wholesome things – the latest letter from one of his absent children, the mild politics discussed last night at the village alehouse, or the meat pudding, piping hot, which his wife will have waiting at home for him.

With the shepherd it is different. His thoughts range earth and skies; he may at any given moment be planning for his own unborn lambs, or dreaming of the flocks kept by the shepherds of Bethlehem; striving to make his own economic ends meet, or yearning over 'them poor mites out in the war countries, without scarce a bite or a sup, poor innocents!'

Although poor and obscure he is not unlearned. He knows each of the constellations by name, and most of the legends concerning them. The night sky is his especial delight, and he has more opportunities of studying it than most men; not once, but many times, between Christmas and Easter, he will be up all night about his lambing duties, and see the marches of the stars from dusk till dawn.

One winter evening during the war I passed him on his homeward way. It was just at the time when the lighting regulations were most stringent, and every cottage window had to be shrouded at night lest some chink should let the light escape. He was so lost in thought that he had no greeting for me, and I missed it.

'A penny for your thoughts, Shepherd!' I called across the road to him.

For answer he pointed to the full moon, riding in a fleece of pearly clouds above the line of the downs.

'They can't put that out,' he said, 'nor the sun, nor the stars, for all their mightiness. To see her shine like that makes you feel that it's only just on the surface that things 'as come to such a pass, and at bottom all is as the Lord intended; and everything will be as it has been again, even though we mid not live to see it.'

For a moment he stood there pointing, his tall, bent figure in its patched earth-coloured clothes, full of dignity, the white light falling full upon his pale, drawn face and patient eyes; then, with a bare 'good-night,' he turned and went. My own heart had been full of bitterness, and I felt rebuked, although comforted. As I walked on I marvelled that such a man should have been born to a life of obscure toil.

I need not have done. His spoken word had influenced me at a moment when the written word of poet or philosopher was but mere paper and printer's ink to me. Others with whom he came in contact must have been influenced even more; and in this way he may, through his whole life, have been working from below, as poet and seer work from above; both he and they being portions of that leaven which, in time, shall leaven all humanity.

Except for the night work in winter, the ploughman's lot is even more solitary than the shepherd's. When ploughing such an isolated upland field as he has today, he must often work the whole day through without hearing a human voice. His midday meal he takes under the lee side of a hedge, eating his bread and bacon and sending up the thrice blessed smoke of his pipe, while his horse munches, and flings up its head, and shakes its nosebag for the last corn, and robins and chaffinches peck round their feet for the modest remains of the feast. These little birds peck up their crumbs with the assured air of welcome guests; but there are other and larger birds in attendance which are scarcely less bold. All day the ploughman and his horse have been the centre of a crowd. Rooks and seagulls have followed them up and down; rabbits and hares scuttered away before them; frogs and toads and fieldmice fled for their lives before the shining terror of the ploughshare.

For the rooks, a field under the plough is a feast spread for their especial benefit. From far and near they flock in a body to spend the livelong day in eating and squabbling. Always a bold bird, the rook at this season grows bolder: the ploughman, he soon discovers, has no wish to molest him, so he edges closer and closer, with that impudent sidelong glance of his, until he struts at the ploughman's very heels, and has his beak in position to grab the prey the moment the share has turned it up for him. The service is mutual. The ploughman saves him the labour of excavating, and he, in his turn, eats up many a noxious grub and insect that would otherwise injure next year's crop.

* * *

It is extremely rare in these days to find mistletoe growing wild. Most of that sold in the shops comes from France and other European countries. That growing in England is usually found upon the apple, the black poplar, and certain firs and pines. In Devonshire orchards a self-set bough may sometimes be seen upon some gnarled old apple-tree – a cherished possession, to be shown as a rarity to visitors.

The plant in its natural state is propagated by birds, which carry the berries from tree to tree, and, to get rid of the sticky white juice which adheres, rub their bills backwards and forwards upon the bark, and in this way drop the seeds into a suitable crevice. As the seeds germinate, roots are sent down into the tissue of the tree, and the mistletoe hangs suspended, a parasite, although a comparatively innocent one, for it causes no discernible harm to its host.

But only a small proportion of the rare wild mistletoe plants bear berries, for the male and female flowers grow upon different plants, and, as they are so seldom found growing near together, the chances of the female flower becoming fertilized are exceedingly small. Like those of the holly and other handsome berry-bearing plants, the flowers of the mistletoe are inconspicuous. Early in February the tiny green clusters appear, to be followed in summer by small, hard, green berries, which soften and grow white as the season advances.

The Norse legend of the mistletoe is a very beautiful one. When Baldur was slain by his blind brother, Hodur, with an arrow fashioned by the malicious Loki, all created things were stricken with grief, and a great cry of weeping arose from the earth. Then the tears were collected and placed in pearly drops upon the plant from which the arrow was cut which caused the mourning, to turn to the pearly, tear-like berries we still see upon the mistletoe today. Then it was decreed that the plant should for ever hang suspended, never to touch the earth, which was Loki's realm; and from this, we are told, came the Christmas custom of suspending a mistletoe bough in our homes that the kiss of good-will may be given under it.

As these last words are written, the early December dusk descends. Soft violet marsh-mists envelop the woods and hills, the stormy red of the sunset dies in a smouldering haze in the west, lights twinkle out one by one from the cottage homes upon the heath, and already the whereabouts of the nearest town is marked by the faint glow of its lights upon the horizon. A deep peace broods over the earth, and a silence only broken by the murmuring of falling water and the far, faint sound of church bells as the village ringers practise their Christmas chimes.

139

Poems

FROM
Bog Myrtle and Peat

To Ronald Campbell Macfie

Yours are the moors, the billowy seas,
Tall mountains and blue distances.
Mine is a cottage garden, set
With marigold and mignonette,
And all the wildling things that dare,
Without a gardener's fostering care.
Yet very well-content I rest
In my obscure, sequestered nest;
For from my cottage garden I
Can see your cloud-peaks pierce the sky!

Flood Time

The floods are out at Welborough:
The encroaching waters creep and moan;
One gaunt old willow stands alone,
Reflected in a steely glass;
And lanes, where we were wont to pass,
And fields where children used to play,
Are water, water all the way.

The floods are out at Welborough:
The house is hushed, the curtain drawn;
The women watch from dusk to dawn,
Because a little child has gone
To walk the meadows all alone.
I search alway, but find him not;
Only a drowned forget-me-not
Mimicks the azure of his eyes;
Beyond the mist, a curlew cries.
O, tell me, sad bird, where he lies!

Heather

You talk of pale primroses,
Of frail and fragrant posies,
   The cowslip and the cuckoo-flower
      that scent the spring-time lea.
         But give to me the heather,
         The honey-scented heather,
         The glowing gipsy heather –
   That is the flower for me!

You love the garden alleys,
Smooth-shaven lawns and valleys,
   The cornfield and the shady lane, and
      fisher-sails at sea.
         But give to me the moorland,
         The noble purple moorland,
         The free, far-stretching moorland –
   That is the land for me!

Home Thoughts from the Desert

In Hampshire now, the woods are brown,
   The heath-sands tawny-gold with rain;
The mist lies blue on Bratley Down,
   The firelight flecks the window pane –
         In Hampshire now!

The wind comes screaming from the sea,
   The wild sea-horses champ and roar,
And every oak on Dudman's Lea
   Echoes the tumult of the shore –
         In Hampshire now!

The 'Wight lies wrapt in cloud and mist,
   Scarce once a week they'll see it clear,
And then it glows like amethyst –
   And Oh, I would that I were there,
         In Hampshire now!

Amidst the desert sand and heat,
   I hear the wheeling seabirds scream,
Scent the good smoke of burning peat,
   Then wake and find it but a dream –
         Ah, Hampshire dear!

August Again

The heather flings her purple robe
   Once more upon the hill;
Beneath a shivering aspen-tree
   My Love lies cold and still; –
Ah, very deep my Love must sleep,
   On that far Flemish plain,
If he does not know that the heath-bells blow
   On the Hampshire hills again!

O, other maids take other men,
   And just a passing sigh
Will not disturb the lightest dream;
   But my poor heart would die
If so very deep my Love should sleep
   Beneath his foreign tree,
That he did not stir at the thought of her
   Who could love so faithfully!

Garden Fires

A drift of wood and weed-smoke
  Floats o'er the garden spaces,
Circling the orchard tree-tops;
    They're burning up the traces
      Of Winter from the earth,
      Now Spring has birth.

Soft showers of snowy petals
  Bestrew the bright, lush green;
Blue smokewreaths wheel and thicken
  As warm winds stir between,
    And living tongues of flame
    Put daffodils to shame.

And men shall make such fires,
  And warm Spring winds blow free,
When all the great desires
  Which rend the heart of me
    Shall dwindle into dust,
    For Time is just!

Flora Thompson in her early twenties

The 'end house' at Juniper Hill

Cottisford School where Flora and Edwin Timms were pupils in the 1880s

Emma Timms, Flora's
mother, in middle age

Old Hill, a broom-
squire of Stoney Bottom,
Grayshott, with his wife
Nancy, about 1892

Fringford post office and forge with Mrs Whitton ('Miss Lane' of *Candleford Green*) holding the carter's horse

The head smith and journeymen, with a customer, outside the forge

Grayshott post office, about 1900

No. 42 Frederica Road,
Winton, Bournemouth,
where Flora lived from
1903 to 1916

Clara Louise Woods (later Mrs Hooker), who worked with Flora at the Liphook post office during the First World War

Flora in her study and her kitchen at Liphook in 1921, when she achieved local celebrity as the 'poetess-postmistress' of *Bog Myrtle and Peat*

Flora's grave in Longcross Cemetery, Dartmouth, Devon

The Earthly Paradise

I desire no heaven of gold harps,
Give me the harps of earth –
Pine trees with red gold on their stems,
The music of the west wind in their branches!

When I am old,
Give me for heaven a little house set on a heath;
The blue hills behind; the blue sea before.
The brick floors scoured crimson, the flagstones like snow;
The brass taps and candlesticks like gold,
And there, in my soft grey gown between the holly-hocks,
Upon a day of days I would welcome an old poet;
And pour him tea, and walk on the heath, and talk
   the sun down;
And then by the wood fire he should read me the poems of
   his passionate youth,
And make new ones praising friendship above love!

Heatherley

CONTENTS

1. *Laura goes farther*

One hot September afternoon near the end of the last century a girl of about twenty walked without knowing it over the border into Hampshire from one of its neighbouring counties. She was dressed in a brown woollen frock with a waist-length cape of the same material and a brown beaver hat decorated with two small ostrich tips, set upright in front, back to back, like a couple of notes of interrogation. This outfit, which would no doubt appear hideous to modern eyes, had given her great moral support on her train journey. The skirt, cut short just to escape contact with the ground and so needing no holding up except in wet weather, was, her dressmaker had assured her, the latest idea for country wear. The hat she had bought on her way through London that morning. It had cost nine and eleven-pence three farthings of the pound she had saved to meet her expenses until her first month's salary was due in her new post, but she did not regret the extravagance for it became her brown eyes and hair and would help her, she hoped, to make a good impression at her journey's end. 'A good first impression is half the battle', she had been told as a child, and she had special reasons for wishing to make a good impression today, for she had lately been somewhat unsettled through taking short holiday-relief engagements at the post offices where she had worked and this new position, she hoped, would prove a permanency. Her people at home were beginning to speak of her as a rolling stone, and rolling stones were not in favour with country people of that day. The plea that to work, even for a short time, in one of the larger post offices was a valuable gain in experience did not appeal to her parents. They looked upon experience as something to be gathered unconsciously, not a thing to be sought. They preferred permanence and security.

But Laura at that moment was not conscious of her appearance and had ceased to care about what impression she was likely to make. Even the uneasy fear that it was due to some mistake of her own that she had not been met, as promised, at the railway station had passed from her mind, for she had emerged from the deep, tree-shaded lane which led up from the little town in the dip, come out upon open heath, and for the first time in her life saw heather growing. She recognized the flower immediately from a thousand descriptions she had read of it in its native haunts which she had supposed to be far north of the Thames, and from earliest childhood had carried with her a mental picture of the heatherclad hills and moors of Scott's novels and poems. Her preconceived idea seemed crude and cold before the living reality.

Pale purple as the bloom on a ripe plum, veined with the gold of late flowering gorse, set with small slender birches just turning yellow, with red-berried rowans and thickets of bracken, the heath lay steeped in sunshine. The dusty white road by which she had come was deserted by all but herself, and the only sounds to be heard were the murmuring of bees in the heath-bells and the low, plaintive cries of a flock of linnets as they flitted from bush to bush. From where she stood she could see, far away on the horizon, a long wavy line of dim blue hills which to her, used as she was to a land of flat fields, appeared mountains. The air, charged with the scent of heather and pine, had the sharp sweetness of wine and was strangely exhilarating to one accustomed from birth to the moist, heavy, pollen-laden air of the agricultural counties. She stood as long as she dared upon the edge of the heath, breathing long breaths and gazing upon the scene with the delight of a discoverer; then with a buoyant floating-upon-air feeling, passed on uphill towards the knot of red roofs which soon appeared among pine trees.

Heatherley, as she afterwards found, was not strictly speaking a village at all, but a settlement of recent growth consisting of a couple of roads with shops, a new model inn with an artistic signboard and a few modern cottages and villas, many of them with an 'Apartments to Let' card in the window. Since a famous scientist had discovered the virtues of the moorland air and a Royal Academician had painted the scenery the place had come into being to serve the convenience of those living in the large houses and staying at the hotels which had sprung up at every favourite viewpoint for miles around. There were other similar settlements in the district, but none of them, so far, had a telegraph office, so, though later it was to be superseded, Heatherley was and remained for a few years the chief postal centre.

Heatherley Post Office was a pretty red-tiled building with wide wooden eaves and a shop window which displayed choice leather goods such as writing and dressing-cases, Bibles and Prayer Books, purses and photograph frames. In the doorway recess was a glass case of the new picture postcards with local views. Views were so far the only subject printed upon postcards; the portraits of musical comedy actresses, the collection of which was soon to become a craze, were as yet unthought of, and farther still in the future was the day of the coloured 'comic'. The modern note of advertisement, however, was already present, as shown by the caption, 'The English Switzerland', beneath a view of some local hill scenery. The view was one of typical English moorland, beautiful on its own small scale but in no way challenging comparison with Alpine grandeur, and the name was probably due to a flight of fancy on the part of one of those out to exploit the place. In other circles the best-known hill near Heatherley was sometimes called the Lesser Parnassus because of the number of poets and other writers who haunted its slopes. But Laura, that afternoon, did not stay to look at the pictured views or to read the captions. She opened the door timidly and made herself known.

As any kind of humble lodging was difficult to find it had been arranged that until she could find a room for herself in the village she should live with the postmaster's family; so she was taken at once to the living-room at the back of the office and handed over to the postmaster's wife. The room in which she found herself was of a different type from those of her recent experiences. This was no ordinary parlour behind a shop, with a sideboard display of silver, linoleum on the floor and framed photographs on the walls; but, as it appeared, the abode of people of some refinement. Yet as it seemed to Laura, if not at that time then later, there was something strange and gloomy, even a little sinister, about the room. The one window, perhaps because it was in a side wall and a path to the back premises ran beneath it, had been reinforced with a screen of painted glass which cast a dim coloured light on the room. A huge, heavily carved oak cabinet, resembling in shape a Jacobean court cupboard, almost filled the wall on one side, and there was a good deal of other heavily carved oak furniture. This, she found later, had been made and carved by the postmaster, who was a cabinet-maker by trade and had a workshop at the back of the house. The walls of the room were plain-washed sage green and the only picture was a signed print of a painting by a local artist.

But Laura, though deeply interested, had no time then for more than a hasty glance round, for her attention was naturally given to the wife of her new employer. Mrs Hertford was as unusual for her time and position in life as was her room. She was tall, thin and faded, with drooping shoulders, a very pale face, and smooth straight masses of dull yellow hair which she wore combed low over her ears. She was in a late stage of pregnancy and wore a long loose green frock with much embroidery about the shoulders. Her voice was melancholy and her movements were silent and slow. Laura thought her face the saddest she had ever seen.

Two children were present, one a small boy, very like his mother in looks and dressed in a little suit which might have been made from the same piece of material as her gown. He was well-mannered, but too silent and grave for his age, and Laura thought he had recently been crying. Both mother and boy looked rather like vegetables or flowers which had been kept in the dark, away from the sun. The baby girl, who had just awakened from her afternoon nap, was a lovely child with cheeks the colour of a wild rose, dark eyes and a mop of fair curls. She was warm from her bed and full of life and laughter and when Laura took her on her knee she at once, without prompting, threw her arms round her neck and kissed her. Her charming welcome was reassuring to Laura, who felt an air of restraint in the room for which she could not account.

When Mrs Hertford heard that Laura had walked up from the railway station she seemed both surprised and distressed. Her husband, she said, had himself intended to drive down to meet her in their little governess-cart. Was Laura sure she had not seen the cart, a little brown turnout with a piebald pony? Laura said she was quite sure, and did not in the least mind not being met. She had left her trunk in the booking office and had thoroughly enjoyed the walk; would not have missed it for anything. Then the small boy, Cecil, came back from the errand on which his mother had sent him and said Miffy, the pony, was out in the paddock and William had told him that Daddy had gone out after dinner, he did not know where, but he had not said anything about meeting the young lady, and Mrs Hertford said that in that case Daddy must have forgotten, he was very forgetful at times, and would Laura like to see her bedroom.

Afterwards, in the post office, Laura took over from the assistant whose place she was taking. Miss Smithers was a woman of forty who had at one time been employed in the Central Telegraph Office in London and had been invalided out of the service with a small pension after a nervous breakdown. Judging by her twitching features and strained, absent-minded expression she was on the eve of a second breakdown. She left Heatherley the next morning, duly driven to the station in the governess-cart by William, the odd-job man, but not before she had told Laura that the household she was leaving was far from a happy one. Mr and Mrs Hertford had what she described as terrific bust-ups. They had had one an hour or two before Laura's arrival, which accounted for her train not being met at the station and for the strained atmosphere she found on her arrival. 'But don't ask me what it's all about,' she added, 'to me there's never seemed any sense or reason in their quarrels. I expect it's just that she doesn't know how to manage him; it's generally the wife's fault in such cases. But they're all right otherwise, rather superior for country people, and I don't suppose their rows will affect you as they do me. I've got a sensitive nature myself. I'm funny that way.'

Laura was to be what was called 'in charge of the office'. That is, she was, with the help of a junior assistant, to undertake all the postal and telegraph duties and make up the daily accounts which had then to be signed by the postmaster, who was responsible to the higher authorities. Beyond guaranteeing the efficient working of the office and the safe custody of the cash and other valuables, Mr Hertford had little to do with the office. But he was no employer of sweated labour; the arrangement was known to and permitted by the authorities, and after he had paid the salaries of his assistants from his official income only a small margin was left to reward him for his responsibilities and to pay office rent. The post-office business was but a sideline to supplement his main income from working at his trade.

Laura's junior, Alma Stedman, was a pretty, blue-eyed, sweet-natured girl of eighteen whose home was in the village. It was one of Laura's duties to teach Alma to manipulate the newly-installed single-needle telegraph instrument. This had been placed in a small passage, a mere cupboard with a window, between the public office and the living-room. It was worked by tapping out the letters of outgoing telegrams in the Morse code and receiving incoming ones by watching, or reading by sound, according to the degree of efficiency of the operator, the single needle, mounted on a green dial, which struck, now right, now left, upon two metal sounders. The striking needle made a pretty, musical tinkling sound which could be heard and interpreted, by those accustomed to it, at some distance from the instrument. Laura's life at Heatherley ran to the tune of its musical tinkling, and the mention or thought of the place in after years brought back its sound, that and the scent of heather and peat and pine, and in the background, the strife and unrest of lives which for a time impinged upon her own.

The old single-needle instrument has long since disappeared from the post-office scene to make way for new labour-saving and easier-to-learn inventions. But at Heatherley in Laura's time it was regarded as a symbol of progress, and the mastery of its mysteries stamped the operator as thoroughly up to date and efficient. After Miss Smithers had departed no one in the village but Laura could work it, and until Alma became proficient her working hours were twelve daily, with no weekly half-day off and two hours' duty on Sunday morning. It had been agreed that as soon as Alma had qualified and could be left in charge of the instrument they should on alternate evenings finish work at six.

Shortly before the office closed on the evening of Laura's arrival Mr Hertford appeared. She had not heard him come into the office; he wore soft-soled shoes which made no sound, and she turned round suddenly to find him standing behind her, laughing silently at her start of surprise. He was a dark, slightly-built man of forty-five who might have been thought handsome but for the peculiar tint of his complexion, which was a deep, dull mauvish-leaden shade, and the strange wild light in his eyes. The silent laughter was a habit of his. He was of a serious, somewhat gloomy nature and seldom smiled, but when anything appealed to his peculiar sense of humour he would throw back his head and go through a pantomime of hilarious laughter without uttering a sound. Another disquieting habit of his was that of quoting texts of scripture or lines from the poets in a hissing whisper. 'Vengeance is mine . . .' or 'To be or not to be . . .' he would hiss under his breath, *à propos* of nothing that had gone before, when taking up the pen to sign the accounts, or even at the family meal table.

But in spite of these and many other peculiarities Laura in many ways liked Mr Hertford. That evening he welcomed her cordially, and he was reasonable in his business relations and an expert at his trade. During the time Laura knew him he did a good business in making articles of furniture which his customers of artistic taste designed for their own homes. He also carved and fitted the woodwork of a private chapel in the house of a Catholic resident, built and fitted with bookshelves a summerhouse for a poet's outdoor study, and framed pictures for an exhibitor at the Royal Academy. He took no part in local affairs and seldom came in contact with ordinary post-office customers, many of whom were under the impression that Laura was postmistress and addressed her as such. But he had a small space at the post-office counter reserved for his intercourse with his own trade customers, and it was evident from the nature of his interviews there that they had a high opinion of his talents and taste. An exhibitor, for instance, had, to comply with the regulations, to have his black and white drawings framed in gilt, which frames, he remarked, would be of no earthly use afterwards. Mr Hertford suggested that ebony frames should be lightly gilded and afterwards sandpapered back to the natural colour of the wood. At such interviews there was no hissing of texts or silent laughter; his was the quiet, helpful, deferential but not too deferential manner of a master craftsman discussing work with a customer.

He had read widely and seen something of the world. In his early twenties he had spent some years in Australia and on his voyages to and from that continent he had taken the opportunity of exploring the Mediterranean ports where passengers were permitted to land. He was a master of debate and to hear him and his brother, who lived near, discuss politics and theology was a revelation to one who had gained such little knowledge as she possessed from the printed word. At such times his face would light up with enthusiasm and his ordinary habit of speech would give place to the clear, ringing tones of conviction.

His brother was a nonconformist in religion, a devoted chapel-goer; Mr Hertford attended neither church nor chapel and, as far as could be gathered from his ordinary conversation, was a sceptic; yet in these debates he would contend hotly for an established Church with a priesthood and bishops and archbishops, while his brother was all for self-government by the congregation. Words such as 'sacerdotalism' and 'hierarchical' flew to and fro between them and feeling often rose to such a point that the brother would rise and leave the house without saying goodnight; but always at their next meeting they were at it again.

During these discussions Mrs Hertford would sit silent in a low chair by the hearth, her pale hair drooping rather untidily over her sewing. She was glad to see her husband interested and occupied, but she herself cared nothing for such subjects. Her passion was music; in her rare hours of domestic peace she would sing or hum airs from the operas or speak of the days before her marriage, when she had heard such and such a famous singer or pianist, or tell of the musical evenings at the house where she had been nursery governess and her services as an accompanist had been much in request. Musically, she had to live on such memories, for she had no piano of her own, and only once during the time Laura knew her did she go out to hear music.

That was when a series of concerts of chamber music was given at a newly-built hall in the next settlement and, as tickets were sold and a plan of the hall was kept at the post office, a two-guinea ticket for the series was sent to the postmaster as an acknowledgement of the service.

Mrs Hertford so seldom left the house, even for an hour, that her going caused quite a flutter of excitement in the establishment. Alma had volunteered to mind the children and get tea ready and, without help, Laura would be especially busy in the post office. Mrs Hertford dressed with care and looked well in black with touches of yellow, her pale hair framed in a black lace hat with bunches of artificial cowslips. All except her husband

161

stood at the window or door to see her off, Alma holding up the new baby. Its mother looked quite happy and cheerful when she turned to smile and wave back to them at the street corner. She returned in a state of exaltation, full of the music she had heard and especially of Miss Fanny Davies's piano playing; but that very evening her husband had one of his wildest outbursts of temper and she went to bed weeping. For the rest of the series of concerts the post-office ticket was unused.

Laura never heard the beginning of one of these domestic upheavals, and for some time their cause, real or imaginary, was a mystery to her. At one meal-time all would be peaceful, then, before the next became due, working quietly at the telegraph instrument where she could not help hearing most of what passed in the living-room, she would suddenly become aware of a deep hissing of abuse on one side and heartbroken weeping on the other. When her husband would permit it, Mrs Hertford was almost slavishly subservient towards him, and after his terrible outbreaks had subsided appeared to feel no resentment, only a pathetic desire to make peace. And a brittle, fugitive peace would be made between them, though it seldom lasted more than a week or two. As the weeks passed Laura became quite accustomed to going indoors for a meal and finding no cloth on the table, Mr Hertford glooming alone by the fireside and his wife and children locked in their bedroom upstairs. Afterwards, for several days, Mr and Mrs Hertford would not communicate with each other directly at table but addressed the remarks intended for each other to Laura, with whom, throughout, both husband and wife remained on ordinary terms. Every few weeks a new small maid would appear to help Mrs Hertford with the housework and children, but none of these stayed longer than a month, some but a day or two. After one of Mr Hertford's outbursts the girl's mother would appear, declaring she was not going to have her child frightened to death by *their* quarrels, and depart with her daughter's belongings in a bundle under one arm and the hand of the other holding that of her daughter, who was usually crying.

The one person who helped to make tolerable those early

days of Laura's life at Heatherley was her junior in the office, Alma Stedman. She was a short, rather sturdily built girl with pretty nut-brown hair and big blue eyes. 'The little blue-eyed girl' was the description applied to her by strangers who wished to speak of her but did not know her name. Although in looks a typical country girl, hers was no common nature. Good and sincere, untouched by the world and its problems and yet no fool, with inborn good taste and a sense of humour, she was one of those rare persons who are happy and contented and wish for no change in their lives. The tempestuous life of the Hertfords affected her less than it did Laura. For one thing she saw and heard less of it, and for another she refused to believe it was caused by anything more than incompatibility of temperament. Married couples, she maintained, were prone to such fallings-out and fallings-in, and Laura, although unconvinced that the Hertford upheavals were mere ordinary married tiffs, for the time being felt reassured and comforted.

But what Laura liked best about Alma was that she was a reader and especially fond of poetry. Not so much the work of the great poets, or that of the more robust type of lesser poet, as smaller, more exquisite things with a touch of magic or faery about them. *Goblin Market, The Forsaken Merman* and Keats's *La Belle Dame Sans Merci* she knew by heart. Christina Rossetti was Alma's favourite poet and it was from her Laura first heard of the work of Coventry Patmore. Alma's taste in everything ran to the small and exquisite. The violet and the snowdrop were her favourite flowers, and, as a view, she preferred some mossy nook with primroses blooming against tree boles to the wide, purple expanse of the heath in its glory. They would sometimes contend a little over their preferences and Laura once wrote a little poem for her beginning:

You talk of pale primroses, of fair and fragrant posies,
The cowslip and the cuckoo-flower that scent the spring-time lea,
But give to me the heather,
The honey-scented heather,
The glowing gypsy heather,
That is the flower for me!

163

Although Alma's good taste was inborn it had not gone uncultivated. She had not had to make her own discoveries in literature, as Laura had done. Her father was a gardener and the lady by whom he was employed held a Sunday afternoon class, or poetry reading, for a few selected girls of whom Alma was one. It also included the lady's two nieces, her parlourmaid, the book-keeper at the steam laundry, and a pupil teacher at the village school. Every week Mrs Camden read a poem of her own selection and commented upon its points of beauty and interest and the girls were then expected to learn it by heart and to repeat it to her on the following Sunday. By this means she hoped to form their taste and certainly in Alma's case her plan had worked very well. The only drawback to the plan that Laura could see was that it rather limited the range of her pupil. What Mrs Camden liked Alma liked so much that she was not inclined to venture further, certainly not to trust her own taste and judgement. She had the advantage of knowing on good authority what books and poems were worthy of her love, but she missed such thrills as Laura experienced when, having come casually upon some book or poem and loving it, she afterwards learned that it was an acknowledged masterpiece.

Alma's was a bright, sunshiny nature. The sorrows, injustices, and inequalities of human life did not loom like a dark cloud on her horizon. When any special instance of sorrow or suffering came to her notice she would grieve sincerely and do all in her power to help or comfort those affected, but every such case was to her an isolated case, not a sign that all was not well with the world. Laura, on the other hand, was, as people told her, too much inclined to look on the dark side of life. Those were the days of the Boer War and she could not help picturing to herself as scenes of suffering those battlefields which, to those around her, were so many steps to final victory, or grieving for the ruined homesteads of the enemy and pitying the Boer women in the concentration camps, mourning their dead or in a state of anxiety for their living, just as the women in this country were mourning or anxious. She was anxious herself about her brother who was out there with his regiment, especially when month after month passed without her or any of her family receiving a letter from him.

When Alma saw her doing what she called 'brooding' she had pretty, innocent ways of trying to cheer her which, though often simple to silliness, would usually raise a smile. Sorting the night mail, she would read out the addresses on the letters, pronouncing the place names grotesquely – Swanage . . . Swanaggie, Metropole . . . Met-ropoly, Leicester . . . Ly-ces-ter, and so on. She would hide Laura's one ring, taken off for hand-washing, or shut up the office cat in the registered letter locker and pretend it was a tiger behind the wire netting. One day she brought a dead bee on her palm and presented it gravely to Laura, saying, 'Is this not a bee you have lost from your bonnet?'

For some time after Laura first knew Alma she hoped she had found what she had not yet had, a close friend of her own age and sex. But no close friendship developed. Alma, living in the village, had her own home interests and friends of long standing; she was also spending much of her off-duty time with the young man she afterwards married, and her life was already full. They remained as they had begun upon friendly terms and, looking back in after years, Laura felt that she owed much to her sweet, wholesome influence.

But even with Alma's companionship for many hours of each day and that of the new friends she was making, hers was an uncomfortable position, and when week after week passed with no early prospect of finding a room for herself in the village she was often on the verge of giving notice to leave her post and seeking a more peaceful life elsewhere. But she was indoors sharing the Hertfords' life but a very few hours each day. With her work in the office she was perfectly satisfied, for she liked the bustle and stimulus of having plenty to do, the new public was interesting and in her off-duty daylight hours she had a new and enthralling country to explore. Moreover she had no money with which to meet removal expenses. Her mother, she knew, would have managed somehow to provide, had she been told of the circumstances, but it would have been at great self-sacrifice, and although she had other relatives who would willingly have helped her, such a horror of borrowing had been instilled into her mind from earliest childhood that she never once thought of applying to them. So she stayed on at Heatherley and gathered there much experience, both pleasant and unpleasant. 'Foolish nineteen and wicked one-and-twenty' was an old saying of the countryside of her birth. A modern author has called the same period in human life Sinister Street. Laura's Sinister Street was, after all, not so very sinister, but, such as it was, she had to pass through it and fate had decreed that that passing through should take place at Heatherley.

11. *The Villagers*

In her early days at Heatherley Laura sometimes felt that she had strayed into a new world. A more prosperous and leisured, a more sophisticated, and on many subjects a better informed, but a less kindly, solid, and permanent world than that of her birth. That impression may have been partly due to the coming and going of visitors in holiday mood, and because, in that new district, few who lived there had been born in the place or had lived there as children. Some of the shopkeepers, married men with families, still spoke of Birmingham, London, or Shropshire as home. Both the Heatherley doctors were new to the village, as was the clergyman, for the church was but newly built. Nearly all the working people had come there simply to earn a livelihood, as indeed had Laura herself. None of these had had time to get rooted in the soil, even if they had had the inclination.

But not all that went to make up the impression was due to locality. The times were changing and people were changing with the times. Of this change Laura had missed several stages. In agricultural counties, such as that of her birth, people were still much as they had been in her childhood. Those born on the land, with very few exceptions, lived and died on the land. New ideas were long in reaching them and were seldom received kindly when they arrived. The old family names survived generation after generation in the villages, and the very fields with their customary rotation of crops helped to confirm the feeling of continuity.

The Heatherley villagers, having broken with their own personal past and come to a place without traditions, appeared to live chiefly for the passing moment. The past, especially the country past, was nothing to them, and if they looked forward to a future it was a future of change, to the comfort and ease of a well-earned retirement for themselves, and more vaguely, for the world at large; to the good time which newspaper prophets assured them was to come with the new century, when new machinery would be invented to do the work and man, with unlimited leisure, would live on a tabloid diet at the cost of a penny a day.

In the meantime new fashions in dress and ways of living, new arrivals in the district with money to spend, new items of local gossip and new ideas culled from the day's newspaper – new today and forgotten tomorrow – were, outside their own family affairs, their main preoccupation. Fundamentally they were much as mankind has always been. They had their hopes and fears, likes and dislikes, they worked hard at their trade, or serving in their shops, or waiting upon the sojourners in their apartments, bearing their troubles and reverses more or less bravely, sacrificing themselves for those they loved or accepting the sacrifice of others, for though manners and ideas may change, human nature is changeless.

Manners and customs were certainly changing. The Heatherley shopkeepers were more independent in their manner towards their customers than the old style village tradesmen, cultivating the take-it-or-leave-it manner which they thought became a free-born Briton. Their shops were smaller and not so well kept as those in the small towns and villages of Laura's childhood and they had not the pride in the quality of their goods and their own ability to oblige which had marked the old-fashioned butcher or grocer. Many of the richer residents had their provisions sent weekly from Whiteley's or the Army and Navy Stores, and some of the poorer combined business and pleasure by Saturday night shopping in the nearest town. Neither rich nor poor felt any moral obligation to deal with local shops. They made their purchases where they thought the goods were likely to be fresher or cheaper.

There was a similar loosening of other relations. The lord of the manor, for instance, who, being untitled, would in a village of the older type have been known as the Squire and reigned more or less beneficently over his small kingdom, was to the Heatherley villagers simply Mr Doddington who lived in such-and-such a large house. He exercised no particular influence upon the villagers, who respected him just as much and no more than any other rich local man who paid his bills regularly. Between his periods of foreign travel he entertained such neighbours as were generally considered his equals, but did not pretend to know everyone in the village or feel it his duty to inquire as to the health and well-being of those who were known to him. He was said to be a good employer to those who worked on his estate and to be kind to them and their families in trouble or sickness, but such kindness, together with his other charities, if he were charitably inclined, were unofficial. He lived the life of a private gentleman, as did the other score or so of private gentlemen living in the neighbourhood, being neither the petty tyrant nor the kindly patron known in less up-to-date parishes as Our Squire.

Between doctor and patient there must always be to some degree a personal relationship, but although both the Heatherley doctors were well liked and their skill respected, the relationship existing between them and their ordinary village patients was not that of the old country doctor and patient. In Laura's childhood, she well remembered, there was in most instances a tie of close affection and, on the one side, of gratitude. An ordinary countrywoman with little of her own in store would when going to the market town to pay her doctor's bill – or more often a small instalment of it – carry with her some little offering, mushrooms, a rabbit, a bottle of home-made wine or ketchup, saying, 'I know 't isn't much and he's got plenty, but I feel that no money can ever pay for what he done for our so-and-so.' In the newer order money was considered a sufficient payment. People received much larger doctor's bills and paid them more or less promptly with no more than the ordinary amount of grumbling, and the obligation was considered cancelled.

At Heatherley the cottages and villas interspersed with the shops were occupied by gardeners, coachmen, and other outdoor workers at the larger houses, by the families of men who worked at their different trades for the local builder, and by widows and maiden ladies who let apartments. There were no really poor people and few who could be called 'country people' in the ordinary sense of the term. To find those native to the place one had to go outside the village. There, tucked away in the long narrow valleys of the heath, were small ancient homesteads, each with its two or three fields, where the descendants of the original inhabitants of the countryside farmed on the smallest possible scale, exercised to the full their commoners' rights and sold butter and eggs and garden produce to the newcomers. They also carried on the old local industry of making the small, round garden brooms called besoms from the long, tough stems of the heather and on that account were still spoken of by the old traditional name of broom-squires.

Laura, on her rambles, was later to see something of the broom-squires' little low houses with ricks built of the few handfuls of hay from their fields and other much larger and taller piles, built rickwise, of new heather brooms with shining white, newly-peeled handles, ready to be taken to market; but when she had first arrived at Heatherley her immediate interest was centred on the celebrities. There were at that time far more of these than of the broom-squires. The widow of the famous scientist who had discovered the place was still living in the house he had built and afterwards fenced on one side with a fifteen-foot screen thatched with heather to hide from view the new houses built by others who had profited by his discovery. A

169

judge who was also a man of letters had a weekend cottage there, an African explorer who had recently been in the forefront of the news had taken a furnished house, and a young publisher whose name was later to be familiar to all readers was a frequent visitor. There were many writers and artists, both well-known and lesser-known, and just at that time it was the writers who were supposed to confer its special distinction on the locality.

On her first Sunday morning walk Laura had seen a tall man on a crutch, with a forked red beard and quick, searching eyes, surrounded by a group of younger men who appeared to be drinking in his every syllable. The tall man with the crutch, she was told, was a writer. He had but recently come there and no-one quite knew what he wrote, but it was known that he was thought a lot of in London. Very clever, they said, very clever indeed. The followers were young men from town who, since he had injured his leg in a cycling accident, came at weekends to visit him. Laura had been a voracious reader from early childhood; most of her adventures so far had been among books, and to see a living author was as exciting to her as a good view of a living film star would be to many girls today. She was to see that particular author again, many times, and to listen with delight to his conversation with friends he met at the post-office counter. Other authors, too, many of whose names and writings were already familiar to her.

One writer especially, who had invented a new type of fiction which is still flourishing at the present day, though the author has, as he himself would express it, long 'passed over'. His was the kind of book which appeals to everybody, young and old, intellectual and simple, and he had then recently scored a big success which had made a great impression on the villagers, not so much as literature as by the big fancy-dress ball he had given at the new hotel on the hill to celebrate it. Scarcely a day passed without his bursting like a breeze into the post office, almost filling it with his fine presence and the deep tones of his jovial voice. As he went about the village he had a kindly greeting for all, rich and poor, known and unknown alike. He was probably the most popular man in the neighbourhood. Practically everyone had read at least one of his books and many of his local readers fully believed him to be the greatest of living authors.

Another resident, also a novelist, though a novelist of a different type, had just caused a sensation by publishing one of the new 'problem' novels which were a feature of the nineties. It was a serious book written by an acknowledged master of style and the situation it dealt with and the method of treatment would appear legitimate and restrained to the novel-reader of today. But then it raised a storm of criticism of its supposed loose morals. Letters were written to the newspapers about it, sermons were preached against it and it was banned by some of the libraries. Everybody who knew the author by sight, or even the outside of the house he lived in, felt a burning desire to read his book and copies were bought and handed round until practically everyone of mature age in the village had read and passed judgement on it. The first reaction to it was shocked but delighted excitement. Whoever'd have thought that that quiet-looking little gentleman with the neat grey beard and the field-glasses slung over his shoulder could think up and write down in black and white such a shocking tale! And would he be prosecuted for writing it? They had heard of Court cases over improper books, and some who had secretly enjoyed reading his novel seemed quite disappointed when the pother it had caused died down and the author still walked at large, apparently unperturbed by the storm he had raised.

Another frequent visitor at the post office was a young poet whose work was then held in high esteem in literary circles. In those days poets still dressed the part. Only a few years before, not many miles from Heatherley, Tennyson himself might have been seen, a noble figure in his black cloak and wide slouch hat, pacing the heath and murmuring aloud to himself the lines he was then fashioning. George Macdonald, in a bath chair, his beautiful white hair set off by a scarlet coat, had been a familiar sight in the streets of the little town in the valley. Theirs had been revered figures in which the whole neighbourhood felt an almost proprietary interest; but the new young poet, who actually lived at Heatherley, was little regarded locally.

He should have attracted more attention, for he raced about the parish at all hours on his bicycle with his halo of long, fair hair uncovered and his almost feminine slightness and grace set off by a white silk shirt, big artist's bow tie and velvet knickerbockers. But he was young. His portrait did not appear in the newspapers on his birthday with a caption claiming him as a national asset, and his works, bound in velvet yapp,* were not available for Christmas and birthday gifts. For the commonalty he did not as yet exist.

These and many other well-known people came to the post office and Laura had her restricted post-office-counter view of them all. Some of them were brilliant conversationalists and when two or more friends or neighbours met there it amused her to listen to their talk. She would sometimes wish that one of those quick, clever remarks they tossed like coloured glass balls into the air could have come her way, for in her youthful vanity she persuaded herself that she could have caught and returned it more neatly than someone to whom it was addressed. In her business relations with them she found as a general rule that those ranking high intellectually, like those of high social rank, were easy and pleasant to deal with. It was those with but some small success to their credit and those who were socially ambitious but of insecure social position that she found self-important and patronizing.

Then there were the Bohemian hangers-on of literature and the arts who, while the place was fashionable, would come, knapsack on shoulder, and put up at a public or an apartment house. A familiar figure for some time in the village was a young man who had taken a room at a public house and given out that he had come there to write a novel. He was a tall, lanky creature who in his black Inverness cloak and soft slouch hat resembled a down-and-out Bohemian artist as seen in a *Punch* drawing. To obtain local colour, as he himself would have expressed it, he associated with the one bad character in the neighbourhood, a

*Name for a style of bookbinding in limp leather with overlapping edges [ML].

permanently out of work ne'er-do-well of about his own age who was suspected of poaching and known to be a foul-mouthed blackguard.

The better-class residents had nothing to do with him, though on account of his peculiar appearance, everybody in the village must have known him by sight. To the ordinary villagers he was a figure of fun to be laughed at and winked over. One of Laura's most painful memories was that of seeing him one evening of rejoicing for a Boer War victory, half drunken and with a girl of about fourteen on his arm. The girl was looking up into his flushed, foolish-looking face with adoring eyes as she guided his unsteady feet towards the inn where he lodged. Perhaps it was well for her that not many days later he was found dead by his own hand with only a few coppers in his possession and deeply in debt to his landlord.

His death made a great impression on the villagers. People were horrified, not so much by the squandering of a young life as because the dance in the assembly room above his bedroom, already arranged for the night after his death, was not postponed. The dance took place. In the room above all was laughter and gaiety, in the room beneath lay the lifeless remains of one whose life, who knows how hopefully begun, had come to nothing.

Laura saw a sad little sequel. A respectable-looking elderly man, a clerk, perhaps, or a small shopkeeper, who was apparently the dead youth's father, came the next day to attend the inquest and arrange the funeral. He came to the post office to send off some telegrams and Laura could not help noticing that, as he stood aside writing them, his tears were dropping on to the telegraph forms and on to his neatly rolled umbrella.

A very different character was the grave, earnest, spectacled young man who, for a whole summer, occupied a room at the house of one of the broom-squires. He had come there in the first place to recuperate after an illness, but he, too, had literary ambitions and was writing a novel. When he called at the post office during a quiet spell he would stay talking to Laura about books, quoting long passages and asking if she preferred this or that, which was flattering to her taste, though it must be confessed that he seldom waited for her answer. Once, while sheltering at the post office from a heavy shower which kept everyone else indoors, he told her about the novel he was writing. He had come to a difficult place, he said, and would like her advice. In accordance with his pre-arranged plot he had now to describe a suicide. The whole story turned on that, but his conscience was troubled lest some future reader should be influenced by the example of his character.

He was so tied to the one idea and yet so distressed about it, and took his future reader so much for granted that his genuine scruple seemed funny to Laura, and she treated the matter so lightly that he was offended. Their budding friendship was nipped for ever. But not before he had done her the great service of introducing her to the work of George Meredith, of which she soon became so great an admirer that she could have passed a stiffish examination in the plots and characters of his novels and could, had she had a listener, have quoted most of his simpler poems. His novels revealed a new world to her, a world where women existed in their own right, not merely loved or unloved, as the complement of man. Diana of the Crossways, Lucy Feverel, Sandra Belloni, Rose Josceline, and dearest of all 'that dainty rogue in porcelain', Clara Middleton, she loved them all and rejoiced in their fine gallant spirit and brilliant wit. She accepted the author's word that there were such women, though she had herself never come in contact with any woman half as delightful, and thought of their world as a paradise of the well-born and well-educated, from which she was barred by her birth.

In time her first fervour subsided, the bright vision of Meredith's world receded into the background of her consciousness, a permanent possession but no longer paramount, and her incense was burnt before other shrines, as is the way of youth. While the fever of enthusiasm was at its height she went one summer Sunday to Box Hill to look upon the outside of Flint Cottage. She had not the good fortune to catch a glimpse of her idol. By that time Meredith was old and an invalid and probably at that hour taking his afternoon rest. But she had the satisfaction of beholding his abode and the view he looked out upon from his windows, with the added enjoyment of exploring Box Hill. Avoiding the many pairs of lovers ensconced in the lower nooks, she climbed to the summit and sat there enthroned to eat her buns and drink the medicine bottle of milk she had brought in the Dorothy bag swinging by long cords from her arm. Then a long, hot walk back to Mickleham station, not unmolested by the proffered attentions of trippers who, as a class, were far more unmannerly in those days than now, and another long trudge after her train journey; then to bed, very tired but blissfully content with her pious pilgrimage.

Meredith's novels and scores of other then modern books were obtained from the library shelves in a shop which stood across the road from the post office. *Madam Lillywhite, Milliner and Costumier, Baby Linen and Real Lace, Lending Library (frequent boxes from Mudie's), Stationery and Artists' Materials* ran the lettering above the door and in white enamel letters on the two windows. Madam Lillywhite was a small, elderly, daintily dressed lady who must have had a passion for her stock of real lace, for she was always adorned with collars, cuffs, jabots and other furbelows of that delicate material. Over her pictures-quely dressed grey hair she wore draped a lace shawl in the style of a Spanish mantilla, a mode of her own which did not, however, appear as freakish as might now be supposed in those days when many elderly ladies still wore some kind of lace headgear indoors. She did a thriving business with visitors to the place and employed several assistants, including at one time a swarthy young man of Indian birth. Madam herself seldom appeared in the shop except to display her treasures of real lace to select customers. Her fellow tradesmen thought her odd, decidedly odd, and they did not like oddness. Above all they resented her styling herself Madam. She did not appear to care in the least for their good or bad opinion, but went her way, doing a good trade with the type of resident and visitor she had no doubt had in mind when establishing her business. Once a month she took train to London and returned with a small selection of fashionable and expensive hats and other goods, many of the things bought on commission for some individual customer. She was indeed a pioneer among the keepers of the exclusive little hat and frock shops we now see everywhere.

Laura could not afford to buy her clothes there, but by means of Madam's shelves and Mr Mudie's boxes she soon got in touch with current literature. There were poems and plays, as well as novels, and copies of such periodicals as the *Athenaeum, Nineteenth Century* and *Quarterly Review*, back numbers of which could be borrowed for a penny. Laura almost 'read her head off', as her mother would have said, getting through everything she borrowed so quickly that she was often ashamed to return a book so soon, but driven on by an unquenchable thirst for novelty.

Sometimes she heard callers at the post-office counter discussing some new book she had read and it interested her to hear their opinion of it and compare it with her own. Literary people at that time, she found, were not enthusiastic about each others' books, unless the author happened to be one of their own circle of friends. Kipling, for instance, then at the height of his reputation and much in the news, was not a general favourite in the colony. At the most his work received but faint praise. Laura heard one lady say that at home she and her husband always spoke of him as 'The Big Noise', and another announced proudly that a certain writer whom she named had in an article criticized his work severely. Time proves all things, and the best of Kipling's work stands firm while the writer of the article has, as an authority, been long forgotten.

Such conversations were diverting when Laura had leisure and peace of mind to enjoy them, but more often than not she had neither. Her work kept her fairly busy, especially during the summer months, and there were worrying difficulties in the course of it. Most worrying of all was the difficulty of getting the telegrams for local delivery out promptly. Five telegraph messengers were employed in the summer, three in the winter, and in theory, these were more than sufficient to deliver forty to fifty incoming telegrams at the height of the season. But in practice it was not so. The distance covered by the delivery was so great and the houses so widely scattered that there was often unavoidable delay. No sooner had Messenger No. 5 disappeared on his bicycle than another telegram would come for the very address to which he had gone, or for another near it, and that had to wait until Messenger No. 1 returned. The post office rules authorized the employment of casual messengers in such emergencies, but no casual messenger was ever to be found, the villagers were all busy with their own more profitable affairs. This local condition the post office authorities could not or would not grasp and often correspondence about a delayed telegram clouded Laura's outlook for days.

One such ever-growing sheaf of papers went to and fro, from London to the local head office, from the head office to Heatherley, and from Heatherley to the head office and back to London, for weeks, and Laura was properly put in her place before the incident closed. It all began by a telegram for delivery arriving during a terrific thunderstorm. The older inhabitants of the place declared that they had never known such a thunderstorm. The thunder was deafening, the lightning terrible to behold, and these were followed by a deluge of rain. A cow was struck dead in a field at the back of the post office, this tragedy being reported by a small messenger boy who came in from his last delivery soaked to the skin and trembling with fear. Laura made a special journey to the postmaster's workshop to consult him as to whether or not the boy should be sent out again in such weather and in his condition, and they agreed that it would be unreasonable to expect him to go and that neither the authorities nor the person to whom the telegram was addressed would wish him to go until the storm abated. Accordingly, Laura sent the boy home to change his wet clothes and wrote upon the back of the telegram as the required explanation of the delay, 'Severe thunderstorm raging'.

Back from Headquarters came the telegram with her endorsement, a stiff letter of complaint about the delay from the addressee, and an official inquiry 'as to the circumstances in which climatic conditions were taken into account'. When writing the 'further explanation' demanded, Laura dwelt upon the unusual severity of the thunderstorm, the condition and age of the messenger boy, and introduced the dead cow as evidence. But if she expected the official mind to be open to such reasoning she was disappointed. 'Climatic conditions', she was told in the next missive, 'are no excuse for the non-delivery of a telegram when a messenger is available. Your reply to No. 18, such-and-such a date, is highly unsatisfactory. You will now return these papers with the telegram properly endorsed and an undertaking that no similar incident occurs in future', and Laura, greatly daring, undertook as directed the control of the elements by writing, 'Error regretted. Care shall be taken that it does not occur again', which meaningless formula apparently gave full satisfaction, for she heard no more of the matter.

At that time the telephone system did not extend to country places and the telegraph was the only quick and ready means of communication. People used it for purposes for which they would now 'ring up' – to send invitations to friends living near them, to inquire as to the progress of invalids, and to give orders to tradesmen. Then telegrams of almost letter length, not at all urgent in appearance, were sent by rich or impulsive people. Some of these last were love letters and many a promising affair took shape and was brought to a happy or a disastrous conclusion through Laura's mediumship.

One outstanding instance may serve to show the almost unbelievable distance we have travelled in the matter of communication since those pre-telephone and pre-motor-car days. A so-far childless couple living in a large country house near Heatherley were looking forward to what was then called 'an interesting event'. They were rich, the lady was not strong in health, their long-deferred hope was about to be fulfilled, and they naturally spared no expense in their arrangements. The first intimation of the expected event at the post office was that for a week, beginning on a stated date a few months ahead, a day and night telegraph service must be arranged. This, as afterwards transpired, was in order that a London specialist could be summoned by telegraph at any hour, day or night. If after midnight, it had been arranged that he should travel by special train from Waterloo.

As it turned out, the well-thought-out programme proved unnecessary, for the baby (good, sensible child) decided to make its appearance at an hour when the telegraph was working and trains were running normally; but that such a programme was pre-arranged, not for the birth of a royal prince or princess but for the child of a plain country gentleman, gives some idea of the great change made in country life by those comparatively new amenities, the telephone and the motor car. Now, of course, in such circumstances, when the hour approached, the patient would either be already in a nursing home or her husband would quickly convey her to one in their own car. Or if, having every comfort and convenience around her, she preferred to remain in her own home, the telephone would soon summon the requisite attendance.

The poorer invalids when they had to be taken to hospital had no smooth, silent-running motor ambulance to convey them. They travelled, often in a sitting position, in whatever horsed vehicle happened to be available. There were no motor buses to take people for pleasure trips or to do their shopping in the nearest town. At Heatherley there were not even horse buses. The poorer went on foot, the richer in their own private turnout, carriage, dog-cart, or governess-cart.

The country roads were not as yet tar-surfaced but left to their natural dust or muddiness. In summer, in dry weather, every vehicle which passed over them moved in a thick cloud of white dust. But no one seemed to notice that or to feel any discomfort. They congratulated themselves on having what they considered good, modern, made-up roads, instead of the former cart-tracks.

By the end of the century, in such modernized parts of the country as the Heatherley district, there was little class consciousness. Except in remote rural villages, the time had gone when every member of the community knew his or her own place in the social system, and their places were exactly defined. Laura could remember hearing the witty old postmistress under whom she had served her apprenticeship lay down a ruling in that respect. A retired tailor from a town who had been but a year or two in the village had been invited to the great house to inspect the squire's collection of coins, in which he had expressed interest. 'But it's such a tremendous place,' he told Miss Lane, 'I've been wondering all the morning which door I ought to go to.' Miss Lane looked him up and down appraisingly; kept silence for a moment, then asked, 'Does Squire send you pheasants or rabbits at Christmas?' 'Oh, rabbits,' said the man, looking rather surprised at the question, 'and I think it's very good of him, being as I am a newcomer.' 'Then,' said the postmistress judicially, 'it's the side door you should go to.' A gift of game, it appeared, implied social, if not financial equality, and such a gift qualified the recipient to mount the steps of the portico, ring the bell, and be shown into the drawing-room by a liveried footman. Rabbits signified not only rabbit pie, but also a middling state in society. If refreshments were offered to side-door callers they were usually partaken of in the housekeeper's room or the butler's pantry; though there was a sub-division of this class: the village schoolmaster, postmaster, or a farmer who was a tenant, would be given a specially set tea in the library, shared only by the gentleman of the house. If Mr Purvis showed an intelligent interest in the squire's collection of coins, he would probably, as he wore a good suit and did not drop his h's, be so honoured.

Ordinary villagers, who received cans of soup as their appropriate share of the bounty, went as a matter of course to the back door and, after their business was concluded, were regaled, according to sex, with a mug of ale and what was known as 'a bite' on the doorstep, or a cup of tea in the servants' hall. None who belonged to the two lower orders felt this grading at all derogatory. Many, if questioned, would have said they preferred to have it so, it made them feel 'more comfortable, like'. And the food and drink were good, even though the democratic spirit was defective.

But times and ideas were changing. By those Laura knew best at Heatherley their richer neighbours were regarded as customers, potential customers, or simply as people richer than themselves who happened to live near. Those poorer than themselves were people who might be glad to earn a shilling or two when they had a job of work to offer. The term 'gentleman' was sometimes defined as one able and willing to pay twenty shillings in the pound, and as those who so defined it prided themselves on being able and willing to do likewise they had no feeling of inferiority. The poor still sometimes spoke of 'the gentry', but having no longer anything to hope or fear from the class so described, they felt little interest in their doings. There was as yet no sign of class hostility; the classes had simply drawn apart, and were as natives of and dwellers in separate countries. The old order with its social prejudices, its assumption of superiority on the one hand and habitual self-abasement on the other, had fallen asunder, and with it had gone the old lavish hospitality and the warm human feeling which had bound man to man as members of one body. Other groupings and combinations of mankind were forming, but these still included only the few; each of the many fought for his own hand, hoping nothing and asking nothing but what he could grasp by his own effort. There was more widely diffused knowledge, though not noticeably more wisdom, and a new sense of independence was growing which was bound in the end to make for human dignity. The old social order had fallen and, though few then living realized it, the long and painful process of shaping the new was beginning. Of the fierce trials they and their children would have to endure before that process was completed the men and women of that day had happily no foreboding.

III. *'Garden of Girls'*

The girl of that day – she then figured as *The Girl of Today* in heavy-type newspaper headings – was said to be mannerless, bold in her dress, speech, and deportment, without respect for her elders and devoid of feminine charm. Some professed to see in this sad falling-off a sign of the times. A dying century, they said, must naturally be a time of expiring virtues. Those whose manners and morals they condemned were degenerate children of a degenerate age. They spoke of modern youth as *fin de siècle*, pronounced in varying ways, but always with an inflection of disapproval.

Youth also applied to itself the term *fin de siècle*, as it did to most other things, for it was a favourite catchword of the day; but, applied to themselves by up-to-the-minute girls and young men, it signified self-congratulation rather than disparagement. New ideas and new ideals were in the air, blowing like a free, fresh wind – as they thought – through the old, stuffy atmosphere of convention, and what to their elders appeared as licence they gloried in as emancipation. In more advanced circles than that in which Laura moved the modern girl had already cast off some of her shackles. She had more freedom to think, speak, and act than her mother or grandmother had had at her age. Before the new century was far advanced, she believed, her freedom would be complete. The vote once secured for her sex, she and her fellow-women would be the equals of men in prestige and opportunity. Woman's position in the home, too, would be a very different one when she was armed to fight for her own and her children's welfare.

But such ideas had not penetrated to country places. The girls Laura knew at Heatherley were *fin de siècle* only in the sense of having been born towards the end of the century. The New Woman, of course, they knew by repute, for she was a familiar figure to all newspaper readers, usually depicted as hideous, in semi-masculine garb with hands extended to grab male privileges, while a balloon of print issuing from her mouth demanded 'Votes for Women!' 'Votes for Women?' fathers and brothers would say, 'I'd give 'em votes if I had my way. I'd give 'em a good slapped bottom and make 'em stay at home, where they belong.'

Mothers and elder sisters described the new women, not one of whom they had seen, as 'a lot of great coarse, ugly creatures who can't get themselves husbands'. 'I'd rather see you in your coffin', parents told their daughters, 'than wearing them bloomers and bawling for votes.' Fortunately, no such choice was necessary. With such a warning before her as the current travesty of the 'new woman' the average country girl determined to abstain altogether from ideas and concentrate upon being feminine.

Frilly muslin frocks, made long enough to sweep up the dust and to catch and tear on the bushes, flower-wreathed hats of floppy straw, long floating scarves, veils and streamers, were her ideal of womanly apparel. In her spare time she embroidered flowers with silks dyed in crude shades on chair-backs, hair-tidies, brush and nightdress cases, tea cosies, hot-water-can cosies and egg cosies, for what was known as her 'bottom drawer', a collection of fancy articles it was then supposed to be the duty of every unmarried girl to amass, 'against the time when she would have a home of her own'. The girl who had acquired the largest and most varied collection of such articles was spoken of by her elders as a good, industrious girl who well deserved a good husband. What special advantage even the most closely packed bottom drawer was likely to be to a man was never stated. Laura was often called upon to inspect and admire the contents of such bottom drawers and she sometimes silently compared their proud owners to hen birds, hoarding straws, before a mate appeared or the site of a nest was decided on.

The girls who were, as people said, 'lucky' in getting husbands, had the satisfaction of using the contents of the bottom drawer to embellish their new homes. But not all were lucky. Laura had one friend who, having reached the age of twenty-six without having had what was known as 'an offer', raffled the contents of her bottom drawer and bought a bicycle with the proceeds. The bicycle succeeded where the bottom drawer had failed. In six months she was married to the proprietor of a bicycle shop where she had stopped on one of her outings for some small repair. Whether or not she regretted parting prematurely with all her beautiful crewel and drawn-thread work nobody knew. Probably not, as she spent most of her married days helping her husband in his new and growing business and was reported to be making a small fortune teaching women and girls to ride their new bicycles.

All the world was awheel in those days. In London, society women and girls rode round and round in the parks in the morning, preferring the more novel form of exercise to riding on horseback in the Row. At weekends the suburbs poured their inhabitants into the country awheel. Sometimes, on a Sunday afternoon, Laura would go with some friend to the turning into the main road and watch the cyclists pass in a continual stream of twos, threes, and companies; the women riders in long skirts, made fast to their ankles with bands of elastic, and blouses with wide 'bishop' sleeves, puffed out by the wind. Occasionally a woman in bloomers appeared, wearing a mannish felt hat with a long quill stuck bolt upright at the side, and a faint murmur of horror would go up from the beholders; but the wearers of bloomers were few, and the garment, which was seldom becoming to the middle-aged and often stout women who most affected it, was soon superseded by the divided skirt, an arrangement which had some kind of cleavage for riding, but fell to the feet in folds when the rider dismounted. The cyclists on that road came from the neighbouring towns. The Heatherley girls – except the engaged ones who, having a male escort, were privileged – did not, as they said, 'go in for Sunday riding'; it was thought 'common', and anything common was taboo.

So, on Sunday between church times, those who were so far unattached took gentle little walks in twos and threes and talked. More talking than walking was done. They would talk themselves to a standstill and find when the subject of their conversation was exhausted it was time to turn back. Those were the girls Laura knew best in the village – the daughters of shopkeepers, shop assistants and other business girls, whose parents kept apartment houses or farmed in a small way. There were also girls from other villages and from isolated homes on or about the heath, most of the girls living within easy walking distance and of about the same age and position in society being included in the set, or, as it was sometimes described, the 'clique'.

Most of them had had more educational advantages than Laura. A few had been to boarding schools; others to elementary schools which, being in the counties nearer London, were greatly in advance of those in remote rural districts, such as the one Laura had attended. They knew, at least by name, a variety of subjects which, as they said, they had 'done' at school. But if such subjects had ever aroused any interest, it had faded, or turned to distaste. Occasionally, in the course of conversation, someone would supply a date, or the name of a city or river, or repeat, parrotwise, a line or two from some popular poem, then exclaim: 'But let's leave that dreary rot to the kids. Thank the gods and little fishes our schooldays are over!'

Home and family life, the conscientious discharge of their duties and loyalty to their friends, were their strong points. There were born nurses among them and clever household managers, and almost without exception they knew how to make the best of their personal appearance and behave in a civilized manner. They were essentially good girls, affectionate, helpful, and unselfish; they were good daughters and good sisters and were prepared to make good wives. They prided themselves upon their goodness, as on their femininity. One of the poetical tags most frequently quoted was Kingsley's 'Be good, sweet maid, and let who will be clever', which was repeated with gusto on relevant occasions.

A good deal of sentimentality figured within the clique. Although friendly with all the circle, many of the girls had one special friend with whom they went everywhere and did everything. These pairs were recognized and seldom spoken of separately. It was always 'we must ask Maud and Fanny' or 'Mary and Isobel'. They walked with their arms round each other's waists, answered questions addressed to each other in conversation, and sometimes even dressed alike. Another piece of sentimentality common to the group was taken from Tennyson's song *Come into the Garden Maud*. 'A garden of girls' was their own private name for their association. 'Another rosebud for our garden of girls' one of them would say quite seriously when some new acquaintance turned up. 'Queen of our rosebud garden of girls!' another would exclaim of the wearer when a becoming new hat or frock appeared. It need scarcely be said that they took no interest whatever in abstract ideas, or indeed in anything which happened or existed outside their own radius. They aimed at being good, rather than intelligent, and in that perhaps they were typical of all but the more advanced girlhood of their day.

Those were the days when the pun still ranked as an acceptable form of humour. A pun, if it were a good pun, could still raise a laugh, or at least an indulgent smile, in circles far more intellectual than those open to Laura. But fashions in wit, like fashions in dress, can never survive extreme popularity, and at the turn of the century the pun had become too cheap to last much longer in favour. All who could articulate punned away merrily. Music hall stars, clergymen, fathers of families, servant girls, shopmen and butcher's boys. Even learned doctors and university dons were known to give way to this form of verbal frailty. From the lips of the girls Laura knew at that time puns dropped as profusely as gold, diamonds, and pearls dripped from the lips of the girl in the fairy tale. One of Laura's lasting memories of Heatherley was that of making one of a cartload of girls returning from a picnic, packed three abreast on the front seat and three abreast on the back seat of an old-fashioned dog-cart; hats wreathed in pink roses, pink faces wreathed in smiles and bedewed with perspiration, and the pressure on each individual body similar to that of a large, warm, enveloping featherbed.

'We travelled at about this rate this morning', remarked one of the girls innocently, and another with a reputation for wit retorted: 'What a tax on the wheels.' That was sufficient to set the whole cartload off wriggling and squealing with laughter, with the exception of one girl, slow at the uptake, into whose ear had to be hissed, 'Rates and Taxes, you idiot; Rates and Taxes!' Her belated screech of laughter set the whole party off again and the cart had to be drawn to the side of the road and the old grey mare stopped while the girls dismounted and threw themselves down on the grass margin to cool off. One of the party, out of sheer high spirits, threw herself down with such abandon that she had to be told she was showing her legs. At that she sat up and clasped her hands tightly around her knees, for as someone remarked, a man might have been coming along the road and seen her. Sobered by the mere idea, they all climbed back to their high seats and the driver chirruped her father's faithful old horse-of-all-work on its way through the dewy dusk, scented with heather and honeysuckle.

That was what now would be called a lowbrow party; one at the other extreme within the range was a book tea to which Laura was invited. The guests, she was told, were to wear or to bear something signifying a book title, and that was rather a worry to her because she knew some of the girls were planning something approaching fancy dress, which she could not possibly afford. Her first idea was to go as *The Woman in White*, but that would not do as her one white frock was a thin summer one and it was winter. Then she remembered she had a little brooch representing a windmill and that, pinned to her breast with a tassel of yellow floss silk, she thought might pass for *The Mill on the Floss*. Nobody guessed what it stood for, but then nobody guessed the meaning of half the symbols. A few were simple enough. One girl carried a small globe and that was plainly *The Wide Wide World*; another kissed and fondled a flaxen-haired doll, and those who had recently read the book exclaimed '*My Little Sweetheart*'. *Great Expectations* was represented by the facial expression of a guest who, on entering the room, pointed to the already laid tea-table and mimed pleasurable anticipation, then turned a little sulky when someone suggested *A Lunatic at Large*.

After an excellent tea in a house where cookery books were the favourite reading the party played what they considered bookish games, such as cross questions and crooked answers. One, probably suggested by the article in the women's paper which had given the hostess the idea of the book tea, consisted of a series of questions to which each guest had to give a written answer.

> Do you prefer Dickens or Thackeray?
> Tennyson or Browning?

it began, then dropped suddenly in altitude to:

> White meat or brown?
> Apples or pears?
> Lilies or roses?
> Dark or fair people?
> Women or men?

which looked rather as if Muriel had substituted some of her own ideas for those of the writer. However, the question game answered its purpose of warming up the company and causing fun, and afterwards they went on to games not so bookish, such as I Spy and Snap.

It was all very pleasant. The creature comforts were maybe superior in quality to the intellectual entertainment. Such a warm, softly padded room, such a glowing fire, such a dainty tea-table, laid with the family's best silver and china, and such superlative home-made pork pies, cakes and scones, and muffins almost melting in the best fresh butter!

Laura must have made special arrangements in order to go to the book tea, unless it happened to be on a Bank Holiday, when she and Alma had a free day alternately. But the girls who lived at home and had no regular business hours went constantly to tea at each other's houses, stampeding from house to house so frequently and with such zest and jollity that they reminded Laura of the curates in *Shirley*. At such times, to all appearances, not one of them had a care in her heart or a thought in her head beyond that of having as good a time as possible. 'A heart like a balloon and a brain the size of a gnat', snapped a cynical old friend of Laura's after she had told him some little anecdote about the giver of one of the parties. But although Laura applauded she knew in her heart that human nature cannot be simplified in that manner. As she came to know the girls better she found that much of their frivolity and apparent brainlessness as a group was a pose, an unconscious pose, due to their determination to appear wholly feminine. They had been told and believed that serious thought was the prerogative of man; woman's part in the scheme of creation was to be charming. Separately, each of the girls had her own life to live, and for that both heart and brain were necessary.

This was proved in after life by the very girl whose character old Mr Foreshaw summed up in a sentence. She was certainly not brilliant, though her unfortunate current habit of giggling made her appear less so than she actually was. When called upon by circumstance she proved capable of running her dead father's little business and supporting her widowed mother in comfort.

Then there was Patience, commonly called Patty, pink and plump and cheerful, who was always the one, when no man or youth was present, to collect the sticks and light the fire at a picnic. The other girls fought shy of this job for fear they should soil their light summer frocks, and before they had finished arguing as to who should do it Patty would have the fire lighted, and with her skirts kilted up, be down on her knees, blowing to encourage the feeble flame with her cheeks puffed out and her lips pursed like those of a cherub. Nobody ever accused Patty of butting in and spoiling their chance of a tête-à-tête with a young man who showed signs of being interested in themselves. Patty, they knew, would be more likely to say: 'Now, you two, you just take a little stroll and leave me to see to these tea-things. But don't go that way. There's some of them having a game of rounders down there and they'll want you to play. You climb to the top of that hill and look at the view. And there's no call to hurry back. It'll take me some time to rinse out these cups and pack them, and when I've done that I shall take off my shoes and rest my poor feet, they do hurt me that cruel.' And, when she had reduced chaos to order, Patty would rest in the shade and probably have a little nap, for she would have been up since four o'clock that morning to milk her father's three cows and earn her few hours of liberty by getting the housework done before breakfast. For Patty was the youngest and the only unmarried daughter of elderly parents and the work of the house and much of that of her father's small-holding was done by her. 'A regular household drudge', was how some of her friends described her; but she did not think of herself as a drudge, she was too sweet-natured and willing.

And there was Edna, more fortunate in her worldly circumstances, but far less contented than Patty. Edna had a voice which her family and friends thought and often declared only needed training to rival that of Madame Patti. As no opportunity to have her voice trained had ever or was ever likely to come her way, Edna had to content herself with singing as leading soprano in the chapel choir and giving piano lessons at ninepence an hour to the village children. She often fretted over what she thought was a wicked waste of her gift; but perhaps she was more fortunate than she imagined, for her singing voice, though capable of taking the high notes, was shrill and without a vestige of feeling. The test by a musical authority which she so much desired might have led to disillusionment, while as things were, her talent was highly esteemed in her own circle and was to herself a priceless possession on which to build daydreams.

Laura could sympathize with Edna, for she had, as she thought, a small gift of her own lying idle. From earliest childhood she had longed to write and, until the age of disillusionment set in, had been a great spoiler of paper. But since she had been at Heatherley and seen, and to some extent known, those she thought of as 'real writers', she had felt ashamed of her own poor attempts and given up trying to write. Even her journal, begun on the day she first left home, had been discontinued. She had destroyed that with her other scraps of writing, saying to herself as they smouldered to tinder that that was the end of a foolish idea. But, after the folly had been renounced there remained with her a sense of some duty neglected which almost amounted to a feeling of guilt, a feeling which persisted throughout her life whenever her pen was idle. She never spoke of this to anyone, but there the feeling was, like a pin pricking at her conscience. As her mother used to say, 'we are as we are made'.

While Edna's ambitions were respected by the other girls, Marion's made her the butt of the party. Marion was a large, serious, moon-faced girl who spent her working hours selling sweets and her spare time furthering a movement known as the Christian Endeavour. A new pastor at the chapel she attended had recently decided that, instead of listening to talks and addresses given by their elders or by some outside local celebrity, the members of the Christian Endeavour should themselves, in turn, prepare and deliver an address. Marion had apparently regarded the speakers at their Thursday evening meetings with awed respect. To speak in public was to her to have reached the very pinnacle of fame, a pinnacle to which she had never dreamed of aspiring. Now greatness was to be thrust upon her. On Thursday fortnight at 8 p.m., instead of merely carrying out her usual prized and jealously guarded office of placing on the table a glass of water at the speaker's elbow, she was herself to remain on the platform, deliver the address and sip the sacred water. It would be the first outstanding event in her life and she could think and talk of nothing else.

As the great day approached she went round with a little notebook and begged her friends to help her with suggestions. What subject should she choose? It need not be a religious subject, though, of course, it must be a serious one. Did Laura think 'Total Abstinence *versus* Moderation' would do? She had once heard an excellent address given under that title at the Band of Hope and thought she could remember most of it. Laura advised something that would be new to her listeners and casually suggested 'The Sweets of Life', thinking she might draw upon her experiences in her sweet shop to provide a little light relief before drawing the moral that the best things in life cost nothing. Marion adopted the idea with enthusiasm. But deciding on a subject, she soon found, was but a beginning; she had still to compose her address. And that was what she could not do. She would write a few sentences, never, even in her large sprawling handwriting, filling more than one sheet of note-paper; hand round what she had written to be read, then alter or cross out according to the advice she received. The fortnight became a week and the week a few days and she had still written so little that it could have been read aloud in one minute. She was a great fat girl whom no amount of worry could have made thin, but her lips began to droop at the corners and her large, round face looked quite woebegone. Laura grew tired of seeing her come into the post office and of having that notebook thrust under her nose. Alma criticized Marion's behaviour as freely as Laura did, but hers was constructive criticism. She it was who put an end to Marion's worry and her friends' boredom by offering to go one evening to Marion's home and help her to write the address.

That done, Marion bloomed again. Her new frock came home in good time from the dressmaker; she resumed her air of importance, practised her gestures, including the sipping of water from an imaginary glass, before her mirror, and finally astonished her friends by ordering a cab to take her from her home to the lecture hall. 'But why a cab, Marion?' said everyone, 'it's such a short walk, and you never have a cab to take you to the meetings, or even to the Annual Social.' But Marion was quite decided on that subject. She had seen and heard speakers from outside the village arrive in a cab and evidently in her opinion the scrunching of cab wheels on the gravel and the gleam of cab lamps through the open door of the hall where the audience was already assembled were necessary to extract the full flavour of the honour and glory of the occasion. And who could begrudge her that last touch of importance on her night of nights? Unless in the same way, she was not likely ever to be in the limelight again, for she was not a marrying kind of girl. 'Too big and clumsy and silly-simple', the other girls decided when discussing her prospects. The last time Laura saw Marion she was closing, with a twirl, a bag of sweets to refresh Laura on a train journey, and she may still be twirling sweet-bags, or she may by this time be a doting grandmother, for when it comes to chances of matrimony you never can tell.

Edna and Marion were exceptions and as such stand out in the memory. The main preoccupation of most of the girls was getting themselves a husband and planning matches for their friends. For, as yet, no ordinary girl was disposed to dispute the general ruling that the success or failure of a woman's life depended on marriage. If a good marriage in a worldly sense, so much the better, but any ordinary marriage was regarded as success in life, and even a poor one as better than spinsterhood. In spite of shining examples of single life in every station, the unmarried woman, or old maid, was looked down upon with mixed pity and contempt. The headmistress of a school, the hospital matron, or the proprietress or manageress of a successful business, if unmarried, was classed among those who had failed in the main object of life; while those without any such abilities would, so long as they wore a wedding ring, speak patronizingly of them.

Laura, like other girls of her time, regarded as a matter of course her marriage some day in the future. From her earliest childhood she had heard people say that, for a woman, a married life was the only natural life. 'Better a bad husband than no husband at all' was a proverb among the countrywomen around her home. While she was still in her teens, when quoting it for her benefit, they would sometimes add reassuringly: 'But you needn't be afraid. You'll get married all right. You're one of the quiet sort men like for a wife', and when in reply Laura would shake her head and declare that she did not mean to marry, 'ever', they would laugh and say, 'All right, my girl. I've heard that tale before. You wait until Mr Right comes along. When he says "snip" you'll say "snap" fast enough, I'll warrant.' When she had turned twenty and still had the appearance of no Mr Right to report, their remarks were less kindly. 'What, twenty, and no sweetheart yet!' exclaimed one old friend; 'You'd better look out for one or you'll be left on the shelf', and when at the age of twenty-four Laura was at last about to be married the same old neighbour said feelingly: 'Well, I am glad! I really am! What a blessing you've been lucky at last! I was really afraid you were going to be one of the leftovers!'

Much the same ideas ruled at Heatherley, though less pointedly expressed, and the girls who had their homes there must sometimes have been, as Laura was, irritated by other people's interest in their affairs. But most of them appeared to take kindly to the notion of marriage as an aim in life, and in the end most of them did marry. Whether more or less wisely for knowing that marriage was expected of them cannot be said.

Those who failed, or failed for some time, to fulfil that expectation, sometimes suffered. There was the case of Izzy. A few years before Laura knew her she had been by general consent the established beauty of the neighbourhood. Her dark, wavy hair, grey-blue eyes, and slim, straight figure still held an air of distinction against the general pink and white plumpness of other girls. But Izzy by that time was twenty-seven and well on the way to old maidenhood. Unless she married Eric. A much discussed question among the girls in her absence was, will Izzy marry, or will her unsatisfactory engagement drag on for years, only to peter out in the end? There were some who said she was already married, that she wore her wedding ring on a ribbon round her neck beneath her clothes and that she and Eric were only waiting for his father to die before proclaiming themselves man and wife before the world. One girl actually said she had seen the wedding ring, or at least a bit of the ribbon upon which it was suspended, peeping out from the neck of her blouse. But Izzy was not married. She would probably have been a happier girl if she had been, even secretly.

Izzy and her widowed mother lived by letting apartments in the neighbouring settlement. In the summer months they took in holiday visitors; one of their front parlours accommodated the village branch of a Bank, and they had, as a permanent boarder, a middle-aged business manager. They were fairly prosperous and Izzy, as a child and a young girl, had been much indulged by her mother, who adored her. While she was still in her teens, her mother had set her heart on 'my little Izzy', or 'my one ewe lamb', as she called her, making a good match. Her favourite idea was that some rich and distinguished summer visitor to their house would fall in love with and marry her. Such things had been known to happen. Not being of a very reserved or a very discreet nature, she had confided her hopes to neighbouring gossips who had soon made them public.

But by the time Laura knew Izzy her mother's hopes of a grand match for her had faded. For Izzy had become what the other girls described as 'mixed up' with a young man whose father had livery stables in the district. In those days, before the advent of the motor car, a livery stable was a profitable and important business. The proprietor would own horses and vehicles, saddle-horses for hacking, horses and carriages for general hire, and often a horse-bus running between the station and town. He would provide, even if he did not actually own, a pair of greys for a wedding couple, or a pair of blacks with flowing manes and tails to draw a hearse. He would employ stablemen and drivers, wear smart, horsey clothes, and often be inclined to look down on the ordinary tradesman. Such a man was Eric's father. Eric himself was a good-looking fellow who, in his smart Bedford cords and well-polished leggings, sat his horse with the air of a gentleman of leisure. Almost daily he rode up to one of the heaths near Heatherley and there Izzy would meet him, when he would dismount, take his horse's reins over his arm and stroll by her side, the two in deep converse. When they first walked so they had no doubt talked of and schemed for their marriage. In hopeful moods they may still have done so, for hope is a perennial plant which can thrive on little nutriment, but in more sober moments they must both of them have realized the hopelessness of their position. For Eric had neither money nor prospects, beyond the far distant prospect of inheriting the family business, which was not one to set up house upon when his father was still in the prime of life and as strong looking and almost as young looking as his son.

Mr Tolman was one of the even then almost obsolete type of business men who expected their sons, and of course their daughters, to stay at home and work in the family business without wages. It was said among the girls that Eric had once asked his father to pay him some stated sum, if but a pound a week, and that his answer had been: 'What the devil do you want with wages? You're master here, as much as I am myself; why want to turn yourself into a stableman! You have the run of your teeth in the house and a first-class suit from my own tailor whenever you need it, and a pound or two here and there to put in your pocket. Where's the need of anything more! What would you do with it if you got it? Go running up to town on a Saturday night, or get mixed up with some hussy! Keep all the money we can get in the business is my motto, as it was my father's and grandfather's before me. Left like that, money breeds money, and it'll all be yours somewhen.'

So Eric had no income at all that he could depend upon. Five pounds from his father when he had brought off a good deal in horseflesh, a pound or two saved by his mother from the housekeeping money and handed to him secretly, and a guinea now and again from a riding pupil, kept him well supplied for his personal expenses. He had money in his pocket to back a horse or to stand a drink for a friend; he gave Izzy some handsome presents and was never wanting in such delicate little attentions as bringing her flowers, or sweets, or bottles of scent. But he could not marry. He was himself of a happy-go-lucky nature, and with good looks, a comfortable home, and money in his pocket he would have been very well satisfied with his lot in life had it not been for his relations with Izzy. He loved her truly and wanted to marry her, but he did not see the necessity for an immediate marriage. 'You've got a good home and so have I,' he told her, 'so where's the hurry? It'll all come right in the end you'll find. You know I'll be true to you, don't you, Izzy?' In the meantime, Izzy's slight figure became angular, her shoulders higher, and her features sharper. Some of the girls began to speak of her as a killjoy at their merrymakings, but she still joined them occasionally and regained some of her old spirits in their company.

In these more rational days a girl in Izzy's position would long before either have made a clean break in the relationship or have cheerfully accepted it as a pleasant friendship, binding on neither. But Izzy was of a loving and constant nature; with her it was Eric or nobody, and it is not at all likely that the thought of mere friendship between them ever occurred to her. At that time and in that class of society friendship between a man and a woman was rare. The very idea was scoffed at by many as something unnatural. A man, it was said, wanted but one thing of a woman and that should be sought by way of wedlock. As to a girl who encouraged such a friendship, she was as bad as the man, or she was a fool, letting her youth and her chances slip by. A hard ruling for the few who happened to have interests outside sex, but one which had to be abided by, for if flouted, there were unpleasant results in the form of gossip and the alienation of friends.

The young of either sex, who naturally inclined towards each other, often by-passed this ban on friendship by entering into hasty and ill-considered engagements and the breaking off of such an engagement when found distasteful by either party was made painful by public opinion. If the man broke it off, and it was usually the man who did so, he was said to be a villain who had jilted the poor girl; if the girl, she was either a heartless flirt or a fool who would live to regret her wicked, unwomanly action. A girl whose erstwhile lover had taken the initiative was in the most unenviable position, for she was the object of a contemptuous kind of pity which was most hurtful to her pride.

In those days breach-of-promise cases were numerous and the newspapers made a special feature of them, reported in detail and embellished with sketches of the principal parties. The hearing of an involved case would often last for days and provide for those following the proceedings in their newspapers both entertainment and a subject for conversation. Many took sides, the men usually sympathizing with the man in the case and the women with the woman. In this way the idea of transmuting injured feelings into hard cash and at the same time avenging one's wrongs by bringing unwelcome publicity upon the offender, became a familiar one. No-one Laura knew personally was ever involved in such an action, but she often heard of the threat of bringing one being held, like a rod taken out of pickle, over the head of a defaulting lover. One unforgettable scene she witnessed was that of seeing a quiet, modest, amiable girl who had been what was then known as jilted, in the midst of weeping into her handkerchief and bewailing her woes, suddenly spring to her feet, cast her sopping handkerchief aside, crying belligerently, 'I'll make him suffer for this, you mark my words I will. I'll breach him! I'll breach him!' The effect was that of a little bleating shorn lamb suddenly ramping and rearing in incongruous rage. But of course Millicent did not carry out her threat. Instead, she mildly and patiently lived down the gossip she had dreaded, and in time found another and let us hope a more constant lover. This might have been expected by anyone who knew her, and the wonder is how the other idea arose in her quiet, gentle mind and was given such fierce expression.

Except for such complications in a few cases, the lives of the Heatherley girls ran smoothly from protected childhood to carefree youth and on to protected marriage, and that, as a general rule, was all they asked of life. But, later, life must have made great demands upon many of them, for the girls of that day became the mothers of the young soldiers in the First World War. How they met the trials which then faced them Laura did not know, for she had long before lost touch with them, but there need be no doubt that their genuine goodness of heart enabled them to bear all that was laid upon them, and that their old gaiety of spirit, by that time sobered to a steady cheerfulness, supported others as well as themselves in the day of trouble and mourning. There is a lot to be said for, as well as a little against, the old-fashioned womanly woman.

IV. *Mr Foreshaw*

The friends thought most suitable for Laura by her elders were those of her own age, sex, and social condition, and at Heatherley she had several such friends, whose company she enjoyed and whose good qualities she appreciated. But like herself, these had had little experience of life, their views and interests were limited, and she often longed to meet someone with a wider mental horizon. Gradually, while still at Heatherley, she did find a few other friends, less suitable for her according to the conventional ruling, but who, she herself felt, gave a new, keen relish to life. The earliest and most memorable of these was Mr Foreshaw.

Laura had often noticed a distinguished-looking old gentleman with snow-white hair and a small, neatly-trimmed white beard at the post-office counter. He was tall and, except for a slight droop of his shoulders, fairly erect; but when seen closely, his great age was apparent in his dark, dried, deeply wrinkled face and forehead, and his eyes which, beneath shaggy brows, were ringed with white round the iris. In winter he wore a long, thick black overcoat and a sealskin cap with ear-pieces tied down under his chin. In hot summer weather he would sometimes appear in a white drill suit of tropical cut. 'Who is the old gentleman in the white suit?' Laura one day asked Alma, who, having her home there, knew most people who lived in the village, and she was told that her old gentleman's name was Mr Foreshaw, and that a year or two before he had had a bungalow built for himself at the end of a little lane off the main road, where he had since lived alone. That was all Alma knew about him, and she was sure to know all that was generally known in the village, so who Mr Foreshaw was, where he had lived and what he had done before coming to Heatherley, and why in extreme old age he had elected to live alone, for some time remained to Laura a mystery. But she, loving a mystery, and being exceptionally fond of aged people, still felt a great interest in her old man, as Alma called him, and would show him any little attention she could when he came to the post office. Disregarding rules and regulations, she would take the letters from his awkward, arthritic old hands and stick on the stamps for him, and soon, if she were on duty, he would as a matter of course pass over to her his unstamped letters. But, beyond thanking her, he said little, and that little was said so gruffly and abruptly that she thought that for some unknown cause he did not like her. One day Alma, who by that time had collected a little more information about him, told Laura that Mr Foreshaw was known to be a woman-hater. He would not have a woman in his house even to clean it and cook his meals, but employed for those purposes an elderly ex-serviceman.

Then one evening after the office door had been locked and while Laura was putting on her hat to go home a telegram came off, addressed to 'Foreshaw, The Bungalow'. From the contents of the telegram it appeared that someone named Roberts was arriving by a late train that night. The telegraph messengers had gone home and could not be recalled as it was past their working hours. Laura should not have taken off the telegram after eight o'clock, but her response to the musical tinkle of Heatherley's code letters had become automatic. Now she had the telegram on her hands. If it had been for any other address she would not have thought twice before setting out herself to deliver it, as she had often before delivered late-coming messages which appeared to be urgent; but in view of Mr Foreshaw's reputation as a woman-hater, she hesitated. He might not appreciate even so small a voluntary service by one of her sex.

But there lay the telegram in its orange-coloured envelope; Mr Foreshaw's visitor was about to step into the railway carriage at Waterloo station; and at the bungalow, Mr Foreshaw was probably thinking of going to bed. The old people she had known hitherto had all gone to bed very early. To save light and fire, they said, and because there was nothing else to do, and they would have been alarmed if knocked up by a visitor at midnight. She slipped the telegram into the pocket of her coat and stepped out into the warm dusk of the August evening.

'At the very end of the lane, standing back in a garden, you'll find it', the man had said of whom she asked the way, and when she came to the gate, she knew she had found it, because in a lighted room, with the curtains undrawn and the window wide open, she could see Mr Foreshaw himself in a grey dressing-gown and black velvet smoking-cap, sitting at a table spread with papers. In response to her timid knock he came to the door. 'What's this?' he said, 'What? A telegram? Ah, now I see who it is. Come in. Come in. I can't read it here in the darkness.' Laura stepped before him into the lighted room and he, after courteously drawing forward a chair for her, sank back into his former seat before the maps, for she saw now that the sheets spread out upon the table were maps, upon which, as she was shown afterwards, he had marked in red ink the course of his many journeys.

As he read the telegram Mr Foreshaw's bushy white eyebrows rose considerably. 'Roberts? Roberts?' he ejaculated, 'Ah, now I recollect the fellow. Saw him last in the Zambesi valley in '84. Good of him to look me up. Don't get many visitors these days. Not that I've got any burning desire for 'em, too used to my own company. Very good of you to bring the wire. You must have a drink now you're here.'

The offer of a drink rather alarmed Laura, for she barely knew the name of any drink other than beer, which she did not like; but interest, or curiosity, made her glad of any excuse to stay a little longer and she said that she would like a little water, or milk, if he had it to spare. At that he laughed gruffly and said that he had not suspected her of being a milk and watery miss, and milk he had not, never touched the stuff, and as to giving her water, he'd leave that sort of hospitality to good Christian people. He's an old pagan, thought Laura, a regular old pagan, and repeated the word mentally with some pride, for she had but recently discovered its modern usage. 'But I've got something here I think you will like', he continued, and he brought a bottle out of a cupboard and mixed her a tumblerful of some sweet syrup and water, which she sipped appreciatively.

Mr Foreshaw sat at the table, propping his head upon one hand, his eyes from beneath their bushy eyebrows regarding her, as she thought critically, though kindly. The fresh night air from without billowed the window-curtains and stirred the papers upon the table, and every pause in the conversation was filled with the loud tick-tocking of the clock in the hall. Laura had never before seen a room at all like Mr Foreshaw's. The light green walls had not a single picture, only framed maps, and here and there long hangings like narrow curtains upon which stiff, angular figures of men and beasts were silhouetted in black on a white ground. On the mantelpiece stood a few pieces of queer foreign-looking pottery and an ostrich's egg upon which someone had drawn a pen-and-ink sketch of an ostrich with a man's face. A tall bookcase stood on one side of the fireplace, the recess on the other side had a stand on which were arranged spears, blowpipes and other weapons, and all about the room stood glass-topped showcases containing specimens of some kind. But that night Laura had time for no more than a general impression of her surroundings, for she feared she was intruding upon Mr Foreshaw's privacy, and after draining her glass she rose and said she was sure he had much to attend to before his visitor arrived. At that he laughed and said, 'Airing a bed for Roberts and getting out the best linen and china you mean, eh? No, no, that's not how we old bachelors manage things. Roberts is an old campaigner like myself and as long as the tantalus and tumblers are on the table he will be satisfied.'

A few days later Mr Foreshaw, handing over his letters to be stamped, rumbled: 'When are you coming to see me again? If you've got nothing better to do come on Sunday and pour out my tea. If anybody asks you where you are going tell 'em to visit your aged grandfather.' Fortunately, Laura had no one to whom it was necessary to account for her movements and she went to see Mr Foreshaw many times. At the time of his first invitation Alma was present and heard what he said and Laura's reply. After he had gone she was a little discouraging. 'You and your old man!' she said, 'I can't understand you, really. If you feel like going out to tea anywhere why not come to us, up home, and go for a walk with Arthur and me afterwards.' But that programme, though kindly offered, did not appeal to Laura, who thought making a third in a lovers' walk a tame prospect compared to a visit to the bungalow. After that, Alma was always a little cold and reserved when any mention was made of Mr Foreshaw, but she was not a gossiping girl and unlikely to have discussed Laura's eccentricity in friendship with others. If anyone else at any time saw her slip up the little green lane and through the white gate at the end of it they probably thought that Mr Foreshaw's great age exempted her from the rule of the day that no really nice girl should ever go alone to the house of a man. But it was far more likely that no-one other than Alma knew of her visits to the bungalow.

Mr Foreshaw

On her second visit to him Mr Foreshaw showed Laura his trophies, including his glass cases of tropical butterflies with wings of the most glorious colours, as bright and fresh as if newly painted, but with wings and bodies so stiff and motionless and so imprisoned under the glass that the sight made her feel sad. 'Pretty things,' he said, 'you like them, eh?' and she, gazing down on them, each one with a pin through its middle and a little label beneath with its name and its species, could think of no better answer than, 'I should like to see them alive.' There were cases of mineral specimens and of arrow heads, stuffed crocodile skins, horns and hoofs, and rugs made of the skins of beasts he had shot in his big-game hunting days. For Mr Foreshaw had for thirty years been a professional big-game hunter in British and Portuguese East Africa. That, he told Laura when he knew her better, was why he had never married. 'Didn't want to leave some poor woman crying her eyes out every time I disappeared into the blue', he said; 'bad for a man, too, cripples his nerve. "He rides swiftest who rides alone", as that new young feller, Kipling, puts it.'

Almost every article in his large collection had a story. There was a tusk of the elephant he had shot that time when the platform of boughs and leafy twigs upon which he was standing collapsed; when he fell to the ground, right in the path of the wounded, charging animal, it had seemed as if, the next moment, he would be trampled to death. His 'boys', as he called his native carriers, scattered in all directions, 'like streaks of greased lightning', he said. But the poor beast, blinded with its own blood, staggered aside as it passed him and, a few yards farther on, collapsed. 'A damned near thing that time,' was his comment when telling the story. He had had numberless such narrow escapes, from wild animals met suddenly in unexpected places, from snake bite, and from hostile native tribes. Once he had been chased by a pack of wild dogs and, having taken refuge in the boughs of a tree, had had to remain there for over three hours, with the creatures leaping and snapping just short of his feet. Twice he was deserted by his carriers, and once, during a great drought, he and his party almost perished of thirst.

He told Laura stories of many such tight corners. When, in the course of their conversation, he said, 'Once, when I was in the Zambesi valley,' or 'in Portuguese East', or 'prospecting for minerals in the Transvaal', Laura knew there was a story coming. Once she ventured to ask him if, after such an adventurous life, he did not find Heatherley dull, and he replied with his characteristic grunt, which by one more experienced than Laura might have been recognized as an exclamation of suppressed suffering, 'Dull? Yes, damned dull. I feel old and cold and as dull as ditchwater and I shan't be sorry to go. Go where? Well, wherever old hunters do go when they die. Pity they can't be like the old elephants who, when they feel their time coming, go alone into the bush, or a swamp, and take what's coming to 'em without a lot of bother and fuss. Did I ever tell you I once found an elephants' cemetery? That was in a swamp. Tons of ivory! I had my boys digging for a fortnight, then made a special journey to Beira to ship off the tusks and to blue most of the proceeds. That was the time I saw with my own eyes the Hindoo kill, pluck and roast a chicken and burn the feathers, then bring it back to life again. Heard the thing's death squawk, saw its blood run when he cut its throat, smelt the roasting flesh and the feathers burning, take my oath I did! Then saw the live fowl running and cackling afterwards. No conjuring about it. Ground as bare as the palm of my hand for yards around and the fellow practically naked. Just him and the bird and a little stick fire. How do I think it was done? Now you're asking something! Some say it's mesmerism. Fowl never killed, and of course never roasted; just a few feathers burnt, and the rest takes place in the imagination of the spectators, suggested by the performer of course. In my opinion it's just pure magic. Yes, I believe in magic, and so would you if you had seen what I've seen. Ever hear of the Indian rope trick? Never had the luck to see that myself, but I've known men willing to swear on the Bible they'd seen it, and not particularly hard-drinking men either.'

When Laura came to know Mr Foreshaw better she rallied him on his reputation as a woman-hater. He laughed, grunted, and said: 'Not a hater of women between the ages of fifteen and fifty, excepting the weasels and quacks, as we used to call 'em, meaning the dried-up, vinegarish sort and the fat white waddlers. Those I never cared for. Girl children I must admit I'm not particularly fond of, and as to old women of either sex, I' (grinding his teeth) 'absolutely abominate 'em.'

For nearly a year Laura went at least once a week to see Mr Foreshaw. On many Sunday afternoons she sat opposite him at the table at which she had first seen him sitting over his maps, and ate guava jelly, dried ginger, or some other dainty he had brought out from his store-cupboard, with cream in her tea, while he drank black coffee and nibbled a dry biscuit.

From the first Laura liked Mr Foreshaw. She liked him for his originality, his raciness, his immense store of experience and his biting wit. As she came to know him better and to realize what a trial it must be to him to live such a quiet, inactive life, after his years of stirring adventure, old and alone and often in pain, her liking deepened to affection. And she thought Mr Foreshaw liked her. The way he treated her was, she knew, partly due to his courteous, old-fashioned manners; but to her, unused as she was to such consideration, it was delightful to have someone take care that she had a comfortable seat, did not sit in a draught, to have her permission to smoke asked at each pipe-lighting, and to have her slightest need elaborately supplied at table. If she called in the evening, when she left he would apologize for not being able to enjoy the great pleasure of seeing her home safely, and even in cold weather he would stand in the doorway until the gate had closed behind her, then raise his hand in a last salute.

On the day of her first visit to tea he had shown her a room, saying: 'Here is a little bower for you if you want to curl your hair or anything. It is a long time since I entertained a lady, so if I have forgotten anything you must put my forgetfulness down to my old bachelor ways; but you will find a looking-glass there, and I've put you out a bottle of eau de cologne . . . .'

'*And* a paper of pins!' exclaimed Laura, 'and it's all just lovely! I feel like Mrs Micawber when she went to supper with David.'

Which was a happy remark of hers, for he was a great lover of Dickens and, he then told her, had always carried his books with him on his expeditions. He showed her the book he had been reading that afternoon before she arrived. It was a copy of *Great Expectations*, and the small round holes like shot-holes which pierced the back cover and tunnelled through the pages had been bored by white ants.

The fiction of Dickens, Thackeray, and a few other Victorians was still his favourite reading, though he also read a good deal of travel and biography and every new book which appeared about Africa. With the one exception of Kipling, whose short stories he greatly admired, he did not care for the modern novelists. 'These new men,' as he called them, 'setting up their Aunt Sallies and shyin' at 'em, and damned clumsy about it, with their little knotty points they call problems, which the older writers would have taken in their stride!'

Laura came to know Mr Foreshaw well and her contact with him, though but of short duration, made a lasting impression on her mind. Yet, looking back in after years, she was surprised that she had learned so little about his life. He would talk freely about his thirty years of big-game hunting in Africa, but of his life before and after that period he said not a word. Where he had been born and spent his childhood, who were his parents, and whether or not he had relatives still living at the time she knew him, she was not told. She did not know if he had loved, or experienced sorrow, beyond the affection he had felt for the lion and cheetah cubs he had reared and kept as pets, and the sorrow he had felt when he lost them, either by death, or by having to ship them off to some zoo in Europe when they became too big and too 'playful' to suit his carriers. All she knew of his private life was that he had, or had had, a sister, and she knew that only because she had read on the fly-leaf of one of his books, *Charles Foreshaw, from his loving sister Clara. Christmas 1880.*

If still living, his sister never came to see him, nor did he ever mention her. Except the doctor, who besides his professional visits sometimes came in the evening to play chess with him, the only visitor he had besides herself while Laura knew him was the Roberts of the telegram, who had stayed two nights and immediately afterwards returned to South Africa, where he had many years before his visit married the widowed owner of a hotel in Rhodesia.

Nor did Mr Foreshaw know much about Laura. She had told him a little about her parents and home and he had seemed interested, and he always enjoyed hearing about any amusing little incident which occurred in her present daily life. But Laura was a listener, rather than a talker, and there were whole tracts in her life and nature that he could not have suspected. They had a similar sense of humour and both thought some things funny which others thought sad, and sad that others thought funny, and that perhaps was the closest bond between them. Only once did she see him moved. Then they had been talking of ghosts and he had been condemning spiritualists and spiritualism, while Laura wavered a little and said that perhaps, after all, there might be something in it. She had heard some strange stories in childhood of people seeing what appeared to be spirits, people she had known and whose word she could believe.

'Ah, there you are,' he said, 'superstition, thy name is woman! I'll bet you'd be afraid to live in this bungalow after I had died in it. Afraid I'd haunt you, eh?' and Laura, a little offended at being thought superstitious, protested that she felt sure she would never fear the ghost of anyone she had known and been fond of. If it were possible, which she doubted, as he did, she thought that she would want to see them.

'But you never will, never! That's the devilishness of death. I knew a man who, towards the end of a trip, sent one of his boys in advance down to the coast to collect his mail. When the letters came, there was one among them – well, someone he knew had died – and I tell you that man prayed all that night, prayed on his knees, mind you, that the spirit of his friend might appear to him, just once. He asked no more than to see her face once again. And what happened? Nothing. Absolutely nothing. Outside his tent in the darkness the palm leaves rattled in the slight breeze that always comes in those parts just before dawn. That, and the loud snoring of his boys huddled round the embers of the camp fire, were the only sounds that he heard. Not a whisper from her, nor a sign to tell that, though unseen, she was near him; only emptiness, emptiness everywhere!'

Mr Foreshaw sank back, his swollen old hands grasping the arms of his chair. Laura said nothing. What could she say? She could only look her sympathy. When he spoke again it was in his ordinary tone about some small everyday matter. But, that evening, before she left him, he said, 'I should like you to live here when I have gone and take care of my things. Shan't be allowed to take 'em with me, and don't like the idea of them being scattered and knocked about by strangers.'

But that was just what did happen to Mr Foreshaw's trophies. One morning the news ran round the village that the old gentleman up at the bungalow had died in his sleep. The ex-service man who cleaned and cooked for him had found him, looking as peaceful as a child asleep, he had told people, and the doctor had said that it was no more than he had expected, as that rheumatic complaint affected the heart.

The doctor and a lawyer from town were the only mourners at his funeral and their two wreaths were the only flowers placed upon his coffin. To those wired, waxen florist's flowers, when they lay on his grave, another friend added a bunch of red roses, chosen because she knew he had loved deep, rich colour in flowers, as he had loved everything strong, warm and positive in life.

After long search, as it appeared, a great-nephew of Mr Foreshaw was discovered in Canada, and as legal heir to the property he gave instructions that the bungalow and its contents should be sold by auction. On the evening of the day of the sale Laura, at the post-office window, watched women passing by carrying curtains, china, lamps, and fire-irons, and men trundling the heavier furniture on wheelbarrows. A boy marched past with a pair of branching antlers held to his own forehead, and two girls swung carelessly between them a clothes-basket containing cups and saucers.

It was some consolation to Laura to learn that his collection of butterflies and some of his native weapons and pottery had been bought by the curator of a museum. Those, at least, would not be 'knocked about', though the story attached to almost every article having now gone to the grave with their former owner, they would become mere objects of interest.

Laura made a timid bid for one of her old friend's books. A woman had come into the post office and placed on the counter while she made her purchases a bundle of books, tied ruinously tightly with string and marked 'Lot 39', which she said she had bought for a shilling, though what she was going to do with them when she got home she did not know, she had only bought them because they were going so cheaply. Laura touched a copy of *Vanity Fair* with her forefinger. It had been a favourite book with Mr Foreshaw, who had always maintained that Becky Sharp would have been a better woman if she had been born to her ten thousand a year. As it was, he liked her for her mettle.

'Would you care to sell me this one for a shilling?' asked Laura, and the woman had replied tartly, 'No. If it's worth a shilling to you it's worth a shilling to me. I'll keep it to prop open my pantry window.'

Although his fears had proved true as to the fate of his possessions, Mr Foreshaw's own ending had been such as he would have wished. Like the old elephant which had staggered away beneath its weight of years to die in the swamp, he also had died alone, without 'fuss and bother'. Laura had lost a kind friend, one whose like she felt she would scarcely meet again, and she was both saddened and sobered. It was the first time in her life that she felt a sense of personal loss. People she had known had died and she had felt sorry, but none of them had been near to her; she had never before faced the great dark, silent abyss which lies between the dead and the living. For weeks after Mr Foreshaw's death, when anything interesting or amusing occurred or was said, she would think, 'I must tell that to Mr Foreshaw', then realize sadly that she would never again tell him anything, or hear his shrewd, spicy comments.

v. *The Wind on the Heath*

Her work at the post office, making new friends and reading new library books in quick succession, did not fill the whole of Laura's life at this time. She had another interest which, though she was able to devote less time to it, lay nearer her heart's core.

Her love of nature was an inborn love and she was quick to recognize natural beauty even in those places where such beauty was not spectacular. In her own county, where the landscape as a whole was plain and homely, there were many sweet scenes which were dear to her. Buttercup meadows set round with dark elms, deep double hedgerows white with may, festooned with wild rose or honeysuckle, or berried with hips and haws and hung with big silvery puffs of old-man's-beard, according to season. And there were little brooks, banked with willow herb and meadowsweet, which meandered through fields where in spring skylarks soared and sang above the young green wheat, or patches of bright yellow mustard; and later in the year when the small birds were silent and coveys of young partridge chicks scurried *peep-peeping* to cover before an approaching footstep on the field paths, those same fields would be golden with ripe grain and there would be poppies in the corn.

And since she had left home, although she had not actually seen the sea, she had seen an Essex saltmarsh bluish-mauve with sea lavender, and a tidal river with red fisher sails upon it and gulls wheeling overhead and seaweed clinging to the stones of its quays. All those things she had loved and would always love. If she had been condemned to live in a great city for the rest of her life they would still have been hers, for nothing could rob her of such memories.

Her love of her own county was that of a child for its parent, a love which takes all for granted, instinctive rather than inspiring, but lifelong. Her love of the Heatherley countryside was of a different nature. It had come to her suddenly in that moment of revelation when, on the day of her arrival, she had unexpectedly come out on the heath and seen the heather in bloom. She had felt then a quick, conscious sense of being one with her surroundings, and as she came to know the hills and heaths in all moods and seasons, the feeling became more definite. It was more a falling in love on her part than of merely loving.

After she had become established at Heatherley her greatest pleasure in life was in her few free daylight hours to roam on the heather-clad hills or to linger in one of the valley woods where trickling watercourses fed the lush greenery of ferns and bracken and mosses and the very light which filtered down through the low, matted overgrowth was tinged with green. She liked best to walk in those places alone, for although she soon made a few friends, a walk in their company, she found, meant a brisk swinging progress from point to point to the accompaniment of much talk and laughter. Such walks could be taken on dark evenings after the office was closed and they were then often taken by Laura with great enjoyment. But she loved best her solitary walks, when she could stand and gaze at some favourite viewpoint, watch the heath birds and insects and quick-darting lizards, gather the heath flowers into little stiff honey-scented bouquets, run the warm, clean heath sands through her fingers and bare her head to the soft, misty rain.

Sunday morning, after the office had closed, was the best time, and in winter the only time for these solitary walks. With good luck in the matter of work, she would have her hat and coat already on when the telegraph instrument ticked out its daily message from Greenwich: '*T-i-m-e —— T-i-m-e ——T-i-m-e*', then, after a few seconds' pause, 'T-E-N!' A moment later she would have locked the door behind her and be halfway down the village street on her way to the hills or woods. During the Boer War, with wireless broadcasts far in the future and only very early editions, printed the day before, of the Sunday newspapers reaching many places, the Government authorities thought it necessary to institute Sunday morning bulletins giving the latest war news. These were telegraphed to every post office to be written out and displayed in the post-office windows. The bulletin was supposed to arrive before ten o'clock, when the offices closed. Occasionally it did arrive before ten, but far more often, at Heatherley, it came a quarter, a half, or sometimes a whole hour after that time. Laura, who had no objection on other days to staying beyond her hours to complete this or that, found this involuntary Sunday overtime exasperating, for it shortened her walk.

When, sooner or later, she was at liberty, it took her but a few minutes to reach open country. Looking neither to right nor left lest she should see some acquaintance who would volunteer to come with her, she would rush like a bandersnatch, as someone once said who had seen her from a distance, and take the first turning out of the village which led to the heath. This led through a narrow sandy lane with high, heather-covered banks on each side to one of the valleys, or 'bottoms', as they were called locally. At one point, close beside the pathway, stood the homestead of one of the broom-squires, a long, low little house with many outbuildings, and often a pile of heather brooms waiting to be taken to market. A wild-looking, hoarsely-barking sheepdog was kennelled near the path in a large beer-barrel turned on its side, and at the sound of a footstep he would leap and bark and rattle his chain like a mad thing. Probably, to some degree, the poor creature *was* mad, for his whole life from puppyhood had been spent on that chain. He was never released even for an hour. What he felt when other, freer dogs gambolled past on their walks with their masters can only be imagined. He had no means of redress in life, poor dog, but in death he had his revenge upon humanity, though not, as so often happens, upon the one who had been responsible for his unnatural existence.

At that time there had been for some weeks an epidemic of dog-poisoning. There were many such barking dogs in the neighbourhood, for at that time and in that district ignorant people thought a watchdog made a better guard if kept constantly on a chain, and one by one they were found in the morning dead before their kennels, poisoned. Great indignation was felt by dog-owners, and it was arranged that a night watch should be kept beside those still living. When it came to our poor friend's turn and the young men, hiding behind a rick, saw a man's form approach in the bright moonlight and place a piece of meat (which afterwards proved to be poisoned) before the dog's kennel, they rushed out from their hiding-place and secured the offender. The dog, meanwhile, snapped up and consumed the meat. The dog died and the men must have had the surprise of their lives when they found they had captured and roughly treated a much respected doctor who had a large house on the border of the heath, a few hundred yards distant from the scene of the crime. He had been running a nursing home for patients with nervous disorders, probably many of them borderline mental cases, for he had male nurses on his staff, and the continual night-and-day barking of suffering dogs had so affected his patients and enraged himself that he had decided to take the extreme measure of poisoning to silence them. He was prosecuted and found guilty, but what legal punishment was meted out to him Laura could not remember, though she remembered well that some of the villagers clubbed together to hire a horse brake to take them to witness his trial. Pity and cowardice combined caused Laura to find a by-pass through a pinewood to avoid what she always thought of as the dog's house, but she could still hear his incessant hoarse barking until she had left the village and its neighbourhood well behind her, and once, when she heard the rattle of a chain among the tree-trunks, her heart stood still, for she thought the dog had broken loose and was about to spring upon her. But the creature that had broken loose and was straying there was only a poor old nanny-goat which, mistaking Laura for its owner, insisted on following her until they came to a stile.

The largest of the green woods was regarded as one of the local beauty spots. It ran for about half a mile along both shores of a chain of three small lakes where low-hanging branches dipped down to the water and the pathways were slippery with tree-roots. In spring the green open glades above the lake edges were crowded with the delicate drooping white flowers of the wood anemone, primroses grew in great tufts by the water's brink, and the flowers and budding trees were reflected in the pale green lake water. In autumn the foliage of the trees, red, yellow, and russet, was seen in duplicate, above and upon the still glassy surface where, later, the many-coloured leaves fallen from the bare branches would float singly and in drifts.

The lakes were one of the sights of the neighbourhood, always visited by strangers staying in the district, and they, with the surrounding woodland, have since been bought by the National Trust. In Laura's time they were a favourite place for picnics, and villagers went there when out for their Sunday evening stroll, but it was seldom that Laura found anyone other than herself there on Sunday mornings. Once, it is true, she disturbed there at his work a photographer who asked her, rather testily, to please move on as he was about to 'take a picture'. He would, no doubt, have described himself as a photographic artist, for he evidently took his calling seriously, dressing up to the part in a velveteen jacket and wearing a vandyke beard. His apparatus consisted of a large wooden camera, the front of which drew out like a concertina, and a heavy wooden tripod. To take his picture he enveloped his head and the back part of his camera in a large square of black velvet.

By one of the paths which led by the lake shores there was at that time a deep sandy basin fed by a spring of crystal clear water which gushed from the bank above. This had been known from time immemorial as the Wishing Well; the local belief was that anyone drinking the water and wishing would have their wish granted, provided they dropped in a pin. In Laura's youth dozens of pins could be seen rusting on the sandy bottom of the well and she dropped in quite a number herself at different times, though what she wished for and whether or not her wishes were granted she could not in old age remember. Twenty years later, when chance brought her to live again in the district, though not at Heatherley, she visited the Wishing Well and found it much altered. A house had been built a few yards from the path and a garden wall stood on the bank. The spring water still had an outlet beneath the wall, though it no longer gushed forth in a crystal stream but fell in a thin trickle from a lead pipe, and the deep sandy basin having been filled in, the little stream wandered aimlessly across the path into the green morass on the edge of the wood. Immediately beneath the pipe there was a small puddle, but no pin, rusted or shining new, was to be seen in it, and strange to relate, no-one Laura ever met in the neighbourhood had heard of the Wishing Well. After its centuries of existence, in twenty short years it had disappeared, and the memory of it had faded from men's minds.

Not far from the well there was a deep dingle, closed on three sides by high sandstone cliffs. Ferns and bracken and small scrubby birches filled the greater part of it, primroses bloomed there in the spring and large moist dewberries ripened in autumn. Crowning the tall yellow cliff on one side was a row of tall pine trees. When Laura first knew it, it was a silent, sequestered spot which seldom knew a human footstep. The story went that, eighty or ninety years before, on a dark windy night a horseman who had lost his bearings in the wood had ridden over one of the cliffs and both he and his horse had been killed. The whole countryside had been searched before the broken bodies of horse and rider were found among the bushes and ferns at the bottom of the dell. From that time it had been a place of ill repute. There were people still living who said that, passing nearby on a dark windy night, they had heard the sound of galloping hoofs, and a crash, then silence. When Laura revisited the hollow she found it had been adopted as a dwelling-place by one of the unemployed ex-Servicemen who for a few years after the 1914–1918 war were to be found living in all kinds of odd places. Some of their improvised homes were wretchedly inadequate, a saddening sight, but the occupant of this one called for no pity. He had the cliffs, steep and tall as the sides of a house, to shelter the lean-to of planks in which he slept and the fireplace of bricks in the open which he used for his cooking, and judging by the sizzling sound and the savoury smell, he had bacon and eggs for his supper. He was singing lustily as he turned his rashers that popular song of those years, 'The red, red robin keeps bob, bob, bobbing', and he looked pretty bobbish himself. A tinker's outfit on a converted perambulator proclaimed his means of living. If he had a wife or

215

children they were not visible. Probably he had no dependants, for there was a jolly, carefree ring in his voice and his face was rosy and unlined. He was tidily dressed, quite a presentable fellow in fact, except that he squinted horribly.

He had probably never heard the story of the dead horseman, for the war years had wiped out many such old traditions in country places, and if he had heard it he did not appear to be a man who would, on dark windy nights, hear the soft thud of a horse's footfalls beneath the trees, followed by the heavy crash of falling bodies, then silence. Horseman and horse had ceased to exist, truly ceased to exist at last. For eighty or ninety years they had survived only in man's memory, from which they had now passed, and the place had become a stage for another scene. Probably today the scene has again changed and has become 'that charming wild bit' in somebody's garden.

But on her Sunday morning walks Laura did not often linger by the lakes; she climbed at once by a little sandy track to the heath beyond. It was then, when she felt the heather brush the hem of her skirt and breathed the honey-scented moorland air, that she was filled with a sense of freedom and detachment from ordinary life such as she was never to know elsewhere.

There was one remote part of the heath where the heather had not been cut or burnt as it was cut or burnt periodically in parts nearer the villages. It was tall and thick and shrubby and its long, dark branches almost met over the paths and inlets of cream-coloured sand. Dotted about it singly were low, stunted-looking trees, some of them with stiff dead branches hung with the smoke-coloured lichen called old man's beard; a few scattered grey rocks were also lichen-coated, and over the whole scene brooded an air of immense age. As far as the eye could see the activities of man had left no impression. There were no prehistoric earthworks or burial mounds; no flint tools or weapons, such as Laura herself was to find on the heaths nearer the sea in the same county, had ever been found there. There was no squared plot, banked round by turf walls, and no marks of the ploughshare beneath heather or bracken to show, as in other places, that although now deserted, man had had his habitation there in times nearer to our own. In its season the heather bloomed purple, then faded through its customary gradations of all shades of pinkish tan to brown and to darkness again, and that was the only visible change in those days, apparently the only one that solitary spot had ever known.

From that high viewpoint Laura would look back on Heatherley and see it as a knot of red roofs, red as a rose against its dark pine trees, and as new to the earth as the rose which had bloomed yesterday, and maybe destined to be almost as fugitive, compared to the continuity of its surroundings. On a morning of April showers and sudden flashes of sunlight she saw the new hotel on the hill beyond Heatherley suddenly stand out from its dark background like a structure carved from ivory. The sun's light had caught its many large windows, which reflected and magnified its beams, and the whole building appeared as though brilliantly illuminated from within. Like a lantern, she thought, like a huge lighted lantern, set down there casually for a moment.

Sometimes she would descend to one of the long, narrow marshes which lay between the hills and explore its pools, standing insecurely on some quaking island of rushes. Newts with smooth dark backs and orange undersides would glide out silently from beneath her feet; frogs squatted sedately, like fat elderly gentlemen, under umbrellas of fern fronds; butterflies hovered in the warm air over the pools, and dragonflies, newly-emerged from their chrysalids, dried their wings and darted away, miracles of blue and silver. In the clearer pools, Laura's own birth plant, Sagittarius, floated its arrow-shaped leaves, and there were other water plants, water-flowers and water-leaves and mosses in abundance. Once she found a few spikes of the bog asphodel, its constellations of yellow starlike blooms shining against the dark rushes, and once, on the heath above, one solitary spike of the rare field gentian, of a heavenly blue. Such were her innocent adventures.

But Laura, though fairly well versed in the ways of the earth, was untrained in the ways of the world. She did and said many things at that time which, to her, seemed natural enough, but

217

which others regarded as doubtful. On the heath, the world forgotten, she was not entirely by the world forgot. Her comings and goings were noted, and those solitary Sunday morning walks were considered by others to be suspicious. One inquisitive person, she was told afterwards, on one occasion took the trouble of following her at a distance, 'just to see who she met'. His curiosity went unrewarded, but the spying on her movements must to some extent have continued, for her later acquaintance with Bob Pikesley and his sister gave rise to some ill-natured gossip which caused her pain.

She came upon Bob one Sunday morning in one of the more remote parts of the heath which she had but recently discovered, herding his three or four cows which were grazing on one of the natural lawns of rabbit-bitten turf among the gorse bushes. He seemed to her quite an old man. He was short of stature and his slightly hunched shoulders, drooping forward, caused him to appear shorter than he actually was; the skin round his shrewd grey eyes was drawn into wrinkles by his outdoor life, and he wore the earth-coloured garments of poverty on the land. He was never seen without a stick in his hand, a stout, rough ash stick, no doubt of his own cutting, and this he used to flourish at straying cows, to walk with, and in leisure moments to trace patterns of noughts and crosses in the sand. When his cows had found a good pasture he would sit for an hour, hunched up on a bank by the pathway, tracing those curious patterns of his with his stick. He said he could read 'at one time', but he had apparently given up reading, perhaps as a bad habit, a waste of time, for at the time Laura knew him he never opened a book and took in no newspaper. Laura at first took him for a labourer, herding the cows of another, but although he lived the life of a labourer, in all essentials Bob was his own master. He was a small freeholder with commoner's rights and lived in his own cottage with a widowed sister.

Their home was so tucked away between two hills that it was possible to pass within a hundred yards of it without suspecting its existence. It was a narrow thatched cottage with outbuildings in a valley so narrow that their three fields were ribbonlike in length and breadth. As Bob said, you could throw a stone from one hill to another right over the chimney and never know that a house was there. As the hills for the greater part of the day kept out the sunshine theirs was a green garden, a tangle of bushes and ferns and shade-loving plants, such as lily-of-the-valley and Solomon's seal, and the roof of the house was hardly less green than the garden, for houseleek and mosses almost covered the thatch that they could not afford to renew. A little brooklet trickled past the doorway, with beside it a red brick path and the white skeleton of a tree with the branches cut down to form pegs on which to hang the newly-scoured milking pails. The fields got more sunlight than the garden, for there the valley became shallower; but the soil was poor and, but for the grazing on the heath, Bob and his sister could scarcely have made a living.

Morning and evening Bob took his churn of milk in a ramshackle old dairy float drawn by a shaggy heath pony to a dairy in the nearest town and brought back with him such household purchases as were absolutely necessary. When about this business he must have had some converse with his kind, but apparently this did not extend to the discussion of the news of the day, or if it did, he never repeated anything he had heard in the town. All his interest was centred upon his beasts, his poultry and fields, and upon the heath, which he regarded primarily as a storehouse from which he had the right to draw forage and firing. When he had driven his cows out to graze and they had come to a likely pasture, he would sit for hours on some grassy knoll where he could keep watch over them; without moving, perhaps without conscious thought.

Whether his remarkable store of heath lore had come from observation or had its source in some instinctive, inborn accumulation of knowledge, was a mystery to Laura. He did not appear to look much about him, in his habitual hunched-up position, his stick either tracing his hieroglyphics on the sand or clasped in his two hands forming a support for his chin, his eyes resting chiefly on the ground. Yet he knew every flower, bird, beast, and reptile upon the heath as well, as he once said in an expansive moment, as the back of his hand. He could in any season at any spot where he happened to be lead the way to the nest and exhibit the eggs or the young of any heath-building bird, or point out the place where any desired plant or flower might be found. He could tell the time by the position of the sun and foretell the weather correctly from the wind and clouds.

One day Laura happened to say casually that though she had been told there were adders on the heath she had never seen one. Without saying a word he motioned to her to follow him to a clump of gorse bushes a few yards away where one of the sandy heath paths took a sharp turn. Still without saying anything, he laid his finger on his lips to command silence. A few seconds later a snake thrust its wicked-looking little head from the heather on one side of the path, halted a second to make certain that no danger threatened, then glided across towards the other side. 'See them marks?' Bob muttered hoarsely, 'Them on its neck and back? They're Vs – V's for Viper. Never you touch a snake with them marks on its skin. They're put there to warn folks.' Before he had finished speaking the tail of the adder had disappeared into the heather on the other side of the path. Much to Laura's relief, for she had feared she would have to witness the sickening scene of its slaughter. As it was, her spine had gone cold and her flesh all goosey, for she had in full measure the instinctive, unreasoning horror of snakes which seems to be a legacy from the days of the Garden of Eden.

'How did I know 't wer' there?' asked Bob when reseated on his hillock. 'Well, I'll tell you; there's no witchcraft about it. While you were talking to me just now, I saw the heather – just over there, see? – ' and he pointed, 'move in a sort of waves, one behind t'other. You might have thought 't wer' two or three little shrews, or summat, but that 't wer' a snake of some sort, I knew, and as vipers are pretty common hereabouts, being high and dry and hot like, I knew 't wer' likely to be one o' they. Them grass snakes like the cooler places and slow-worms travel so close to the ground they don't make much stir when they move. As to knowing 't would cross that path, any fool could have told that by the direction in which it was going. No, I never trouble to kill the poor things, unless I find one near the cowhouse. They don't hurt me, so why should I go out of my way to hurt them? Besides, I should have my work cut out if I went running with a stick every time I saw a wriggle in the heather.'

On another occasion Bob and she had taken cover from a sudden heavy shower in a small pine-clump topping a knoll a few yards from the pathway. Like birds in a cage, Laura thought, as she stood watching the long, silver bars of rain streaking down all around, especially as a flock of linnets had also taken refuge there and were flitting and twittering among the upper branches. Bob stood on the outer edge of the little wood keeping watch on his cows and the weather. He had flung the old sack he had brought to sit upon over his shoulders and, leaning forward upon his stick, looked more the old country-man than ever. Presently he straightened himself and looked up at the sky. ''T won't hold up yet a while,' he said, 'that cloud from the west's getting right overhead. Why don't you sit down and rest yourself?'

Laura looked down at the pine-needles, wet and slippery from previous showers, and shook her head. 'Too wet for 'ee?' Bob chuckled, 'deary, deary, what a helpless crittur you be. Don't you know that there's always a dry seat under pines in any weather?' And forthwith he stooped and raked aside the top layer of pine-needles and made her feel the warm dryness of those an inch or two beneath. 'There!' he said, 'just sit down and lean your back against that trunk and you'll have a seat fit for a queen.'

But although Bob talked to Laura occasionally, he was by nature a silent man and often their converse was limited to a 'good morning' and a few remarks about the weather. Laura, who had an idea that he preferred his own company to hers, would often pass him by at a little distance without speaking. Or she would look down from some hill and see him, sitting in his usual hunched-up position with his eyes on the ground, and wonder what his thoughts were. When she first knew him she thought he might be engrossed in some deep mental speculation. He might be a peasant philosopher or a mute peasant poet with ideas he was unable, or unwilling, to put into words. But that thought, born of her own fancy, was far from the truth. Bob, she found when she knew him better, was a man of limited ideas and as nearly devoid of human feeling as a human being can be. When, very occasionally, he mentioned one of his fellow men he spoke of him gruffly and shortly. Sometimes he would refer casually to his sister. 'Jeanette's done this', or 'Jeanette says that', but never, as it appeared, with a spark of human feeling.

Once only were his lips unlocked as to any human contact of his, and then a smouldering sense of injustice was responsible for the outburst. Two or three years before Laura came to Heatherley a sanitary inspector, new to the district, had visited Bob's holding to inquire into his dairy methods. He had at once decided that the water supply was inadequate, being at that time obtained from one of the natural valley springs around which the earth had been banked up to form a shallow well. Bob had pleaded that the spring had served his family for their own drinking as well as for dairy purposes for his own lifetime and that of his father before him and that nobody had ever been a ha'porth the worse for the use of it. But his pleading availed nothing; he could not put back the clock; new times had brought new ideas, and what had served in the past could not be permitted to serve a new germ-conscious generation. The ultimatum was that he must either provide a new water supply or sell no more milk.

So a new well had to be sunk at the cost of eighty pounds. If he had possessed that sum or had to borrow it, Bob did not say, but as he accused the inspector of having put him in chains for the rest of his life he probably had to borrow it. Having a load of debt on his shoulders may have accounted for the bitterness of his tone when telling the story of 'that dressed up, la-di-da young devil who came from God knows where and went back to the place he belonged to'. For the bitter irony of it all to Bob was that the inspector held but a temporary post in the neighbourhood, and before the new well was ready for use he had gone. 'Seems he wer' just sent here by the devil or somebody just for the purpose of making me sink that well. Never interfered with nobody else as I ever heard of. I'd well him if I had my way! Put him down a well and make him stay there. But there wouldn't be water in that well. Oh, no! there'd be fire and brimstone.'

Laura, as in friendship bound, agreed that it was 'hard lines' on Bob that the inspector should ever have come there; but secretly she suspected that the new water supply was necessary, for like others of her generation who read the newspapers, she was acutely germ-conscious.

She only once saw Bob's sister Jeanette. Then Bob had wanted to send her a message and had asked her to call as she passed near the house and deliver it. He asked this simply, not as asking a favour of a grown-up person, but as though speaking to a child. Laura almost expected him to conclude by saying, 'you run along quickly now and I'll give you a penny'. No penny was mentioned or produced, but she had her reward.

The inside of Bob's house was plain to primitiveness, with a big open fireplace, whitewashed walls, and a brick floor where the feet of passing generations had worn on the soft surface a pathway from doorway to hearth. Of furniture there was but a table and chairs with one corner cupboard from which Jeanette brought forth a glass to fill with milk for Laura. Jeanette looked older than Bob, her hair was quite white while his was brindled; she was tall and upright and had fine dark eyes which, far from being shrewd and even a little cunning, as Bob's were, had a distant, abstracted expression. A listening look, Laura thought, as of one whose ears were astrain to catch some far-away sound. Her accent was better than Bob's and she used no dialect words, as he often did, and her clothes, though simple, were neat.

She told Laura that she got up at four o'clock every morning to milk the cows and prepare Bob's breakfast before he left for the town with the milk float. Bob, meanwhile, had the cowshed to clean and his horse to feed and get ready. In addition to these and other regular duties, he would often put in an hour in the fields. When Laura remarked, 'It is a hard life for you both', she gave her a quick, penetrating look, as though suddenly aware of her presence, and said, 'It might seem so to some people, but there are lives harder.' Except for a few commonplace remarks about the weather and the cows, that was almost all the conversation that took place between them, for it was getting late and Laura had to be in punctually for the Sunday dinner. Jeanette did, however, rather to Laura's surprise, ask her to look in and drink a glass of milk whenever she happened to be passing. But Laura never went there again, though at the time she fully intended to do so, for almost immediately afterwards she heard of the gossip about her solitary walks, and curtailed them. She did not give them up entirely, for she could not bring herself to do that; all the while she remained at Heatherley the heath formed what she felt to be the foundation or background of her life; but thenceforth she walked more circumspectly and more in the beaten track instead of ranging where she would, over the hills and far away.

Twenty years later, when living again in the neighbourhood, she discovered by chance that the woman who came in to clean for her was a native of Heatherley. When asked if she knew Bob and his sister, she said she had known them as children, but later in life they had 'turned sort of queer' and nobody had had much to do with them. They were both dead. They had died in that influenza epidemic, as they called it, just after the war. Both down with it at the same time and nobody to look after them. They might easily have died and nobody been any the wiser if the man who had bought their milk had not sent someone to see what had become of Bob and his churns. They took them off to the Cottage Hospital, but it was too late to save them and, in her opinion, hospitals never were much good to those wild kind of people. Look at the gipsies, they always said that to be taken to hospital meant death to one of their tribe.

When gently urged back to the track she said that Jeanette, unlike Bob, had not lived all her life upon the heath. As a girl she had been away in service. Then, for a few years, she had been married to the captain of a small coasting vessel and had accompanied him on his voyages. Mrs Judd said she remembered her coming home for her holidays, 'dressed up to the nines' and almost too proud to speak to her old schoolfellows. But pride comes before a fall and she had a fall, poor thing, in the long run.

She really did not remember all the ins and outs of what happened, for it was all years ago and she herself at the time had been living up country, married and having an increase every eighteen months, as regular as clockwork. They seemed to manage such things better in these days. But what was she saying, Oh! Yes, well, the husband's ship was wrecked in a storm, off Land's End or somewhere, they were going from Cardiff to London, and Jeanette's husband was drowned and Jeanette herself had some sort of narrow escape. She did remember that much for it was all in the newspapers and someone at home sent her a paper and she read about it. And she thought, though she could not be sure, that Jeanette lost her reason for a time. She was either in an asylum or a hospital, she couldn't say which, and, after all, it didn't much matter. Anyhow, it was a long time before she went back to her old home and then only to wander about the heath like a ghost, never looking at or speaking to anybody. But when her mother got old and ill she seemed to have buckled to again, saw to the house and dairy and nursed her mother through her last illness, and afterwards stayed with her brother. Folks said they were both a bit touched, and she could quite believe it for it would send her stark, staring mad in a month to live out in the wilds as they did.

Poor Jeanette! If that story were true, as no doubt it was in essentials, though vague in the telling, it accounted for the strained, listening expression which had puzzled Laura in girlhood. Above the murmuring of bees in the heath-bells, the soft sighing of pines and the pattering of raindrops, she perhaps sometimes heard the booming of Atlantic rollers above an unmarked grave.

VI. *The Hertfords*

In some ways Laura had never before been so near happiness as during her first few months at Heatherley. She had work she enjoyed, a new countryside to explore, plenty of books to read, and some interesting people to observe. The one disadvantage was her position as one of the Hertford household. It was distressing to one of her age and disposition to be a silent and uninvolved but embarrassed third when disputes arose between husband and wife, and still more distressing when, as occasionally happened, one or other of the contending couple would appeal to her to bear witness as to some point under dispute. When this happened her usual good sense would desert her and, quite unintentionally, she would say something which would be seized upon by one or the other as supporting evidence on their own side and so add fuel to the flames. Or she would say, often untruthfully, that she did not know, or could not remember what had been said or done a day or two before, which had the effect of offending one or other or both of the disputants.

The brief intervals of reconciliation were almost as trying to witness, the husband's attitude towards his wife being then one of patronizing forgiveness and hers towards him one of almost fulsome adoration. Mrs Hertford's attitude towards her husband at such times was sincere, however unwise. In her happier moments she would often declare to Laura that, in spite of his treatment of her, she loved him devotedly. On his side such kindness as he might show towards her appeared to be due to nothing more than a momentary feeling of pity, perhaps of remorse. At other times it was quite obvious to an onlooker that he was only acting a part which happened to suit him at the moment. One evening, on coming into the living-room to bring the office cash for safe keeping during the night, Laura found Mrs Hertford reclining on the hearthrug with her head on her husband's knee, while he, sitting in a low chair, was stroking her hair. The scene, embarrassing enough to one who knew the ordinary relationship of the couple, became for Laura one of horror when the husband, over his devoted wife's head, treated Laura to such a grimace that it sent a cold shiver down her spine.

Then Laura would sometimes wake in the night and hear soft, padding footsteps on the stairs or in the passage outside her bedroom, and more than once or twice she awoke suddenly with the impression that someone had been standing beside her bed. Once she thought she heard the door close softly. She had no key to her door and did not like to ask for one as she was only sleeping there on sufferance and was never sure that she might not have been dreaming; but the idea of that lurking presence by night caused her great uneasiness and she wished that she had some friend, older and wiser than herself, to whom she might go for advice. There was no-one in the village she could confide in without exposing the Hertfords' affairs and it all seemed too indefinite to tell in a letter to her mother. She had not told her anything of the state of unrest in the Hertfords' home for she knew it would worry her and she had worries enough of her own.

Laura was very much alone in the world at that time. She was far from her home and her childhood's friends and, having but recently arrived at Heatherley, her new friends there were as yet scarcely more than acquaintances. They were, moreover, mostly young people of her own age, pleasant enough to talk to on ordinary subjects, but too unknown and untried for confidences. Nor did she for some time visit her home. Until she had been at Heatherley for a year no holiday was due to her and it was not before her second summer there she could hope to see her family again. And naturally, she could not go to Mrs Hertford with the story of her night fears. She, poor soul, had enough to bear without being troubled by what, after all, might be purely imaginary. By the light of later events she learned that while living under the Hertfords' roof she had been in some personal peril and that her presence there had intensified the strife between the unhappy couple; but of this she had no idea at that time and, no outside accommodation being available, she remained there all through her first winter at Heatherley.

One day in a burst of confidence Mrs Hertford told Laura the story of her marriage. Previously she had been nursery governess to some children whose parents, one summer, had taken a furnished house in the Heatherley district. While there she had met her present husband who had recently undertaken the care of the newly opened post office, which was then a very small one with no telegraph and insufficient other business to require a trained assistant. His housekeeper had so far sold stamps and weighed parcels during the day and he himself had made up the one bag containing the night mail after working all day at his 'trade. But the housekeeper was leaving and Mrs Hertford, then Miss Mosley, agreed to take her place. Six months later they were married.

Of what led up to the marriage she gave a probably unintentional hint when she said that there had been gossip about them in the village and that she herself had given notice to leave. He had then asked her to marry him and, at the same time, told her the story of his life which she repeated to Laura. It was the kind of story beloved of minor Victorian novelists and turned upon a father's pride, an obedient daughter's broken heart, and the faithfulness of a lover. Even to Laura, herself a Victorian, it seemed at the time she heard it to belong to some distant period, for by the beginning of this century the old ideas of parental authority and daughterly submission had become greatly modified.

George Hertford had been born the son of an innkeeper, had had a grammar-school education and been apprenticed to what in those days was considered a superior trade, that of cabinet-maker; but when in his late teens he had fallen in love with the daughter of a well-to-do farmer, her parents had forbidden the match as most unsuitable and derogatory. The girl – her name was Letitia, or Letty – must at first have defied her parents to some extent, for George, when telling his future wife the story, had said that it was only by ill usage they had been able to get her to agree to not seeing or writing to him. The form the ill usage took he did not say. They would surely not have used personal violence to their only child, 'the apple of their eye', to use

228

George's expression, and it was probably mental, or they may have locked her in her bedroom, though such a measure would be out of date in the eighteen-seventies At any rate, by some means they prevailed upon her to promise to have no more to do with her lover.

But Letty, although outwardly acquiescing in this arrangement, did contrive to meet George once more and to tell him that her feelings for him were unchanged and unchangeable. They could not elope and get married as they wished, for neither had money, but at that last interview they came to an agreement. George was to emigrate to Australia where men of his trade were said to be making fortunes in the large towns. Their plan was that, having saved a sufficient sum from his earnings, he should return to England and claim her hand from her father. The father, they hoped, when convinced of George's improved prospects in life, would consent to their marriage and either take him into partnership on the farm or help him to found a substantial business in his own line as cabinet-maker. If he still withheld his consent to their marriage they would make a runaway match. No letters were to pass between them; Letty was firm on that point, for she had given a solemn promise to her parents; but they would hear of each other from time to time through George's parents. In old country fashion they clasped hands over running water and vowed to be true to each other, then parted, sadly enough no doubt, but buoyed up by their hopes for the future.

George had booked his passage to Sydney where he had an old workmate who he had hoped would put him in the way of employment, but at Adelaide, where the passengers were permitted to land for a few hours, he was stopped as he left the ship by a stranger who asked him his trade and, when he told him, forthwith offered him employment at high wages. The reports which had reached him in England had not been exaggerated. In the Australian cities there was a great shortage of skilled craftsmen, and cabinet-makers able to make and carve heavy, elaborate pieces of furniture were in special request to meet the demands of those who had made fortunes in gold-mining and were bent upon furnishing their newly-built houses in what they called tip-top style. For three years George, as he said, had only to stoop to pick up money. Laura often heard him tell that part of the story himself and some of his adventures at that time were odd ones. The new millionaires, many of them simple, generous men who had come by their fortunes easily, had, as we should say in these days, money to burn. Not content with paying a high price for an article which pleased them, they would insist as well upon making a handsome present to the workman who had made it. They were fond of large, ornate pieces of furniture, richly carved, and liked to stand by and watch the work in progress. George Hertford had a notable talent for such work and some of his pieces are probably still treasured possessions of antipodean families who point with pride to the interlaced initials of their grandparents, carved by his hand.

From time to time his mother mentioned Letty in her letters. At first there were messages from her, she sent her love and was living for the day of his return. Then the messages became fewer, her parents kept her very close, his mother thought, for she seldom came to the village, but she had seen her in church last Sunday and she had turned round in her seat to smile. She was wearing the sweetest bonnet, kingfisher blue velvet, which suited her fair hair to a T. Her face looked a little peaked and his mother thought she looked thinner, as if she might have been fretting, but nothing for George to worry about; she just mentioned it to let him know that his Letty was not the sort to gad about and make merry during his absence. Then, for one whole summer, Letty was away at the seaside. She had not been very well and the doctor had ordered sea air and sea bathing. But George was not to worry about her, for not much could be wrong; she had had a lovely colour last time his mother had seen her and the sea air would soon set her cough right. Three months later she was back at home, for George's mother had met her in Cudhill Lane and she had sent her love, her dear, dear love, to Georgie. Such meagre news must have been poor fare for a lover, but if it did not satisfy fully, it satisfied the better because the end of his exile was in sight.

He was twenty-two and Letty would be about the same age when, the stipulated sum of money in hand and his passage home already booked, he received a cable from his parents: 'Return at once. Letty ill. Her father consents to marriage.' It was during the hurry and excitement of the few following days that he had the heat-stroke which so sadly affected his after life. He should have had rest and treatment, but that was impossible, for the ship upon which his passage was booked was about to sail. He got safely on board, then collapsed and lay in his bunk for·the greater part of the voyage. By the time he landed in England he had apparently recovered, and had not another and greater shock been awaiting him he might not have felt any serious after-effects.

He had come too late. His father met him at Southampton and somehow and somewhere broke the news to him that Letty was dead. She had died two days before his arrival and he had returned, not to a marriage, but a funeral ceremony. She had never been a robust girl, and after his departure her health had deteriorated. The villagers said that her parents had worried her into her grave by constant reproaches about her engagement, but there was no proof of that and George himself had not believed it after her mother had told him of her own surprise when Letty, upon what proved to be her deathbed, begged her and her father to send for George. She said Letty had not spoken at home of George for months, and they had concluded that time and absence had done their work and that the memory of her love affair had faded. It may have been so, or it may have been that suppressed grief had hastened, or even caused, her decline. George, of course, believed that she had died for love of him and grieved wildly. During the twenty years which elapsed between Letty's death and his meeting with Mrs Hertford he had twice been back to Australia, drifted from one part of the country to another, and finally, taking the advice of his brother who was in business and doing well there, had settled at Heatherley.

He had probably made some vow to himself never to marry

but, as the romantic novelists of that time would have expressed it, to remain true to the memory of his lost love. At any rate, Mrs Hertford told Laura that when he proposed to her – she used the term 'proposed' – he told her, 'I'll marry you if you will have me, but my heart is buried in poor Letty's grave.' 'But,' she added, when telling the story, 'I did not mind that, I felt so sure of winning him over.'

That was the story which at the time she first heard it touched Laura to tears. How irrational it sounds in these days and how far away and faded, as faded and out of date as the photograph of the slim, sloping-shouldered girl with a pork-pie hat perched on a chignon of fair hair which hung on the wall of Mr Hertford's bedroom. For he had his own bedroom, that was one of the reservations he had made at the time of his marriage, though the arrangement did not appear to interfere with the regular arrival of his children. There were a boy and a girl when Laura first knew them, a girl was born while she was there and two other children after she had left.

As far as Laura was concerned, things came to a climax one night after she had gone to bed and heard a loud bang which she thought at first was some kind of explosion. Rushing out on to the landing she found Mrs Hertford, in her nightdress, coaxing her husband back to bed. He held a small revolver in his hand and Mrs Hertford afterwards told Laura that he had thought he heard whispering beneath the landing window, and thinking it was burglars, he had fired his revolver to scare them away. Whether or not the shot scared anyone below, it certainly scared Laura, and she was not at all reassured when, thinking the proper time had come to tell Mrs Hertford about the footsteps she thought she had heard at night and of her impression that someone had been in her room, she was told that it was one of Mr Hertford's habits to prowl about the house at all hours of the night, opening and shutting doors and looking into dark corners with the idea of finding some unnamed enemy he believed was lying in wait for him. He had sometimes been in Laura's room at night for it was one of his ideas that Laura might be in league with the enemy. When he had this idea he would call his wife up from her sleep to play propriety, and while she stood at the door, he, with a shaded candle in his hand, would creep softly into the room to see if anyone beside Laura was there. Laura, of course, was always alone and in bed with her hair screwed up in Hind's curlers and her face thickly cold-creamed, and so obviously asleep that, for a time, he was pacified. At other times it was his wife he suspected, or her and Laura in collusion, and he even accused his little children of carrying messages from one to the other. The reason for this strange behaviour was that the poor man's mind was affected. His wife must already have had some suspicion of this, for she told Laura that she had begged him, time after time, to consult a doctor about the violent headaches from which he suffered; but the mere mention of seeing a doctor threw him into one of his rages and she dared not herself take steps to have him medically examined. A few years later he totally lost his reason and ended his days in Broadmoor Criminal Asylum.

After that night of terror Laura felt that she could not remain under that roof a day longer than was absolutely necessary and made such a determined effort to find herself a room outside that, in less than a week, she had removed herself and her belongings from the house. Not without an uneasy feeling that she was deserting Mrs Hertford, who, however, seemed rather relieved than otherwise when told of the new arrangement. Her husband, she said, was always at his worst when anyone outside his own family was present. Their most innocent actions provoked his suspicions and the effort to find out where they were and what they were doing kept him in a constant state of excitement. Alone, she said, she could manage him better. Before Laura left Mrs Hertford adjured her solemnly not to say a word to any living creature about anything she had seen or heard while living with them. She promised willingly and kept her promise, and as far as she ever heard, no-one in the village, with the exception of herself and Alma, had any idea that the relationship between the postmaster and his wife was other than normal. Then, gradually, as Laura came to see less of the

Hertfords' home life and her own outside interests increased, their affairs no longer troubled her to the extent they had done. Sometimes, indeed, seeing Mr Hertford stand, calm and collected, coolly discussing some trade order with a customer and drawing little pencil sketches to illustrate his suggestions, she felt that she must have imagined that pistol-shot. But there were other times when, sitting at the telegraph instrument, she heard the old sounds of strife within doors, or when some confidence of Mrs Hertford's would bring to her mind the old fears and misgivings and she felt she was treading on treacherous ground. During the whole of her time at Heatherley, even in moments of personal happiness, she was aware, if but dimly, of a sinister cloud in the background.

As may be imagined, it was not easy to find a cheap lodging in a place where cottage front rooms could be let for a couple of guineas a week in the season. For a few weeks Laura lived as a boarder with a retired business couple and their grown-up daughter in one of the villas just beyond the village street. There she had a bedroom with the whitest of stiffly starched counterpanes on the bed, framed texts upon the walls and a looking-glass draped with lace and blue ribbon; plenty of good, solid food, her laundry done for her free of charge and even her stockings mended, for the inclusive charge of ten shillings weekly. One thing only was denied her; there was not a shred of privacy. If she came downstairs dressed to go out she was expected to say where she was going and why, and, if for a walk, she was bidden to wait 'just a tick' while Clara got ready to accompany her. 'I know she'd like a walk,' her mother would say, 'for she said just now she wouldn't mind one, only, of course, she'd got nobody to go out with', and Clara would come sailing downstairs in her fine clothes and high-heeled town shoes and the two would saunter along the main road, stopping to hold long conversations with anyone who was known to Clara. If Laura went to her bedroom to write a letter or to read she was seldom there more than ten minutes before there would come a tap at the door and a cheerful voice outside would call out: 'Whatever are you doing up here by yourself! There's a fire in the parlour and Clara's just going to try over her new piece on the piano and she wants you to come down and hear it', and if that invitation failed to allure, Clara's own refined Cockney accent would be heard on the stairs, calling: 'Come down, you poor lonely little thing and let's cheer you up a bit!' Laura felt bound to comply for she knew such invitations were kindly meant, but for her, the walk was ruined and the evening downstairs not only wasted, but unutterably boring.

Though kind-hearted, Mrs Binks had not much delicacy of feeling. She several times pointed out to Laura what a great advantage it was to be permitted to share such a home as theirs, and for such a small sum weekly. 'But', she would add, 'we can well afford to take you at that price and we like having you, reely, for you're company for Clara and it's been dull for her since we retired and came to live in the country. In London, of course, she had troops of pals, she was the life and soul of the company wherever she went, but here, the people are either stuck up or such as we couldn't let her associate with, so we thought if we could get a business girl such as yourself of about her own age she'd feel more happy and settled like.' So, Laura noted, she had been taken in as a companion for Clara, and being companion to Clara was not a position she enjoyed, for although Clara was all very well in her way, her way was not Laura's way and she had no wish to be forced into it. Yet they were all so well-meaning and kindly disposed that when she heard of a room such as she had really wanted she was hard put to it to find an excuse for leaving them. Mrs Binks begged her to say if there was anything she did not like in their arrangements, 'because, you know, if there's anything different you'd fancy to eat we could get that for you, and if you'd like your breakfast a mite earlier, and I know you've had to run for it at times, I'll make that girl put on the kettle before she takes off her hat in the morning and you shall have your breakfast without waiting for us, for as you know, we're none of us very early risers.' Laura caught at the idea of having to start work early and said she wanted to live nearer the post office, which reason for leaving could not have been very convincing, coming from one who made nothing of a ten-mile walk, but it served, although there was ever after a pained, disappointed-in-you expression on each of their three faces whenever she happened to meet them.

VII. *Living alone and liking it*

Laura never forgot the feeling of exaltation she experienced when, her day's work done, she for the first time approached her new dwelling, saw the flicker of firelight on an upper window and knew the room in which the fire had been lighted was *her* room, in which she could shut herself up without fear of intrusion. After she had had her evening meal and arranged her few possessions she sat on long after her usual bedtime, enjoying her first taste of freedom for months. It was a wild March night with the wind blustering round the outside walls of the house and rattling the none-too-well-fitting windows, and as long as the fire lasted puffs of smoke came down the chimney into her face; but far from causing her any discomfort the storm made her situation more pleasing for in contrast with the outer world, her room seemed to her a little haven of peace.

The house had been built by a speculating builder with the idea of attracting a superior type of purchaser or tenant; but as it had a very small garden and was closely neighboured by a group of poor cottages, he had for some time been unable either to sell or let it. It had then been let to two working-class families, one occupying the rooms on one side of the house and the other those on the other side, and with one of these it had been agreed that Laura should rent their front room upstairs. It was a fair sized room with two windows, one of them with a view of the heath with, in the distance, the long wavy line of blue hills she had seen on the day she reached Heatherley.

The room was but poorly furnished and its two or three threadbare rugs were islands in a broad expanse of scrubbed boards; but it was clean and cheap at the rent of four shillings a week, which included some attendance. It would probably have been let to summer visitors had the landlady possessed better furniture and a smaller family of her own to attend to, but as that was out of the question – for what well-paying visitor would have tolerated uncarpeted stairs which children of two families used as a playground, or patched sheets and hastily prepared meals? – it was reserved for 'a young person in business. Out all day preferred', and, for more than two years, that young person was Laura.

It would be possible to write a pathetic account of Laura's life at that time with its long working hours, poorly furnished bed-sitting-room, scrappy meals, absence of opportunity for organized recreation, inferior social status. But though correct in the main as to facts, such an account would not be true to life, not to Laura's life at any rate. The bare room did not strike her as particularly bare: it had a clean bed, a table, primarily for meals, at which she could write, shelves in a recess by the fireplace for her books, a shabby but comfortable old easy-chair, patched on both elbows, and a paraffin lamp which her landlady had bought at an auction sale. Laura thought the lamp, when lighted, gave quite an air to the room with its red, crinkled silk shade and embossed figures on its silver-coloured base. It certainly smelt a little, but when she remarked upon this her landlady told her that she used for it only the best tea-rose lamp-oil and after that, the name of the brand of oil seemed to sweeten the scent.

A friend who once called to see Laura told her that she should 'go balmy on the crumpet' sitting up there with nobody to talk to, but the quiet and solitude which would have been poison to Kitty were spiritual meat and drink to Laura. As to poverty, she had been born to that, and to her social inferiority she gave no thought for already, as in after life, it was, to her, the individual who counted, not his or her place in society. Though not what is now called 'a good mixer' in general assemblies, she was in the course of her life to find friends in all classes except the most exalted and the most depressed, and might possibly have found them at both of those extremes had opportunity offered.

As Laura's salary was but one pound weekly she had, after her rent was paid, to keep down her living expenses, including laundry and coals in winter, to ten shillings a week, and it may be of interest to hear of the prices which made this possible. The South African war, already in progress, was to send prices up to a level from which they would never descend but, on the contrary, rise to what were then almost unbelievable heights as the years went on. Already, before the war had affected them, food and other commodities were much dearer than in Laura's childhood. A pint of new milk cost three halfpence, fresh farm butter from a shilling to one-and-four a pound, new-laid eggs from tenpence to one-and-two a dozen according to season. The best back rashers of Hampshire bacon cost eightpence a pound, a small lamb chop or cutlet fourpence or fivepence, and a small dab or plaice about the same amount.

As long as no-one but herself was qualified to work the telegraph instrument, Laura was unable to leave the office for her midday meal and, for a time, had fetched for her by a telegraph messenger one of the ninepenny dinners which were a feature of the new model inn. It was an immense ninepennyworth and included a thick cut off the joint, two or more vegetables, and a wedge of fruit tart or a round of roly-poly, sufficient for three dinners for one with her appetite. Mrs Hertford kindly stored and heated up for the next day what was left, but Laura soon tired of such heavy and monotonous food and preferred to bring with her bread and cheese and an apple, or to send out for a glass of milk and a bun, and to wait for a more substantial meal until she reached home in the evening.

After the inn dinners were discontinued the foundation of her diet was a pint of milk daily, and weekly, a half-pound of farm butter and a dozen new-laid eggs. These were local produce brought round on a donkey-cart by an old countrywoman known as Mammy Pasfield who wore a big white apron and a sunbonnet. She was a kind old soul who always apologized for what she considered the high price she had to ask for her produce, and to salve her own conscience and to please her customer, always threw something in – an apple or a bunch of flowers, and once an immense savoy cabbage.

Laura's chief meal of the day was what is, or was, known in Scotland as tea with an egg to it. Sometimes, by way of variety, she would have her egg fried with a rasher, or a little fish or a tiny chop, with plenty of bread but no vegetables, not even potatoes, because it was not in the bond that her landlady should cook for her what she called a full meal. She was supposed to get her dinner out. And no jam, cakes, or pastry because Laura did not care for sweet foods. She ate a good many apples and other fruit when obtainable. Upon this diet she lived in the best of good health for two years and a half and indeed, although there were some deficiencies according to modern scientific ideas, she had most of the foods regarded today as essential to healthy living. She had not as yet become a cigarette smoker, but had she been, a packet of five woodbines would have cost but one penny. One of the saddest features of later life is the knowledge of such lost opportunities!

Clothing was more of a problem than food. In those days there were no attractive little ready-made frocks to be bought for a few shillings. Ready-made frocks were certainly obtainable, but they fell into one or other of two categories – what the shopkeepers called models on the one hand, and on the other the cheap and nasty; and Laura, who was not at all handy with her needle, had to pay a dressmaker to make her frocks, and consequently they were too expensive to have more than one a year. Cotton blouses and serge skirts were her ordinary office wear; the blouses made with stiff, stand-up collars and worn with a tie. In this attire she flattered herself that she looked very neat and businesslike, but she often longed for something softer to the touch and more becoming. Her hair she wore twisted into what was known as a teapot-handle high up on the back of her head, with a heavy curled fringe on her forehead; topped, when she left the office at night, with one of the stiff round white straw hats known as sailors, which for several years were the universal everyday wear of women of all classes. But even this fashion in sailor hats did not remain static. One year there would be broader or narrower brims than the last or the crown would be higher or lower, and the angle at which the hat was worn varied from year to year. At one time it was worn tilted over the nose of the wearer, at another it had slipped down to the back of the head and formed a kind of halo. Unbelievable as it may appear, the sailor hat, with its stiff outline softened by the curls on the forehead, was not at all an unbecoming fashion to most women, and another recommendation was that a good quality sailor hat could be bought for two shillings; an inferior copy cost eightpence.

For better wear, before she went to Heatherley, Laura in a reckless hour had had a grey coat and skirt made for her by a tailor, for which she had paid two guineas in instalments, and a kind aunt had by a coincidence sent her for a birthday present a perfectly toning muff and fur necklet of the then fashionable grey, silky, thickly-curling fur called Thibet. These, with a white muslin frock for hot Sundays, or a white blouse worn with a white piqué skirt, served her all the time she was there. Her best hat in winter was a close-fitting affair puckered up by herself from a square of black velvet; in summer, a large, floppy white straw trimmed by herself with a wreath of artificial roses which figured on hat after hat. Shoes and shoe-mending, stockings and underwear, soap and tooth powder, writing and sewing materials and an occasional book had to be contrived from an income of one pound a week.

Nothing was spent on amusements. There were no amusements to spend money on, except, once a year, the one-shilling entrance fee to the parish social evening, by that time known as a *soirée*. This was held in a neighbouring settlement in a newly-built hall belonging to a religious denomination which, when not using it for its own purposes, was willing to let it for any public event. In that hall Laura several times heard Mr Bernard Shaw lecture on Socialism. He was freely interrupted and questioned by his audience, to which at that time the initials G.B.S. had no special significance. On one occasion a working man stood up in the body of the hall to argue some point with the lecturer and, being absolutely unselfconscious and unimpressed by a reputation of which he knew nothing, acquitted himself very creditably. On another occasion an elderly reporter on one of the local newspapers engaged in a long and heated contest with the same distinguished lecturer about unearned increment; but as the term was new to him and he had failed to grasp its exact meaning, the debate ended with his collapse and apology. Other speakers expounded their views on Spiritualism, Vegetarianism, Unrest in the Balkans, different aspects of the Boer War, the duties and limitations of womanhood, and other subjects.

Laura also attended one of a series of readings of their own work by living writers. That evening Ian Maclaren, the Scottish novelist, read from his then very popular book, *Beside the Bonny Briar Bush*. More exciting was the occasion when a travelling troupe of actors in Elizabethan dress entertained the company with hand-bell ringing and Elizabethan part-songs, with quips and anecdotes by the leader, who also sang as solos most of the songs from the plays of Shakespeare. It was a simple enough performance but there was something about those who took part in it, especially about the leader, which gave an almost perfect illusion of Elizabethan reality. There was gusto and such an apparent joy in life that, together with the period dress and a remarkable resemblance in the features of the leader to Shakespeare himself, gave at least one of the audience the sensation of having been magically wafted back three centuries in time to Elizabethan London. Laura never heard the cognomen of the troupe or the name of its leader, nor did anyone else in the audience ever mention the performance to her afterwards; but to her, for life, the memory of it remained, not as an entertainment but as a magic glimpse of the past.

Then later, the famous Cappers came to the hall and read everyone's most secret thoughts, after they had been written down and the paper folded. Or husband and wife would retire from the hall, come back blindfolded and discover some small article concealed during their absence. It was a clever display. The written, but concealed, thoughts were with one or two exceptions more or less accurately deciphered and the hidden articles found, but there was an expression of great strain and tension on the faces and in the movements of the thought-readers, who seemed to divine at too great a cost of physical and mental effort such questions as 'Wonder what I'll get for my supper?'; and the husband, led by his wife by the hand, straining, like a hunting dog on the leash, should have had something more important to find than a thimble or a match-box. Still, the Cappers were all the rage in London at that time and it was something for country mice to be able to say that they had seen them, especially for those who had had their thoughts read by them.

As the hall belonged to a religious body it was not available for dancing. But the new dancing era had begun; there was in the parish a large wooden hut which had once been used as a temporary church, and there cheap, popular dances took place whenever anyone could be found to organize them. There were also public dances in a large room over one of the inns which were well attended by the young people of the village. These were not the old, informal country dances of Laura's childhood, but more sophisticated affairs; there was a Master of Cere-monies, a piano and a violin to play up-to-date waltzes, and most of the girls and young women who attended made some attempt at evening dress.

As Laura had no latchkey, when she took part in any such evening diversions her landlady or her husband would sit up for her, and when she came in, say at eleven, their tired faces would silently reproach her for keeping late hours. She knew better what was expected of her than to stay out after ten on ordinary evenings. On one of the very few occasions when she transgressed this unwritten law, although she was barely a quarter past the hour, she was received with cold looks and sundry hints as to what was and was not becoming in an unmarried girl.

That evening she had had one of those small, curious experiences which, though nothing much in themselves, seem to us afterwards to have a hidden significance. It had been a lovely May day and when she left the office and breathed the soft, lilac-scented air and saw all the signs of spring around her she had felt the folly of going immediately indoors. It was the

242

season of nightingale song, and as this was never heard close around Heatherley, perhaps because most of the trees were pine trees, she thought she would walk a mile or two out on the main road to one of the known haunts of the bird. She had not gone more than a mile when, coming to a bend in the road, she saw before her a thicket of tall old thorn trees in full bloom. Sheeted in snowy blossom, they stood in a semi-circle on the edge of the heath and she turned aside and stood for a long time among them, looking up through their glimmering branches at the stars twinkling out, one by one, in the grey-blue twilight. Petals drifted down on her face, light as snowflakes, and the air was faintly sweet with the scent of the may. Although but a few yards away from one of the main arteries of traffic to the coast, the spot was at that hour deserted and the silence profound. She heard no nightingales. It was evidently not one of their concert nights, or perhaps the sight of the blossoming may and nightingale song together would be too much of beauty to be vouchsafed to one poor mortal.

She heard no nightingales, but while standing there, concealed in the shadow of the trees, she heard, approaching her on the road, the soft, slithering sound of deflated bicycle tyres. The bicycle and its rider came slowly into her view, still with that heavy, slithering sound, and she saw in the dusk the silhouette of an ordinary sailor on the saddle, an ordinary bell-bottomed bluejacket. But his behaviour was not at all ordinary for, leaning forward over the handlebars, he was sobbing brokenheartedly. He approached and passed her, unaware of her existence, and she, knowing nothing of the cause of his grief, grieved with and for him as she came out of her hiding-place and walked soberly home. She had gone out to hear nightingales and heard instead the desolate sound of human suffering, and that against a background of pure loveliness.

When Laura first went to live in her house her landlady, Mrs Parkhurst, was about forty-five, a tall, massively built woman with dark hair and eyes and well-defined features. Occasionally, when some passing excitement brought a faint flush to her sallow cheeks and caused her dark eyes to kindle, she might still

have been thought a handsome woman, but constant childbear-
ing and the strain of bringing up a large family on insufficient
means had lined her face, sharpened her voice, and destroyed
the contours of her figure. In her person she was scrupulously
clean and fairly tidy. Her dress was that of all overworked
working-class mothers of that day, patched and faded old
garments of nondescript hue partly covered by a large white
apron.

She had seven children still living at home, and with washing
and ironing and cleaning and cooking for ten people her life was
a hard one. At an hour when more privileged housewives were
enjoying their evening amusement or evening repose she was
cooking a hot meal for her husband and two sons who had been
away at work all day and she had yet to wash up, pack their
meals for the morrow, get her younger children to bed and do
what was necessary for Laura. Sometimes, when asked if she did
not feel tired, she would say: 'I do. I don't believe I've sat down
a moment all day, except to meals.'

The couple who rented the other part of the house had three
small children, and with those and Mrs Parkhurst's own three
little girls running in and out, or playing in the hall or on the
stairs in wet weather, the view of the interior of the house from
the front doorstep was often far from attractive. The stairs
being used in common by both families, neither housewife felt
inclined to provide a stair-covering, and the bare boards, though
frequently scrubbed, gave the place a poverty-stricken appearance to those who came no farther than the front door. That
entrance was perhaps one of the reasons why Mrs Parkhurst's
reputation was not as good as it should have been with district
visitors and other kind ladies who visited the poor in their own
homes. One of them once commiserated with Laura for being
obliged to live in such a poor lodging. For they felt it their duty
to keep an eye on Laura, too, though their good intentions
towards her were fruitless. They had parties and dancing classes
for their own young people and ran a club with a gymnasium for
those they called working girls, chiefly for those working in a
large steam laundry in the district; but for neither group was

Laura qualified. She did not seem to fit in anywhere, as one lady regretfully told her. A state of things Laura acknowledged with alacrity.

Apparently Mrs Parkhurst did not fit in either. She had no time to attend Mothers' Meetings, even had she wished to do so, and indeed was not even a churchgoer, so all they could do was to bring her a copy of the Parish Magazine, spy out the land while inquiring about the health of her family, and go away shaking their heads. None of them liked her; she was too independent and forthright in her manner to please their taste, and calling as they did at odd hours and seeing her blowsed from housework, they put her down as a slattern. Yet Mrs Parkhurst did not strike Laura as a common woman. Her height and bearing may have had something to do with that impression, but there was something more – a core of integrity, of good breeding, a positive note of personality – which distinguished her from the mass of humanity.

With so much to occupy and harass her, her voice was sometimes raised in anger, and that, as she herself said, was bound to be just as one of the visiting ladies came knocking at the door. But, even in anger, she never attacked the offender by making the wildly exaggerated charges or by using the threats and expressions which, though meaningless and generally understood as being so, made hideous the domestic life of some such families. Her ordinary manner towards her children was kind and motherly. She appeared to understand and to make allowance for their varying dispositions; was not too hard on her elder boys when they stayed out late in the evening, and bore patiently such trials, caused by the younger children, as broken crockery, torn clothing, and muddied floors.

Her husband was a tired-looking, ageing man, smaller and weaker physically than herself and inferior in type. As a wage-earner he was a hard-working and trustworthy man, though not a skilled one, and they counted as one of their chief blessings that he had not been unemployed for a day since they married. Mrs Parkhurst loyally held him up to her children as the head of the household. 'We must ask your father', she would say, or

'We'll see what your Dad says about it'; but, in fact, she was in every way the leading spirit and shouldered his share of responsibility as well as her own simply and naturally. He, for his part, was well contented that it should be so and regarded her with the same loving admiration, mixed with tolerance of 'her little ways', as that shown by her grown-up sons.

The Parkhursts belonged to an obscure dissenting sect which had no meeting place nearer than that in a market town seven miles distant. As there was no public conveyance between there and Heatherley, Mrs Parkhurst and her younger children were unable to attend the services. Her elder boys had no wish to attend; one of them went to church with his girl, the others had their own ways of spending the Sabbath, and it was left to Mr Parkhurst to represent the entire family. Once a month, early on Sunday morning, he would come downstairs, dressed in his best and newly shaved, and set out on his long walk with a packet of bread and cheese in his pocket to eat between services, if none of the brethren invited him to dinner. More often than not he received such an invitation, for, though all of them poor, they appeared to live up to their watchword, 'Let brotherly love continue'; but there were occasions when no one thought of him and he stole away by himself to eat his humble provender. Those were known in the family as 'Dad's chapel Sundays', and on those days, after the huge Sunday dinner had been eaten and the washing-up done, Mrs Parkhurst would dress herself more carefully than on ordinary Sundays, gather round her her younger children and read to them from a monthly tract she received called *The Young Believer*. The children would probably have been better taught at the church Sunday School, and she would certainly have been more in favour with the visiting ladies had she sent them there, but such was her idea of her duty to her children, and she carried it out to the best of her ability.

As far as Laura could judge from what she heard, the tenets of their sect were harsh and narrow. Theatre-going, dancing, and novel-reading were counted as sins and those who indulged in those pastimes were bound for perdition. Laura's own diversions must often have shocked her kindly landlady, though she never openly censured them. Perhaps she regarded them as she did those of another person of whom she once said with a sigh: 'Well, we can only pray for him.' But the way of the congregation was not too strait to leave room for warm human feeling. On one occasion Laura happened to be present when Mr Parkhurst returned from chapel with the news that one of the sisterhood had died, evidently one who had taken a prominent part in the life of the community, for, after a moment of shocked silence, Mrs Parkhurst exclaimed: 'Oh, she'll be missed! She'll be missed sorely! Who's going to take the Women's Bible Readings, and look after the sick and the out of works in winter and see that the rent of the chapel is paid! Whoever does it, and the Lord'll raise up some friend, we shall never see her like again. She was a Mother in Israel! A real Mother in Israel!'

Twice a year the minister of the denomination cycled over to pay Mrs Parkhurst a pastoral visit. With commendable delicacy he always let her know beforehand when to expect him, and, in consequence, found Mrs Parkhurst dressed in her best, the parlour swept and garnished and a suitable tea prepared. After one of his visits, when Laura came home in the evening, she found Mrs Parkhurst in a cheerful, almost exalted mood. 'I've had a blessed time,' she said, 'a truly blessed time, and I feel a new creature for it!' After another of Mr Lupton's visits, Laura said she hoped the children had been good and not bothered her by running in and out of the room. She said they had been good enough, and well they might be, for Mr Lupton had insisted upon having them in to share with him the dish of small cakes she had made specially for his tea. Afterwards he had told them about Our Lord when He said 'Suffer little children to come unto me'; then he had laid his own hand on their heads and blessed them and sent them back to their play.

With so much to do for her own numerous family Mrs Parkhurst had little time to devote to her lodger, but she did faithfully all she had undertaken to do, and a little more. The fires she lighted always burned up brightly, the meal she had cooked was served to time, and often, as a freewill offering, there would be on the table a few flowers of her own growing, or a freshly baked scone or bun. Sometimes, when she knew Mrs Parkhurst had had a hard day at the washtub, Laura would have liked to relieve her by lighting her own fire and getting her own meal, but she had by that time gained enough knowledge of the world to know that for her to go in and out of the kitchen at odd times would either be looked upon as an intrusion, or, on the other hand, that it would soon lead to her being expected to take her meals there as one of the family. So she did what she could to help by getting up early enough to make her own bed and leave the room tidy, and by doing any oddments of shopping to save Mrs Parkhurst the walk to the village, so that Mrs Parkhurst, who hitherto had had only young men lodgers, was pleased with what she called a helping hand.

But Mrs Parkhurst was no saint; she could, at times, be very irritating. She was not an intrusive or a talkative woman and did not pry unduly into Laura's affairs, but their respective ages and their position as landlady and lodger gave her, as she thought, some right of censorship. When she did not approve of Laura's proceedings she would be more than habitually reserved, or she would throw out hints, ostensibly general hints, as to her own standard of behaviour for young women living away from home. She did not, for instance, believe in such young persons having friends of the opposite sex; or, if they had one such friend, he must be the only one. Of girls who were seen home from an entertainment by one young man one week and the following week by another she did not approve, and when Laura suggested that there was safety in numbers, she told her she was one of those who go round and round the wood and bring out a crooked stick in the end.

Her ideas on dress differed greatly from Laura's. She did not presume to criticize openly any of Laura's belongings, but seeing her attired for some special festival in white muslin and a rose-wreathed hat she would remark, somewhat sourly, that in her opinion nothing was more becoming to a girl than a neat costume and sailor hat. She could go anywhere in that dress and be respected, for it always looked good. She never had held with a lot of finery. This was vexing to a girl who had thought she looked both suitably and becomingly dressed for a fête where there was to be outdoor dancing. On the subject of dancing she was surprisingly broadminded. To her and her co-religionists dancing was a sin, but she admitted that she knew that many truly Christian people saw no harm in it.

When she approved of Laura's behaviour she would signify her approval by a warmer welcome than usual, or by some small act of kindness such as washing for her, free of cost, some article of apparel. At such times, if she had a few spare moments, she would stay for a chat when she cleared away the tea things, and in that way Laura came to know something of her life.

She had been born and lived as a child in a hamlet near Selborne, Gilbert White's Selborne, and was proud of her birthplace. 'You should see the Hanger at Selborne', she would say when Laura brought in wild flowers. 'You should see it in spring, when the primroses are out, you could sit down and pick your hat full without moving.' Her father had owned or rented a little land and they had kept fowls, geese, and a pig or two, and he had, in addition to his work at home, put in a day here and there working for wages. Every year at the beginning of the hop-picking season the whole family had been packed, bag and baggage, into a little donkey-cart they had and had gone to work in some hop-gardens near Farnham, leaving only the old grandmother at home to keep house and attend to the animals.

She looked back on those hop-picking days as the happiest of her life; ''Twas a regular holiday for us children,' she declared, 'though every one of us big enough to stand on our two legs had to work hard. But if we worked all day we had plenty of fun playing round the fire with the other children in the evening while our mums cooked our suppers and washed our clothes, and a fine hearty appetite we had all of us, for the smell of the hops was as good as a medicine. "I'm that hungry I could eat a child dead of the smallpox", our dad used to say, but that was only his fun, you know. He liked good food and he got it when hopping, great big stews cooked in a three-legged pot slung over the fire, with young rabbits and mushrooms and a nice bit of bacon we'd brought with us from home, and the men clubbed together to buy a barrel of beer for themselves and, after supper, they'd all sit round the fires and sing. Everybody in the villages round went hopping in those days. The farmers gave as many men as they could spare a holiday and the few left at home did for themselves while their wives and children were away. The houses were all shut up in the daytime and not a soul to be seen in the place, excepting a few old grannies left behind to feed the cats and the pigs and so on. Now, of course, there's all this riff-raff from towns in the hop-gardens and nobody who thinks themselves respectable goes any more; but, then, it was a holiday for the whole countryside. And when settling-up time came there was a present for every one of us children. 'Twas supposed to be a prize for those who worked hardest, but though some worked harder than others, as is but human nature, nobody was ever left out that I can remember. My father bought me a doll one year, and a beautiful doll it was, that opened and shut its eyes and squeaked when you pressed a spring in its chest. I wish I could give a doll like that to our young Ivy, but times have changed and such a doll would cost nine or ten shillings now; and there's no chance of going hopping either, a man who works for wages in these days can't take a fortnight or three weeks off to go hopping or somebody else would soon be stepping into his shoes on his job. Then the farmers were glad to let men off after the harvest was carried. It saved them paying out wages when there was nothing much doing for a week or two. The gipsies do a lot of it now, them and that rough lot from towns, and the hop-gardens aren't what they were when everybody under gentry thought it no come-down to lend a hand with the picking.'

When Laura asked if she had in her childhood heard of an old-time curate of Selborne who had written a book about birds, she said she thought she had heard the name of Gilbert White mentioned at some time, but she was not sure. Which was disappointing to Laura, who had hoped to glean some local traditions of the celebrated parson-naturalist. But although disappointed she was not surprised, for even in her own time, thirty years later than that of Mrs Parkhurst, not much attention was given to local history in elementary schools. One of her own regrets in later life was that in her childhood she had not known that the poet Pope had visited the local mansion near her home and had actually written part or the whole of *The Rape of the Lock* there. When she learned this in middle life she had long left her old home and had little prospect of seeing it again, and though she was still able to picture the frail, crooked little figure in a black cloak pacing the beech avenue which had been her own favourite haunt as a child, age and distance took off the edge of the delight she would have experienced had she known that she was treading in the footsteps of a real poet.

Laura thought of the Parkhursts as elderly people. Their eldest son was the same age as herself; they had a daughter away in service, who was soon to be married; and they often spoke of themselves as getting on in years and said that, as the younger children grew up, they hoped for an easier time for themselves. That hope was not soon to be realized. At the age of forty-seven and while Laura was still living with them Mrs Parkhurst once more found herself pregnant. It was a difficult position for her, surrounded by her grown and growing-up family, and she had physically a miserable time in the early months. Her face grew yellow and thin and the hitherto faint lines became wrinkles; but only once did Laura know her to make anything approaching a complaint. Then she had been speaking of babies' clothes and had said that all she had were worn out or had been given away long before, and how to get new ones she did not know. 'I did think I had done with all that', she said, and tears welled into her eyes as she said it. She wiped them away with a corner of her apron and added: 'But I know it is God's will and I must be patient, though I do dread the time when it begins showing.'

When the time came she had a long and difficult confinement, with two doctors in attendance. The district nurse told Laura afterwards that her fortitude was wonderful. 'And what do you think she said when she came round from the chloroform? You'd never guess in a month of Sundays. "I know that my Redeemer liveth!" says she, "I know that my Redeemer liveth."

I didn't know she was a religious woman, did you?'

A few days later Laura said good-bye to Mrs Parkhurst, as she thought then, for ever. She was resting peacefully in bed with her youngest daughter on her arm and her eldest, aged twenty, in attendance as nurse. She said it was the first good rest she had had since Ivy was born and she meant to make the most of it. 'You'd better! for it's the last you'll get of this sort, my lady!' laughed her grown-up daughter who, in view of her new responsibilities and her own approaching marriage, was indulging in the airs of mature womanhood. She took the gurgling morsel of humanity from the bed and, patting it vigorously on the back, assured it that it should have its nicey-picey dilly-dilly-dilly-water in a little min-min, when brother Herbie came back from the chemie's, and that nursey-pursey would soon be coming to give baby its bathie-pathie, while her mother looked proudly on, exclaiming 'How natural it all comes to her!' The old freemasonry of sex was working. Mrs Parkhurst's husband had gone out that morning looking as if the cares of the whole world had suddenly rolled from his shoulders. A plate of grapes which one of her sons had walked miles to obtain for her stood on the table beside her bed; she pressed Laura to take some of these as she dared not eat them herself for fear they should make her milk disagree with the baby. Husband and sons had been unexpectedly helpful and sympathetic and she had been touched to the heart by their anxiety and their care for her; but for all that, she had felt relieved when she saw them depart for their work in the morning, leaving her with Mabel who, by virtue of her sex, could sympathize understandingly and give real practical aid.

When on that sunny, misty August morning at the beginning of the century, Laura said good-bye to Mrs Parkhurst and to all her other Heatherley friends and took the road over the heath to the railway station she thought the farewell was final. But Laura had not seen the last of her old landlady. Twenty years later, when she returned to live in the district, one of her first callers was Mrs Parkhurst. A more cheerful, comfortable-looking and a much better-dressed Mrs Parkhurst than the one she remembered, but otherwise little changed. When Laura had formerly known her she had looked older than her years, but the time between then and their second meeting had adjusted that matter and at sixty-five she looked much as she had at forty-five.

She had brought with her an intelligent-looking, smartly-dressed girl of twenty whom she introduced as 'My youngest daughter, Elsie; the one you saw last as a tiny long-clothed baby in bed. Do you see any change in her?' she asked, and her eyes dwelt proudly on the short-skirted, shingled, and pleasantly smiling figure at her side. Laura quite truthfully declared that had she not been told who she was she would never have recognized her, which caused some merriment and put all on a comfortable footing. They had come by bus, for buses were by that time running. Mrs Parkhurst had somehow learned that Laura was again living in the district, and when Elsie had suggested taking her mother for a trip somewhere she at once thought of Laura, 'for,' she said, 'I have never forgotten you. You ask Elsie here and she'll tell you how I've always talked about the way you used to run upstairs, two steps at a time, very often, and what a one you were for your books and for bringing in great bunches of wild flowers.' But it was not about Laura's youth she was longing to talk; that was over long ago and here she was, sitting at her own table with her own children around her, pouring out tea for her visitors, an accredited matron; but ready, as ever, to listen and be interested.

Elsie – 'my daughter Elsie' – was Mrs Parkhurst's chief topic of conversation. Elsie had been a wonderful child. 'The flower of the family', her poor dad used to call her. He had been dead these five years, poor dear soul; he made a truly Christian end, so patient under suffering; and the boys were all married, and Mabel too, of course; she herself had been a grandmother for these seventeen years, and with the older children away from home, what she would have done without Elsie she did not know. Elsie was the clever one of the family. She had won a scholarship and been to a secondary school, and now she was book-keeper at one of the hotels, getting good money, and so good and thoughtful she wouldn't let her mother want for a thing. And she herself had not done too badly either; when the children had got up a little she had moved into a better house, one all to themselves, and had let the two front rooms to summer visitors, and since poor dad had been gone she had been drawing her little pension. 'Thank God,' she said, 'I've got much to be thankful for.'

VIII. *'I have had playmates, I have had companions . . .'*

One winter afternoon when the oil-lamp which swung over the post-office counter had been lighted at half-past three and all who had no urgent business to compel them to face the east wind were enjoying their tea and muffins by the fireside, the office door suddenly burst open to admit a young man. He was a stranger to Laura, but nevertheless welcome, as anyone else would have been who brought a little variety into a dull day. He was a large young man, both tall and thickset, and the shaggy grey overcoat he was wearing made him look larger than he would otherwise have done. A snub nose and remarkably clear bright grey eyes were the only noticeable features of a face whipped into rosiness by the wind and rain. His small fair moustache and the shaggy grey surface of his overcoat were beaded with raindrops and he carried a stout walking-stick of some natural wood. A farmer, or a game-keeper, thought Laura.

Her guess was wide of the mark. Richard Brownlow, though not a Londoner by birth, had spent almost the whole of his life in London, the last few years employed by one of the big cable companies in the City. He had come to Heatherley to stay with some connections by marriage who had recently settled there. He was evidently a cheerful and communicative young man. As he handed in his telegram he remarked that he knew his mother would not rest until she had heard of his safe arrival, and added that he had walked the last ten miles of the way and had enjoyed the wild weather. 'This east wind which shrivels most people up is the breath of life to me,' he declared.

When Laura returned to the counter after sending off his telegram he was still there, examining a showcase of picture postcards with local views. Alma being away for an hour, Laura should have summoned Mrs Hertford to attend to him as a shop customer, but having nothing to do herself at the moment and perhaps wishing to see more of him, she helped him to select and took the money for his purchases. The discussion of picture-postcard views led to the discussion of the scenes represented, and it was not until another customer claimed her attention that he made his exit.

Alma had by that time returned to duty, and when Laura said that she did not think she had seen that young man before, she answered thickly – she was sucking a sweet at the time – 'You'll see him again.' Which was odd, because, as Alma afterwards said, she herself had never seen him before and did not know him from Adam. She had concluded from his appearance that he was on a walking tour. The term 'hiking' was unknown in those days.

Laura did see Richard Brownlow again. During his first short visit to Heatherley he called at the post office several times daily, and after that he was frequently down for weekends and longer holidays. The friendship which was soon established between them grew rapidly, for it was founded on mutual liking and similarity of taste. Everything in literature Laura admired, Richard admired. If one of the two began to quote poetry, the other capped the quotation, or held out a finger to link and called out the name of a poet to signify that their thoughts had been identical. And often the old childish proceeding did not end there, for the poet's name which first sprung to the lips of one would spring to the lips of the other. 'Burns!' 'Browning!' or 'Keats!' they would cry simultaneously, and instead of linked fingers there were clasped hands and laughter.

Richard had an only sister named Mavis who sometimes came with him to Heatherley. The two were devoted and their tastes

255

were alike. Both were fond of ideas, especially ideas for reforming the world; both loved the country and both were well read. In appearance the two were very unlike, Richard being large, and Mavis a slender graceful little creature with dark red hair, eyes the colour of autumn beech leaves and a velvety cream complexion. She was so small and dainty of build and so quick and bird-like in her movements that beside her Laura, herself neither large nor inactive, felt clumsy. She had mental qualities to match her physique; she did not reason things out to a logical conclusion as Richard did, but reached her conclusions by flashes of insight or by wheeling and dipping in a kind of swallow flight which, light and casual as it might appear, was certain. Laura was delighted with her new friends. She would have liked them in any case for what they were in themselves, but an added attraction for her was that they were modern. They had the latest ideas, knew and sometimes used the latest catchwords, and had read and could discuss new books by new authors whose names, to Laura, were but vaguely familiar. At last, Laura thought, she had friends who were truly *fin de siècle*.

On dark nights, after the post office had closed, they would take long walks, swinging along the highway, Mavis on Richard's arm on one side, Laura on the other, chanting in unison the quatrains of Omar Khayyám, or a chorus from Swinburne, or talking sense or nonsense. Often they were in melancholy mood, as they imagined became children of a decadent day, and a silent passer-by who had happened to overhear their outpourings might have pitied them. How many times did Laura exclaim tragically into the night:

> What shall I be at fifty, if God should keep me alive,
> Who find my life so bitter before I am twenty-five?

or 'thank whatever powers there be' that

> No man lives for ever,
> That dead men rise up never,

in pure innocent ignorance of bitterness of spirit, or the terrible finality of death. May the sins of youth be forgiven! Mavis, equally inexperienced, would cry aloud in tragic tones such lines as,

> Would to God I had never known you, sweet,
> Would to God we had never met,
>   To steer a way for our erring feet
> To the sad shores of regret!

while Richard, tall as a cliff and firm as a rock between them, preserved the mental as well as the physical balance by keeping mainly to passages from Milton or Shakespeare.

One night when they had climbed to the summit of a hill where a tall granite cross marked the spot where had once stood a gibbet, Laura dropped to her knees on the turf and, pressing her ear to the cold stone of the shaft, recited in trance-like tones an imaginary conversation between two malefactors who she asked them to suppose had once suffered there, an effort which was applauded as worthy of Poe.

On Sunday afternoons and light summer evenings Laura showed Richard and Mavis some of her moorland and wood-land haunts. Some, not all; there were a few spots she reserved. One of these was the place she had named 'the heart of the wood', where an oblong of lawn-like turf, threaded by a little stream, was shut in on every side by trees and thick under-growth. Ferns grew beside the stream and on one side a spreading beech tree cast in summer a cool green shade. Laura had often gone there on summer evenings, to think her own quiet thoughts, to read – although when she took a book there she seldom opened it – or simply to steep herself in the beauty and peace of her surroundings. There had been a time when she had hurried there with hot, angry tears in her eyes, caused by the slighting remark of a chance-met acquaintance. The remark was probably unconsidered and in no way intended as an insult, but it is mortifying to youthful pride to be reminded that one has neither the birth, education, nor any personal quality to justify the holding of an opinion differing from those held by the majority. But there, in the wood, was healing for sore eyes and hurt pride. 'Wood-sorrel and wild violet' to 'soothe the heart's fret', and what drooping spirits can long remain sullen within hearing of a blackbird's evensong?

But although Laura held inviolate this and one or two other

257

secret sanctuaries, she admitted her new friends to all her ordinary haunts. She showed them the view from the pine-clump, Bob's valley farm, and many woodland nooks other than her own special retreat. They loved the country and never tired of exploring its beauties, though, as she soon found, their love of nature, though perhaps equal in degree, was of a different kind from her own. To her the country was an enveloping atmosphere from which she drew strength and delight; they studied it consciously, as an open book, naming each bird and flower, or never resting until they could name them, surveying prospects in detail to discover what in its contours gave charm to the view; examining the ferns, lichens, and wildflowers and looking them up in their little books which gave the names of the species in Latin. Their interest was intelligent, Laura's instinctive.

She showed them one day, far out on the moors, a patch of heather which, seen from a short distance, looked stunted and blighted and had a reddish tinge. When closely examined every individual plant was seen to be netted and dragged down to earth by the thin, red, threadlike runners of a parasite. They were horrified at the sight and asked the name of the plant with the stranglehold. Laura told them it was dodder and said that, if she were a novelist, she would write a book with that title. It would be the story of a man or woman – she thought a woman – of fine, sensitive nature, bound by some tie – probably marriage – to one of a nature which was strong, coarse, and encroaching, and would tell how, in time, the heather person shrank and withered, while the dodder one fattened and prospered.

It was not a cheerful idea, but it pleased them, and they sat for some time on a grassy knoll overlooking the heather patch, eating from a bag of cherries Richard had produced and discussing Laura's plot. Then one of them spoke of the dodder husband as the villain of the piece. 'No!' cried Laura, quite warmly, rushing to the defence of her newly-born character. 'The dodder cannot help being dodder, it was made that way, and must act according to its nature, and in the same way, the dodder man has no evil intentions, he may even be kindly disposed; it just happens that his close proximity is ruinous. He thrives and becomes more and more bumptious, important, and respected – I think he must be a stockbroker, with a white waistcoat and a thick gold watch-chain – she – she painted quite good watercolours when a girl, you know – she withers and shrinks into the mere wraith of a woman.'

'Jolly fine!' said Richard. 'But who is going to write this story?' 'Laura, of course,' said Mavis, 'she knows all about people.' At that, Richard looked a little taken aback, for he, as the man of the party and a man with known literary tastes, was obviously best fitted to deal with the delicate situation. But though touched with the sense of masculine superiority (for how could he help it, being a child of his own day?), he was touched but slightly. He sprang to his feet, seized Laura's hand, and having heaved her up, waltzed her round and round on a patch of sand, singing, 'She knows about it all. She knows! She knows!'

Their more serious talk was in essence not unlike that of young people of their type today. They had theories about many things of which by experience they knew nothing, and their theories did credit to their hearts, if not always to their heads. They hated the oppressor and pitied the oppressed. The miseries of the women chair-makers of Cradley Heath, then much in the limelight, or those of the sweated seamstresses of the East End of London, moved Richard to wrath. The mention of the shoeless, ragged, half-starved children of the slums touched Mavis and Laura to tears. They called it a burning shame that human beings should be compelled to live in houses no better than cattle byres, and that workers should be under-paid, ill-fed, or suffer any kind of injustice. So far they resembled the young of today in their ideas, but only so far, for although they were aware of and deplored social ills, they had no plan for their redress. The mild Liberalism in which they believed would in time, they hoped, ameliorate the lot of the poor and oppressed; but when and to what extent they had no idea. With old Omar they longed to grasp this sorry scheme of things entire and shatter it to bits, but they possessed no blueprint by which to remould it nearer to their hearts' desire. Had they been born half a century later, how they would have enjoyed helping to plan the New Order!

But though, as is the way of youth, they were inclined to take themselves seriously, there were times when they talked sheer nonsense. They were fond of limericks and other nonsense verses, and between them had a good stock of these. Richard knew several of the *Bab Ballads* by heart and could, and would, fill up a blank space in the conversation by declaiming *The Rival Curates* or *The Precocious Baby*, often with Mavis trying to stuff her handkerchief into his mouth to stop him. When other entertainment failed they would relate anecdotes. Laura had her country childhood to draw upon for her stories and her 'Lawk 'a' mussy O's and 'Where be 'ee a-gooin's provoked peals of laughter. Richard's and Mavis's stories were more sophisticated, with a sting in the tail. Brilliantly clever, thought Laura.

The truth of the matter is, though no one would have attributed it to such a cause at that date, that those bubbling high spirits, that love of childish nonsense, that reeling with laughter without cause, were due to a rebound; in Laura's case from a somewhat harsh and restricted childhood, and in that of her friends, from experiencing a great shock, followed by a prolonged ordeal. Laura had not known Richard and Mavis long before she surmised from chance words that there was, or had been, some shadow upon their home life, and when the time was ripe for confidences, Mavis, who had come to her room one night, told her the whole story. Laura had said that her people were poor, and when Mavis retorted, 'Well, all the best people are poor, aren't they?' she had answered, 'But not poor in the way I mean. We live in a tiny cottage and my father is a working man.' Mavis said in a subdued voice, 'But how lucky you are to have a father.' Then she had told her the main points of the following story.

Richard and Mavis had been well educated and had had a happy, comfortable home with kind parents in childhood and early youth. Then, five years before Laura knew them, their father had died suddenly in bed by the side of their mother, who had known nothing of his collapse until she woke up naturally, and touching his hand, found it cold. The shock had shattered her nervous system and left her more or less an invalid. For a year after her husband's death her reason had been feared for and she had been taken from hospital to hospital and from nursing home to nursing home in the hope of a cure. The only near relative of the family then living was a sister of Mrs Brownlow who lived far up in the North of England and whose husband was then in delicate health. After she had done all she could to help the young Brownlows to settle their affairs she had been obliged to return to her own home, and the two, Richard at that time not quite twenty and Mavis eighteen, had been left alone to face hitherto undreamed-of responsibilities.

At their father's death the greater part of the family income had ceased, but they were not left utterly destitute. Richard was already earning a small salary. Their father had insured his life for a fairly substantial sum, and his late employers, a City firm, generously paid his widow a sum equal to a full year of his earnings. The greater part of this small capital went in specialists' and nursing-home fees, but it also sufficed to keep the home going until Richard was earning enough, though barely enough, for them to live upon. Since then he had had annual increases, although his salary, according to their standards, was still but a modest one. At the time of her father's death Mavis had begun a course of art training with the idea of taking up the new poster and advertisement work. She had a gift for drawing and her teachers had a good opinion of her as a colourist; but her training then came to a premature end and she had to turn housekeeper. It may be supposed that a girl of eighteen, without any previous experience beyond that of the light, ornamental duties of an indulged only daughter in the school holidays, found housekeeping difficult and housework drudgery. Richard, at twenty, had not only to undertake the full financial responsibility of the home, but also that of his mother's illness. Mavis told Laura that he would sometimes sit at the table the whole evening, half the time adding up totals and pencilling columns of figures, and the other half with his elbows on the table and his head in his hands.

It must have been a hard life for two young things who had hitherto been spared all responsibility by loving and protecting parents; but when their mother had recovered sufficiently to return home, their position became even harder, for Mrs Brownlow's recovery was but partial. The kind mother they had formerly known had become a capricious, fractious, self-centred semi-invalid, what we should now call a nervous wreck, and although they knew that this sad change in her was due to the shock she had experienced, and never failed her in their love and sympathy, they must have suffered severely. To her duties as housekeeper Mavis had added those of nurse. The management of their slender resources still devolved upon Richard.

For more than a year their lives were overshadowed. Then gradually Mrs Brownlow's condition improved. She became able to dress herself without help, to do a little in the house, to go for a walk in the park, or to look at the shops, and although she was still at times irritable and capricious she was not more so than the ordinary nerve sufferer. Small pleasures again brightened the lives of her children, they could go to a lecture, or to the theatre, or on Sunday take train for some wayside station in Surrey and tramp back over the hills. Both had always been great readers and even in the thick of their troubles reading and discussing the books they read had been one unfailing resource. Now they found friends of their own age who shared their interest. They had gained experience, too, and felt more sure of themselves; they had accepted their position and learned to get the best out of it. In short, they had grown up.

A few weeks before Richard's first visit to Heatherley Mrs Brownlow's sister, recently widowed, had come to live with them and it was arranged that she should relieve Mavis of the housekeeping, leaving her free to learn shorthand and typing with a view to a post in the City. Mavis would have preferred to resume her art training, but that would have been longer, more expensive, and less certain as a means of livelihood. Their Aunt Maggie, they both declared, was an angel. As soon as she had taken the household reins in hand everything seemed to go smoothly, and as the elder sister, she had great influence on their mother who, under her care, became more like her old self. As soon as she had taken stock of the situation, Aunt Maggie suggested that Richard and Mavis should have some little change of air and scene occasionally. Neither had slept from home for one night since the last family holiday in the Isle of Wight the year of their father's death. Aunt Maggie said that such a closed-in life at their age was unnatural. A nephew of her late husband had recently gone to live at Heatherley, there was lovely country round there, and his wife took in paying guests. Why should not Richard go there for his next long weekend? Richard went.

Both Richard and Mavis were anxious that Laura should get work in London. They sketched a delightful programme of theatres, museums, and picture galleries and of country outings on Sundays, with themselves as companions, and for a time Laura was persuaded that the change would be wholly delightful. She even went so far as to obtain a syllabus of some Civil Service examination, to pay her fee of one guinea to a Civil Service college, and to begin studying the subjects. But she knew from the first she could not hope to win even the lowest place in a competitive examination, no matter how hard she studied. Her education had left too many black spaces and, apart from that, she had not a competitive mind. The correspondence course only served to reveal to herself her abysmal ignorance. Having never learned the rules, she had to leave most of the arithmetic problems unsolved. Her geography was a little better because she had read a good deal about foreign countries; but even so, she had not read the right books to enlighten her about imports and exports, or industries or distances. In essay-writing she was able to reach the average number of marks, sometimes a little above the average, though her paper often came back to her marked in red ink, 'More facts, please', or 'No purple patches'. Her handwriting alone was pronounced 'satisfactory'.

Her inborn peasant thrift, however, forbade wasting the guinea paid in advance and she persevered in at least conscientiously attempting to answer the questions and work out the problems. The guinea, which seemed quite a large sum to her, was of course very little as a fee for what the advertisement of the college termed 'individual tuition', and the comments of her coach were naturally brief and not very enlightening. But there was on one occasion a human touch. Then the subject set for the essay was: 'Give an account of a book you have read recently', and Laura, who at that time was enthralled by the work of Henry James, took for her subject *The Portrait of a Lady*. When her papers were returned to her, below the official red-ink assessment she found written, 'A curious choice. Don't care for James's work myself, but almost thou persuadest me!'

When Alma had mastered the telegraph instrument and could be left in charge for the two hours on Sunday morning, Laura had the exciting adventure of a trip to town. Richard and Mavis met her at Waterloo, and each of them seizing an arm, dragged her through the, to her, immense and confusing crowd on the platform. They appeared to be as much at home in the press as she was far out on the heath, but she, as they passed out of the station into the crowded gas-lit streets, had a dreamlike feeling of unreality.

It had been raining; the inside of their bus was choked to the doorway, and Richard assisted the two girls up the steep steps to the outside seats on the top of the vehicle. 'Now we can talk', he said, as he turned back the tarpaulin which protected unoccupied seats from the rain, and they did try to talk, but the others soon saw that, with the roar of the traffic in her unaccustomed ears, Laura could not hear one half of what they were saying. So, huddled together for warmth, they sat in silence, smiling into each other's eyes when they happened to meet, while the horse-bus went, clopping and grinding, with many stops and much pinging of the bell, through lighted streets thronged with people, though the hour seemed quite late to Laura.

It was the first time she had seen London or any large town by night and, after her dark walk to the railway station and her hour in the dimly lit carriage, the scene she beheld from between the rails at the top of the bus was at first dazzling. But she soon found herself gazing down with deep interest on the flaring shop-fronts and the crowds surging before them, looking like crowds of little black ants against the brightness. In the roadway passed other buses with brightly lit interiors where the large, feathered hats of the women eclipsed the bowlered heads of the men, and the driver, sitting aloft and aloof on his high perch in front in his shining black macintosh cape, cracked his long whip and craned his neck to shout in a voice like a fog-horn to some passing fellow-driver. And there were hansoms, jink-jinking as they threaded the heavier traffic and outstripped it, and a one-legged man playing an accordion outside a public house, and children playing in the gutter, actually playing, with so much traffic about, and at that hour! And the smell and taste of the thick, moist air! What was it? It appeared to be a blend of orange-peel, horse-manure and wet clothes, with a dash of coal gas.

So this was London at night. And this noisy, hustling life beneath the street lamps was going on only a few miles away from the dark, silent, deserted heaths, fields, and woods she had left so recently. She had of course known that London was thickly populated, that it was brightly lit at night, and that night crowds congregated, but it was not until she saw it with her own eyes that she fully realized the contrast between town and country. She fancied herself caught in a great sparkling net hanging amidst miles and miles of surrounding darkness.

'We shall soon be there. Only one other very short ride after this,' said a voice in her ear, and she found that Richard had changed seats with Mavis and was sitting beside her. 'Cold?' he asked, pressing her hand. 'What do you think of London?' asked Mavis, and when Laura said that she thought it was wonderful they laughed and called her their little country mouse.

Richard and Mavis lived with their mother and aunt in a flat, or rather the upper floor of a house, in a pleasant suburban road. In the small plot in front of the house the leaves of wet evergreen shrubs reflected the light from a near-by lamp-post. The sound of the traffic in the main streets was subdued by distance to a dull roaring, against which their own footfalls and those of the few passers-by rang out sharply. Laura compared herself to some storm-buffeted ship which had reached a quiet harbour.

Richard and Mavis thought and sometimes spoke of themselves as poor, and Laura knew they must be much poorer than they had been in their father's lifetime, but their poverty was different in kind, as well as in degree, from that to which she had been accustomed. Some of the furniture in their rooms was shabby, because, as they explained, nothing had been renewed and very little renovated for more than five years, but it was good and substantial and tastefully disposed; the rooms had a look of inevitable rightness. They had treasures, too, which had belonged to former generations of their family. Oil-painted portraits of their grandparents hung on either side of the fireplace; blue and white china and a carved ivory pagoda brought home from abroad by a seafaring great-uncle were displayed in a cabinet, and a musical album, purchased by a great-aunt at the Great Exhibition, was brought out from a cupboard to play its little tinkling fairy-like tunes for Laura's amusement. Between its pages were tinted photographs of chignoned and crinolined ladies, their gold chains and lockets and wide, flat bracelets picked out with gilding; untinted photographs of whiskered men in dark cut-away coats and pale, wide trousers, their top-hats and gloves reposing beside them on elaborate studio tables.

This background reminded Laura of her father's family, but it was far removed from that of her own cottage home, and when she went to bed in Mavis's room, Mavis sleeping with her aunt that night, and found a fire burning and a hot water bottle in her bed, her surroundings seemed positively luxurious. By that time it was Sunday morning, for after the mother and aunt had retired the three friends had sat talking and Richard had read aloud stories and poems which fairly scintillated with brilliance, from some back numbers of *The Yellow Book* he had picked up on a second-hand bookstall.

To be actually in London for a night and a day in the

company of her brilliant friends was exciting to Laura, and to be cared for and made much of, as they cared for and made much of her, was comforting to one who lived far from her own home and was dependent on herself alone for her well-being. The aunt, as they had said, was a perfect angel. She took care of them all and obviously enjoyed seeing their enjoyment, so that Laura would have had a weekend of unalloyed bliss, had it not been for the disquieting presence of Mrs Brownlow. Her affliction had by that time taken the form of a constant twitching of the features and a restlessness which would not allow her to sit down in one chair for more than a moment or two. She would come into the room where her children and Laura were talking, wander from chair to chair, complain that the fire was too large, or too low, then drift out again. If anyone spoke at all loudly she would remind them of her 'poor head', if she required anything and no one had noticed her requirement, she complained that no one ever did anything for her.

Her manner towards Laura was polite, though by no means cordial, except on one occasion when Laura was relating some trifling experience which the others found amusing and she, with a shrug of impatience, audibly muttered 'What nonsense!' Richard, who had been present and seen Laura's embarrassment, said to her afterwards, 'You mustn't take any notice of Mother's little ways. She's been ill so long, I'm afraid we have spoiled her', and Mavis sighed and said, 'If only Laura could have known her as she used to be when we were children! She'd have loved her then.'

Early in the afternoon Richard suggested that he and Mavis should show Laura the City before seeing her off at Waterloo, and after some bus rides and tea at a tea-shop they walked through silent Sabbath streets, the names of which were familiar to Laura through her telegraph work, but which, until then, had been but names. Now she saw Fleet Street and Johnson's Court, passing without the faintest anticipatory thrill the office of the magazine whose editor would one day accept her first shyly-offered contribution; then on to Threadneedle Street to gaze on the outside of the Central Telegraph Office, familiarly known to

Laura as 'T.S.' and figuring in her world as the centre of the universe. Now and then a horse-bus trundled through the main streets and a few passengers were seen on the pavement; the side streets were deserted. And, strange as it seemed to Laura, although Richard and Mavis had lived all their lives in London, neither of them had ever before seen the City on a Sunday afternoon. They had known it only as the thronged hive of weekdays, and the hushed calm which seemed positively to brood over the empty ways appeared to amaze them almost as much as it did Laura. They wandered on, walking leisurely and stopping to look at this and that in places past which on an ordinary day they would have been carried by a swift tide of humanity. They passed through narrow passages between high blocks of buildings where their footsteps rang loudly on the pavement and the sky, tinged with sunset, showed like a rose-coloured ribbon between the tall roofs.

That walk through the silent, deserted City was one of the richest memories of Laura's later years. She would not for anything have missed seeing it as it was then; nor would she have willingly missed seeing the very different Saturday night scene in the shopping quarter, or the suburban home of her friends; and still less would she have cared to miss the sensation of freedom and home-coming she felt when, at the end of her train journey, she came to the heath and once more breathed the odours of heather and pine and saw the starry heaven above the pine-tops.

It had been delightful to visit her friends in London and to obtain a brief glimpse of town life. She would like to go often. If ever she became rich she would have a flat of her own to go to for a few days whenever she felt inclined. But never to make her home there, shut away by miles and miles of bricks and mortar from the green earth and the changing seasons. To see the first swallow skim the fields and streams, to hear the first cuckoo call from the woods, to see the apple trees in blossom and the other flowers as they appeared, from the earliest snowdrop through all the pageant of spring and summer to the golden-green ivy bloom, alive with bees and hovering butterflies, was, she felt instinctively, essential to her bodily and spiritual wellbeing.

When she had left London the weather, though no longer wet, had been moist and mild. The Hampshire night was clear and frosty and when she reached the higher ground she found a light sprinkling of snow. She breathed in the pure, invigorating air with conscious enjoyment and rejoiced in her sense of release from the flaring lights and eddying crowd to the freedom of her natural environment.

The next day she wrote to the secretary of her Civil Service college saying that, since she had little chance of gaining a place in the examinations and had a fairly good post where she was, she had decided to discontinue her course at the end of that session. And so ended Laura's one bid for worldly advancement. Her compensation for failure in that respect was a whole lifetime spent, if not all of it actually in the country, never too far from it to be able to reach it easily. During many years of her later life she had both sea and country just beyond her doorstep.

She never visited Richard's and Mavis's home again. They often asked her and she sometimes thought she would like to go, but was kept back by a feeling that, on her last visit, Mrs Brownlow had looked on her as an intruder. Every month or two Richard and Mavis would come to Heatherley for a weekend, or Richard would come alone on a Sunday and return the same night. Their walks and talks went on and they still delighted in each other's company, but there was a slight, indefinable change in their relationship, a shadow, the shade of a shade, had crept between them. Her friends, as she had expected, were sorry when she told them she had given up the attempt to pass the examination that was to have brought her to live near them, and when she tried to explain the motives which lay at the root of her decision she was told, for the first time in her life, though not the last, that she cared more for places than people. And it was no good her trying to get them to laugh it off by saying that she had been a cat in a previous existence and that it was always places not persons to which cats were attached, for they were really grave and a little hurt. And it hurt Laura to know she had disappointed them. However, one article of their belief which they had frequently rehearsed and Richard now repeated was that we all have to live our own lives and must be left free to make our own decisions. After a little more discussion the subject of Laura's projected promotion to town was dropped. But the slight shadow remained, and on Laura's side the feeling that, between herself and her friends, all was not quite as it had been.

Then, one winter evening when it had been dark for hours and Laura, already muffled up for a dash for home through the darkness and cold, was locking the post-office door on the inside, she was surprised to see through the glass upper panel Richard standing outside on the pavement. Against the dark background of the unlighted street, with the faint rays of the office oil-lamp falling upon it, his face looked unnaturally pale. His coat collar was turned up against the cold, which made him look hunched up and dejected; but he smiled his old smile when he saw her and signalled to her to make haste and come out, and the first words he said when she had come round from the back of the house were, 'I want to talk to you.'

She had nowhere indoors to take him to talk. Her room, having a bed in it, was out of the question at that date, and her landlady's front room, which she sometimes borrowed when she had friends to tea, would not be available with no previous notice. So they walked off through the village and out on the main road. The weather that night was depressing; there had been snow which the raw, cold thaw was rapidly turning to slush; fog made the darkness darker, and the few people they met were obviously hurrying home. They alone were making for the open country.

Mavis had been unwell with a cough left behind by one of the chest colds to which she was subject and one of Laura's first questions was 'How is Mavis?'

'Not at all well,' he said, 'that is one of the things I want to tell you about', and, after Laura had said how sorry she was, not another word was spoken until they reached the crossroads. Then he felt for her arm, and as they moved slowly along the main road, enclosed and cut off from the rest of the world by a curtain of mist, Richard told Laura that Mavis had been examined by a doctor who had told their Aunt Maggie that, although there was no positive symptom of the disease, he felt he ought to warn her that her niece's condition showed a marked tendency to tuberculosis. She certainly ought not to remain in London this cold, foggy weather. He supposed the South of France was out of the question? Ah, yes, of course, he knew something of the family circumstances. Then some sheltered place in the south of this country, Bournemouth, perhaps, or Shanklin.

'Oh, poor, poor Mavis!' cried Laura, appalled, 'and just as she was doing so well in her new post! Isn't she terribly disappointed – and frightened?'

'Disappointed, of course, but not at all frightened. Says it's all nonsense, the doctor has made a mistake; except for a bit of a cough, no worse than she has had other winters, she feels perfectly well. At first she flatly refused to be packed off, as she calls it, to Bournemouth.'

'But she is going?'

'Going? Of course she's going,' he said, and he went on to explain that such symptoms as those the doctor had discovered in Mavis were taken seriously nowadays and had to be dealt with at once, while there was still ground for hope that the patient would throw them off entirely. There were sanatoriums where rich patients were sent, where they lived practically in the open air and were placed on a diet, and homes for the poor who were similarly affected were being established all over the country. Even fairly advanced cases, he said, responded to the new treatment, and there had been some almost miraculous cures. Laura, who had read all this in the newspapers, and felt sure that Mavis would recover – she must! – knew also that a long stay at Bournemouth or Shanklin would be expensive. 'And it can be managed?' she asked.

He then told her that their Aunt Maggie had a little money of her own, not enough for her to live upon, but the interest brought her in a few shillings a week, enough for her clothes and personal expenses, and after her talk with the doctor she had

271

determined to realize sufficient of her small capital to give Mavis three months at Bournemouth. Aunt Maggie had a friend there, a trained nurse, who kept a boarding-house for delicate people, many of whom came there in winter, and Aunt Maggie had written to this friend and arrangements had been made to place Mavis under her care.

'I hate taking her money from her,' he said, 'it's robbing the widow of her mite; but what can I do? I've been able to save nothing. Though, in any case, Mavis would have gone there. She's going to have the best possible treatment, if I have to borrow the money from a moneylender. I've often been tempted to borrow from one in the past and may come to it yet. One day you'll read in the newspaper, 'Young man in moneylender's clutches!' and you'll find you know that young man. Oh, Laura, you don't know, you will never know, what I have gone through. I've been like someone trying to climb up out of a pit who, every time he came near the top, was knocked on the head and fell back to the bottom again. And so it will always be with me. I can never marry, you know that, don't you, Laura?'

Laura stiffened inwardly. Some mean little spirit said in her heart, 'Good Heavens! surely he doesn't think I want him to marry me!' but another voice which was also her own told her it was no time for silly pride, and she said, as lightly as she was able, 'But you don't want to marry anyone, do you? And perhaps by the time you do you'll have made a fortune.'

Pacing to and fro, enclosed in the fog, Richard opened his heart to Laura as never before. He spoke of their happy home life when Mavis and he were children; of how fine and generous a man his father had been; his mother, how gay and charming; of their seaside holidays, their Christmas parties, and of all the other pleasures he had shared with his little sister. Then of the sudden blow which had put an end to his happy, carefree youth and brought him, all unprepared, face to face with a man's responsibilities. He said the few friends who had rallied round them in their trouble, business friends of his father and their wives, had told him he was wonderful, that very few youths of his age could have acted as he did; but he himself had known all the time that, far from being wonderful, he was but a poor sort of creature. He had sometimes cried into his pillow at night, 'blubbered' was the word he used; 'I blubbered like a kid when an unexpected bill came in, or a letter came from mother saying she hated her new treatment; or, if nothing of that kind had happened, I lay sweating with fear lest the next day should bring some demand upon me to which I was unequal. Mavis never knew this, no one knew it, I always managed somehow to keep up my spirits before others, and Mavis herself was truly wonderful, you should have seen her down on her knees scrubbing the scullery, or counting the pennies left in her purse when she had been shopping, without a word of complaint – did I say without complaint? So far from it that she would make fun out of what must have been hardships. Oh, my poor Mavis!'

Laura told him, as any other comforter would, that he was feeling so discouraged because this latest trial had followed so many other trials and followed them when, at last, they had seemed at an end. He must try to take this new trouble separately. Mavis would recover, of course she would; indeed, the doctor had not found anything definitely wrong with her: he had advised that she should winter in a warmer climate merely as a precaution. Mavis had wonderful spirit, he had just said so himself, and Laura knew it, too. In the mild, pine-scented air of Bournemouth she would soon throw off her cough and grow stronger, and in six months' time he would look back on his fears of tonight as part of a nightmare.

When he had become more cheerful and hopeful they parted, for he had at last agreed to Laura's suggestion that he should leave her at the crossroads and take a shorter and more direct way to the railway station than the one through Heatherley. By doing so he would catch the ten-thirty train and so secure some of the rest he needed before going to his work in the morning.

Still enveloped in the fog, they stood beneath the signpost, her hand in his hand. All had been said that could be said and their few moments' silence was filled by the sound of water dripping, *drip*, *drip*, from the boughs, and the humming of

273

telegraph wires. Then, to relieve the tension, Laura said, without much thought, 'I suppose it will be some time before I see you again?' and he answered, very sadly, 'I'm afraid it will, Laura. There will be no holidays for me, not even weekends, until Mavis is better.'

They parted and she stood for a few seconds listening to his retreating footsteps. Then the sound ceased for a moment; he turned and came back at a running pace, but all he had to say when he reached her under the signpost was a last 'Good-bye, Laura'.

Mavis went home from Bournemouth apparently restored to her usual health. Her post in the City had been filled during her absence and she found one, less exacting, as secretary to a lady in Surrey. It was such a post as is seldom found in real life, with light work in luxurious surroundings. Her employer was an unmarried woman, a writer of stories for children, who, living alone, except for a houseful of servants, wanted a secretary who would also be a companion. Mavis was taken for carriage drives and had the run of a beautiful garden and well-stocked library and had plenty of leisure to enjoy them. The one disadvantage of her position was that she had no regular, specified whole days off and could seldom go home; but even for this there was promised compensation in the way of long holidays whenever her employer was travelling abroad. The time for that had gone for that year, but she had one week at home during the summer and, for the weekend, came with Richard to Heatherley. That time theirs was a farewell visit, for Laura was leaving Heatherley to take up a post fifty miles farther from London. They would have no more weekends together, but Richard and Mavis planned to spend some part of their future summer holidays near Laura's new abode.

As it turned out, the three friends never met again. Mavis's cure had not been complete and she spent the next winter at one of the new sanatoriums. While she was there Laura heard from her often and her letters were teeming with fun and fancy and brimming with affection. She still would not believe that there was anything serious the matter with her and declared that she was getting all this attention, 'petting' she called it, under false pretences. Laura had also letters from Richard. His were not so gay as those of Mavis, though he was no longer as despondent as he had been at the onset of her illness.

Mavis again recovered and went back to her post in Surrey, and Laura heard with delight that her kind employer had promised to take her with her to winter in Rome. Later, there were letters and picture postcards from Italy, and once, a long flat basket of glorious spring flowers came by post from the French Riviera.

Then, gradually, the letters which passed between Laura and her two friends grew fewer and farther apart. Time and distance are great separators, especially when, as in this case, they are aided by circumstances. Laura still wrote to and heard from Richard occasionally up to the time of her marriage, when the correspondence ceased. But though separated from her friends and plunged deep into the absorption of living her own life, Laura never forgot or ceased to be grateful to them for the happiness they had once brought into her life, and the time she had spent in their company came to signify to her in retrospect the high-water mark of her youth.

What happened to Mavis she never knew. It is to be feared that that bright, high-spirited young life was not a long one. Of Richard she did hear once more. Many years after he and Mavis had passed out of her life, Laura's youngest son, then an engineering apprentice, passed to her over the supper-table one of his technical journals for her to look at the illustration of a new liner which had just been launched, and there, on turning the page, she read an account of a presentation to Richard on his retirement from the service of the cable company.

A portrait of the once familiar face looked up at her from the page. It was that of a prosperous, kindly-looking middle-aged man, clean-shaven and a little inclined to plumpness; but the eyes which gazed straight out of the portrait at the beholder were Richard's eyes, keen, steadfast, and slyly humorous, and the smile on the lips was Richard's old smile.

According to the letterpress which accompanied the portrait

he had had a distinguished career. He had been on the company's business for some years in China, and other sojourns of his in the Far East were mentioned. He appeared to be still unmarried, for there was no mention of a Mrs Richard Brownlow, and the farewell gift of his colleagues, instead of taking the form of a piece of plate for domestic use, was a portfolio of old prints, of which, it was stated, he already possessed a notable collection. Mention was made of the cottage on the east coast where it was hoped he would spend many years of well-earned retirement, 'with his books, antique furniture, and old prints about him'. A wish that found an echo in one reader's heart, mingled with some regret that their ways in life had been so far asunder.

IX. *The Village in Wartime*

The outbreak of the Boer War was a stirring event to a people who for two generations had been involved only in minor warfare with those described by Kipling as 'lesser breeds without the Law'. The elderly, of course, remembered the Crimean War. Veterans of that war still came to cottage doors, hawking bootlaces, or were seen pushing barrel organs about the streets. Others, with pensions, had settled in neat little cottages and were still fighting their battles over again in fancy upon benches they shared with other elders on village greens, or by alehouse fires. Laura herself knew several of these, and she also knew a quiet little white-haired old lady who had been one of Miss Nightingale's nurses. But that war had been over long before the majority of those living at the end of the century had been born, and to those of the younger generation it was as much a matter of history as the Battle of Hastings.

When the new, exciting conflict broke out in South Africa it was welcomed with flag-waving and other rejoicings. For some time stories had been appearing in the newspapers of diamond merchants and other business men of British nationality being insulted and, in some cases, suffering personal violence at the hands of the original settlers on the Rand. 'The cheek of it! The confounded cheek of it! It's as good as an insult to the British flag. We shall have to give these Boers a lesson, that's certain!' People living in sequestered English villages who had hitherto scarcely known of the existence of such a people suddenly acquired an intimate knowledge of the nature and habits of the Boers. They were filthy in their persons, addicted to brandy, shared their wives with any chance comer, let their hair and beards grow longer than was decent, and, above all, were wily. Their President Kruger, more familiarly known as Oom Paul, was pictured in newspaper cartoons as a huge, hideous old man brandishing a Bible in one hand and in the other a brandy-bottle. That such a nation with such a president should dare to defy our Government made the ordinary Englishman's blood boil. 'We've got to have a slap at them if only to put them in their place,' was the general conclusion, often expressed with the rider, 'The pity of it is that they'll cave in before our troops have time to get there.'

Others, who from superior education and more exact information as to the events which had led up to the climax were better qualified to judge, rejoiced that, after long years of lethargy, our country was once more about to assert her authority as one of the greatest, some said *the* greatest, of world powers. We had been too modest, too lenient, they said, and see what had come of it; now, once for all, we must give such small upstarts a lesson. That done, no other small community would ever dare to endanger the peace of the world. It was really a war to prevent future wars.

There were, it is true, a few who maintained that the Boers were an honest, hardworking race of farmers who had as much right as those belonging to larger nations to manage their own affairs in their own way; and though doubtless they had been misled by their leaders in the present instance, they did not deserve half the obloquy which was being heaped upon them. These persons were known as pro-Boers and were most unpopular. The windows of their houses were smashed by stones after dark, boys called rude names after them in the streets and burned their effigies in bonfires. Down at Hayling Island the shrubs and flowers in Mr Stead's garden were uprooted and his garden roller was run out to sea. But, apart from such petty acts of mob violence, the pro-Boers were left severely alone. There was no 18B. They were at liberty to express their opinions in public, as in private, if they could find listeners. Heatherley had its pro-Boer in the person of Mr Hertford's brother, who proclaimed his principles by growing a beard and wearing a wideawake hat, similar to those worn by the Boers in pictures. The only effect of his unpopular attitude was a mild sending to Coventry. Nobody who was not obliged to do so on business spoke to him in the street or visited him at his home; but, as one half of the villagers were employed by him and the other half employed him, this was scarcely noticeable. Neither those who looked to him for their weekly wages, nor those who had pipes liable to freeze and roof tiles which might need replacing at short notice, could afford to ignore him. Mr Hertford himself, rather surprisingly, had come out as an ardent supporter of the war, so the two brothers had plenty to argue about at their evening sessions.

The section of the general public with which Laura came most into contact were wholehearted supporters of the war. Few, indeed, expected it to affect them in any way personally. No young wife looked at her husband and no mother at her big schoolboy son with the unspoken prayer that the war might be over before their turn came to take part in it, for there was no conscription and no talk of conscription and it was supposed that, like previous wars, it would be fought to a finish by the standing Army. When, afterwards, volunteers were called for, the number required was comparatively small. All ordinary men had to do was to pay their taxes while their womenfolk rolled bandages, made shirts, and knitted socks for 'the Tommies', as the private soldiers were called. Men, women, and children alike waved flags, sang patriotic songs, and cheered the soldiers on to victory.

'Tommy', or 'Tommy Atkins', after years of being regarded as the dregs of society, suddenly became a hero. When the early contingents of the 'fifty thousand horse and men' set out for Table Bay, crowds lined the streets to see them march past. Tommy was dragged from the ranks to be kissed by strange girls, gifts of sweets and tobacco were showered upon him, and he was given the addresses of complete strangers wishing to boast the distinction of receiving a letter from the Front. Other crowds lined the quays to wave and cheer as his transport moved out to the strains of *The Soldiers of the Queen*, *Dolly Gray*, or *The Girl I Left Behind Me*.

Tons of white enamel buttons with portraits of the popular generals printed in colours were sold in the shops and worn as brooches or lapel ornaments. With the older people Lord Roberts led as first favourite; the younger generation favoured Baden-Powell, and Generals Buller and Kitchener had their supporters. Children let loose from school ran about shouting:

> Lord Roberts and Kitchener,
> Baden-Powell and White,
> All dressed in khaki, all going to fight,
> When we catch Kruger how happy we'll be,
> We'll have a tug at his whiskers and have a Jubilee.

That dashing new colour, the khaki of the soldiers' field uniforms, became the rage for womens' coats and costumes. Red, white, and blue striped bands were used to bring the somewhat outmoded sailor hat up to date. Concerts and other entertainments were got up, the proceeds to benefit the troops, and altogether, as one of the girls said, the time was thrilling. Women of all ages knitted comforts for the soldiers. Many had first to learn to knit, for knitted garments had long been out of fashion and the old, homely craft of knitting was almost a lost art. But all went to it with a will, and cargoes of khaki socks, scarves, kneecaps, and Balaclava helmets were soon being despatched to the Front. Later on, soldiers invalided home reported that in some places the veldt was strewn for miles with these votive offerings which, though kindly meant, were less in demand in the South African climate than they had been in the frozen trenches before Sebastopol. The workers then concentrated on knitting socks and making shirts, which were more in demand. Laura's contribution to this movement was a long, wide scarf of scarlet wool, knitted on wooden needles, which she worked on behind the post-office counter. The colour of the wool was not her own choice, it had been provided by some organization, and she had to repeat this many times to callers who had remarked that it would make a good mark 'for one of these here snipers'. It was her first piece of knitting since she had left off wearing homeknit wool stockings in the winter and she grew very tired of it before it was finished. Had anyone then told her how many miles of knitting she would do in her lifetime and what a great solace it would become to her she would not have believed them.

Another wartime occupation was making flags for decoration. Every victory, even the smallest, was celebrated at home. Every house put out at least one flag, the streets were festooned with bunting, and the village or town brass band was called out to play patriotic airs. The stock of flags on the market was soon exhausted and homemade flags had somehow to be contrived from lengths of red, white, and blue sateen. There was soon a shortage of material in those colours, and those fortunate enough to secure material for their flag or flags still had another difficulty to contend with, how to shape their work and blend the three colours to avoid solecism. On one occasion the rumour went round that a certain householder was flying the French flag. France was then regarded in this country as a potential enemy and those who were told that the French flag was floating over their village street were so horrified at the idea that several of them went to the house to expostulate with the offender. They found the report was true; the tricolour was indeed floating from the bedroom window of a respected old dressmaker who had never before been suspected of French sympathies. But it was hauled in with great haste when its maker was made aware of the enormity she had unwittingly perpetrated. 'You'll be flying the Boer flag next, if you're not careful,' she was told by a friendly critic.

As well as the victories there were reverses for our troops. Many and unlooked-for reverses, Laura learned afterwards, in the early months of the war. In this country at large, in better informed circles, one week of bad news which caused general depression was known as the Black Week. The intellectuals living in the neighbourhood no doubt shared this anxiety, but no depression was felt by the ordinary villagers; their confidence in our troops and their leaders never wavered for a moment. If the report of some set-back appeared in the newspapers, it was speedily explained as a 'dodge' of 'Bobs', or Buller, or White to deceive the enemy. Of the prolonged siege of Mafeking Laura heard one man say: 'Our troops'll break out when they're ready, you'll see. Baden-Powell's only keeping 'em shut up to draw on them old Boers.'

The calling-up of the Yeomanry and the forming of various volunteer regiments brought the war a little nearer home, though the number of families affected was still very small in proportion to the population. The majority of the volunteers were young, unattached men; farmers' sons and others who could already ride and shoot were supposed to be the most desirable recruits. But clerks and shopmen in towns also crowded the recruiting offices and at one time there were many of these stranded at Aldershot, unable to begin their training until horses could be procured. 'My God,' said one of these to Laura, 'the bally old war'll be over before we even embark', and he looked so romantic in his new khaki uniform and smart slouch hat, turned rakishly up at one side, that Laura felt almost as sorry for him as he did for himself. But he and his comrade yeomen had ample time in which to get there and to see some hard fighting, for the war lasted three years, and soon the first question on meeting a friend was, 'Have you anyone out at the Front?' The few, it was still but a few, who could answer 'Yes', answered proudly.

With the appearance of the smarter looking Yeomen and C.I.V.s [City Imperial Volunteers] poor Tommy Atkins suffered an eclipse in popular esteem. In the country towns which had a Yeomanry Headquarters even the yeomen who had enlisted only for home defence were treated as heroes. Laura had one amusing little experience of this. In one of the war years, during her holidays, she went for a weekend to visit some friends living in a small Bedfordshire town and on the Sunday evening was taken to the railway station to witness the return from camp of the local Yeomanry troop.

What was, for such a small town, a huge crowd had gathered in the street leading to the railway station, not only of townspeople, but also many from neighbouring villages, and there was shouting and cheering and waving of hats and handkerchiefs when the train steamed in. The road was so choked with sightseers that it was only with difficulty that a stretcher-bearing party could force its way from the station entrance to a waiting ambulance; especially as, on the appearance of the stretcher, the crowd rushed forward in great excitement. 'Good old Sergeant! Good old Sergeant!' was the cry, 'Glad to see you safe home again, old fellow!' Then someone suggested, 'Let's give him three times three,' and the three times three was given and many times repeated.

Laura concluded that the prostrate warrior waving his hand weakly over the side of the stretcher had been invalided home from the Front, probably after distinguished service; but, afterwards, when hoping for some story of heroism she inquired into the matter, she was told that the invalid was just an ordinary Home Defence man who had been ill in camp – with pork poisoning.

For the first few months of the war a small crowd gathered on Sunday mornings outside the post office to read and comment upon the bulletin of war news posted in the window, and 'Any news?' was a frequent question at the post-office counter on other days. A few of the more prominent residents had private bulletins of war news telegraphed to them from London nightly, but the contents of these, like other telegraphic communications, were inviolable, and Laura, in possession of the very latest news, found these questions embarrassing until she invented the formula, 'No *official* news', which satisfied everyone.

In those pre-broadcasting days many well-to-do country dwellers had the late news of any happening which stirred public interest telegraphed to them. Election results, the verdict in murder trials, closing prices on the Stock Exchange and other such matters. During the Rheims court-martial of Captain Dreyfus a priest – judging by his appearance a Catholic priest, and by his accent, a Frenchman – called every evening for a telegram addressed to him at the post office. Often his telegram would not have arrived and he would wait, sometimes for the better part of an hour, pacing to and fro on the pavement outside the door, or standing, a dark figure in the background, while others came and went about their business at the counter. No-one who came in appeared to know him or even to notice his presence and Laura had not seen him before and never saw him afterwards; but she never forgot his face and expression when, one evening towards the end of the trial, she noticed that the hand he held out for his telegram was trembling and that beads of perspiration stood upon his brow. She often wondered afterwards who he was, where he came from, and if he had any personal connection with those involved.

When known names began to appear in the casualty lists and men who had suffered from that scourge of the war, enteric fever, were invalided home, pale and emaciated, those who had friends or relatives serving overseas began to realize the grim reality of the war. Among those whose own lives were unaffected enthusiasm declined. There was no food shortage or rationing or billeting of troops to remind people that there was a war on, and of course there were no evacuees, for no part of the homeland was threatened. Between the Relief of Ladysmith and that of Mafeking ordinary country people appeared to forget the war, or, if they thought or spoke of it, it was as something dragging on, far away in a foreign country, not as any great concern of their own.

Laura sometimes almost envied those people their detachment. She had had almost from the beginning 'someone out at the Front'. Her brother Edmund, next in age to herself in her family and her childhood's playmate and closest friend, had, at the outbreak of war, been staying with some relatives in Yorkshire. He had enlisted at once as a regular soldier in the West Yorks Regiment and at barely nineteen years of age went overseas as one of a draft. Laura said goodbye to him on a snowy Sunday morning at Aldershot railway station. The train by which she had to travel back to Heatherley was an hour late, for the war and the snow together had upset the timetable, and they walked together up and down the cold platform, talking: she with the forced cheerfulness which marks all such partings; he, flushed with excitement and his blue eyes glowing with enthusiasm as he tried to impress upon her his great good luck in getting out with the draft.

He went gaily, for to him, nurtured as his spirit had been on the tales of old romance and chivalry they had devoured together as children, war was one of the greatest possible human adventures; one which he had never thought to see in his lifetime, but one in which now, as it seemed miraculously, he was to take part. But Laura was full of fears and misgivings. He looked so young, and as she thought, tender, with his slight, boyish figure encased in ill-fitting wartime khaki, and she dreaded for him the hardships as well as the dangers of war.

They were practically alone on the platform, for the other passengers had crowded into the warmer waiting-rooms, and Edmund, after remarking on this, began to repeat one of their old favourite passages from Scott's poems. It was the Death of Marmion. Laura had loved that passage in childhood, but she loved it no longer. The very sound of the word 'death' made her heart feel cold as stone. But she managed to smile until the train pulled out and from the carriage window she had waved a long farewell to Edmund. Her last view was of him standing erect at the end of the platform, his hand raised to his forehead in a military salute. In the railway carriage she found other women and girls who had been to Aldershot on similar errands, and her silent tears were unnoticed in the general weeping and comparing of experiences.

There followed for her days of anxiety and nights when she would lie awake picturing Edmund alone and wounded on the veldt. She never once imagined him dead, but always wounded and alone beneath the strange, bright stars he had written of in his letters. Actually, he came through his three years' service in South Africa without any serious injury, his destiny being to die in 1916 on a more fiercely contested battlefield. Once during his South African service he was taken prisoner while scouting and carried off by a party of Boer horsemen who at last, finding him an encumbrance, stripped him of all but trousers and shirt and abandoned him on the open veldt.

They had carried him miles into wild, desolate country on which the fierce sun poured down by day and the night air chilled to the bone. One of the horsemen, as they were riding off, had turned in the saddle and flung back to Edmund his water-bottle, but there was little water in it and he had no food. After many turnings and twistings, for he had little sense of direction, he did at last reach an English camp, steering by the sun by day and the stars by night. On the way he had but one adventure. His own store of water was soon exhausted; it was a waterless country and he was suffering agonies of thirst when, on the third day, he came to a Boer homestead, the first human habitation he had seen. No human being or domestic animal was in sight; there was no smoke from a fire, the only window he could see was boarded over, and he thought the place was deserted. But he could not be sure of that, and said afterwards that he loitered for what seemed hours in the vicinity, lurking behind tussocks and patches of scrub, afraid to approach the dwelling lest the men of the house should be hiding there. In his weak state he would easily have been overpowered, and yet he was so drawn towards the house by the pangs of thirst and the certainty that water must be there, that he found himself insensibly edging nearer.

Presently a Boer woman, coming round the corner of the house from the back, came face to face with him. She was old and stout and unkempt, the very image of old Nancy Baines, he said, naming an old woman at home; and like Nancy, she had a pleasant, good-natured expression. When she realized that the ragged, half-naked stranger was an enemy soldier, she naturally looked startled. But she did not spit at him or shout abuse, as the Boer women were said to do to their helpless and unarmed prisoners of war, and when he pointed to his baked lips and held out his water-bottle, she took the bottle and filled it. Not one word passed between them, for neither knew the language of the other, but human compassion and human gratitude can be expressed without words.

When Edmund, on reaching an English camp, told others of this incident, to which, as he thought, he owed his life, he was told that the woman was probably alone in the house. The Boers left their old people to shift for themselves when they flitted, and being alone, she was of course afraid to offend one who might prove troublesome. But Edmund himself did not accept that explanation. He firmly believed that the woman had acted from pure human kindness.

*　　*　　*

After his South African service Edmund's regiment was sent direct to India, where he served a further five years before returning to this country. Then, after a year or two at home, he emigrated to Canada. He had been on the eve of emigrating there when the war broke out and he had enlisted. Had not the war and his long foreign service intervened he would have begun life in his new country as a boy of eighteen with the vigour and adaptability of youth; when he actually went it was as a man of thirty who had seen something of the world and who, had it been possible, would have preferred to settle down at home. He still loved the land and wished for nothing better than to spend the rest of his life working on it; but to farm on his own account without capital was impracticable, and the wage of a farm labourer at that time was not a living wage. Being unmarried, he had managed to live fairly comfortably at home on his earnings during the interval, but even he, the least ambitious of men in a worldly sense, had realized at last that, if he was to live a full life, he must go further.

Laura had married early in the century and her new home was

a hundred miles from that of their childhood; she had her house and a young family to care for, and during all those years she saw her brother but once. That was when she spent a few days with her children at her old home a fortnight before Edmund emigrated. During the short time they spent together Laura was much taken up with the care of her children, Edmund was working on a farm and did not return till evening, and they had but one walk and confidential talk together. Then they had been, late in the evening, to see a younger sister off by train from the nearest town. It was September, a moist, dark night of soft winds blowing over the stubble of the stripped fields, and they took their return walk of three miles easily, once talking themselves to a standstill by the roadside pond into which Laura had fallen through the ice when a child. As they stood there, talking of this and that, of their childhood days and some of the queer old characters they had known; of Edmund's travels (York Minster and the Taj Mahal were the sights which had most impressed him), and of Laura's home and children – somewhere, a field or two away in the darkness, a man's voice was suddenly uplifted in song.

'Old Buffy,' said Edmund, 'going home by the fieldpath and singing to keep up his spirits in the dark.' The old country songs were no longer heard there and the one old Buffy was singing was but a popular music-hall song of the moment, but he had a pleasant voice and the soft, warm darkness lent enchantment. The brother and sister stood, listening and savouring the good earthy smells of the fields. Then, as they turned to go, Edmund said, waving his arm to include the fields and trees and hedgerows they both knew so intimately, 'I've seen a good bit of the world, but I've seen nothing I liked better than this. It takes some beating. Yes, it takes some beating.' Laura said, 'Yes, I know how you feel. Other places are richer and finer and more exciting to see, but to us, this is somehow more satisfying – more real – more solid – it has the goodness of bread.'

Edmund liked his new life in a new country and his friends thought he had settled there for life; but a year or two later he was back in England, again a soldier, and on his way to his last war. He had one short home leave early in 1916, but at the time Laura's children were down with whooping cough and she was unable to go to their old home to see him. Although it was March the weather was wintry, snow lay over the whole country, and the night Edmund set out on his return journey to the trenches in France the Oxfordshire roads were barely passable. But when duty calls a soldier must obey and Edmund shouldered his pack and rifle and went down the old path from his mother's cottage, 'loaded up like a horse', as she said afterwards.

He had no-one of his own kin young enough or strong enough to accompany him to the railway station, but a kind neighbour volunteered to see him off and to help him on the way with his baggage. He stayed with him till near midnight at the station, waiting for the overdue train; then, having the long tramp back through the snow before him and fearing his wife might be anxious, he wished Edmund goodbye and good luck and left him alone in the fireless waiting-room. The train, as it turned out, was not running, the line was blocked with snow and the night of that freezing vigil was the last the soldier was ever to spend in his own beloved country. Three weeks later he was killed in action.

The morning on which Laura heard of his death was one of glorious April sunshine. Larks were singing above her sub-urban garden and she noticed as she shook out the crumbs from the breakfast-cloth that the lilac was budding. Her children had recovered from their illness and she was rejoicing that her troubles were over and that summer was coming, when the letter arrived. It was one of her own letters to Edmund, returned to her, marked in pencil, 'Killed in Action', the first intimation of his death because the official letter which should have told of it had been mis-directed.

Returned to her with her letter was a broadsheet copy she had sent enclosed in it of Wordsworth's *Happy Warrior*, and she came to feel in later life that in the matter of his death Edmund was indeed happy, for he was a soldier by his own choice and he died a soldier's death on the battlefield. Unlike some who fall in warfare, he had not to relinquish life before he had well tasted it, and unlike others, he left behind him no brood of young children to face the world fatherless. He went the way of the old heroes of his childhood, in the prime of his manhood, fighting for a cause he wholeheartedly believed in, and went swiftly and suddenly in the heat of a battle, a happy warrior.

*   *   *

The Boer War ended, again there were scenes of rejoicing, but rejoicings of a quieter and more sober kind than the outbreak of almost delirious joy which had distinguished Mafeking night. For the war had proved more serious and lasted longer than people had anticipated. It had brought anxiety and bereavement to some families and, to all, a depression of spirits, changes in the way of living, increased taxation, the rise in prices inseparable from war. When at last the long-drawn-out struggle ended in victory for our troops there was heartfelt rejoicing, but it was a rejoicing best expressed by the frequently heard exclamation, 'Thank God it's over!'

At Heatherley, when the news came through, flags were flown, people wore red, white, and blue rosettes in their buttonholes, cheers were heard in the streets and the public houses did a brisker business than usual; but beneath this surface gaiety people were more thoughtful than they had been at the outbreak of war. A local landowner with a fine estate had lost both his heir and his only other son, and from two or three humbler homes in the district one member of the family had gone overseas in the flower of his youth to return no more. Life, people told each other, would never be quite the same again. Of course there would be no more war in their lifetime. For one thing, this war had been a lesson to the world, and for another, in future not many nations would be inclined to face the cost of a war. Look at the cost of the one now ended, thousands of pounds a day! And how prices had risen, all due to the war, it was said; though why eggs laid and eaten in the same parish should go up threepence a dozen was a mystery that most speakers declared was beyond them.

Fortunately it was also beyond them to see into the future or to know that the war so recently ended was but as the first faint tremor presaging an earthquake.

x. *The New Century*

The old century waned. 'It came in with wars and it's going out with a war,' people reminded each other, not pessimistically but hopefully, for there was a general idea that the war then in progress would be the last war. If not peace over the whole earth, it was confidently expected that there would be permanent peace wherever British influence extended.

And the new century would bring other blessings. The old century had been a marvellous one. Look at the new inventions! Look at the progress! they said as they counted their blessings – railway travelling, the telephone and the telegraph, even the humble bicycle. And the march of civilization, the putting down of the slave trade, free State education for children, the reform of prisons and criminal laws, the advance in science and medicine. Why, at the beginning of the century they hadn't any chloroform even, and people had to lie and look on while their legs were sawn off! In the year 1800 a child of ten or twelve might be hanged for stealing a few apples, and until well into the century even younger children were working in factories and in dark underground mines. The nineteenth century had altered all that; it remained to be seen what new and astonishing developments the twentieth would unfold.

That the developments would proceed along much the same lines nobody doubted. The newspapers foretold that our exports, already stupendous, would continue to increase and that higher wages and a better standard of living for the masses would follow; that there would be new and still more marvellous mechanical inventions which would relieve man of the necessity of working more than two or three hours a day. As well as these material advantages, it was hinted that a new era of human happiness was at hand. People were going to live longer and healthier lives, science would see to that, and extended leisure would provide an opportunity for mental and spiritual cultivation. That a new century would bring a new and better way of living was taken for granted.

People began to look forward to the exact moment when the change would begin. Did the old century end with the year 1899, or with 1900? There was a good deal of controversy on that point, and although the authorities decided that not until midnight on December 31st 1900 would the new and better time begin, general opinion inclined to the earlier date. Both New Year's Eves were kept by their respective supporters with more than ordinary festivity. Children of families, down to the youngest who could be supposed to comprehend the importance of the occasion, were allowed to stay up to see in the new century, for, as their parents told them, even they, young as they were, could not hope to see another such New Year's Day.

The first notable event of the new century was a sad one. In January 1901 it became known that the revered, beloved old Queen Victoria was failing in health, and on the twenty-second of that month she died. The nation was touched to the heart. People of mature age went about with tears in their eyes, saying, 'Our poor old Queen! We shall never see her like on the throne of this country again!' On the gloomy January morning when the news of her death reached Heatherley many who had never before made any show of their loyalty mourned for the queen sincerely. Early in the day a poor working man, a fish hawker, came into the post office. 'This is sad news about our queen,' he said, and astonishingly, there were tears in his eyes. 'What's Hecuba to him, or he to Hecuba, that he should weep for her?' asked Laura, as the door closed behind him, and then felt ashamed of her levity when she saw that Alma's big blue eyes were brimming over. For a day or two there were many such incidents, not always, not often tearful, but always expressive of sincere personal sorrow. Faces were sad and voices grew tender as callers spoke of the nation's great loss and retold the many little stories current which illustrated the goodness of nature of her whom they spoke of as Victoria the Good, the Mother of her People.

Then the new king. When the war had begun there had been a queen on the throne; when it ended, as it must soon end, there would be a king. This perfectly natural circumstance had for many people an almost mystical significance. Kings had hitherto, to the vast majority of those then living in this country, been but names in history, part of the romance of past ages; and now to have a living king, and another Edward, on the throne was an exciting experience. And, all in good time, there would be a coronation. That was an event very few then living could remember, but upon which all could speculate.

But now, first of all, there was mourning for the queen to be contrived, for the whole nation went into mourning dress, probably for the last time in history. Women of means ordered new all-black outfits; those whose means did not permit this expense ransacked their wardrobes for something black to wear, a less vain quest than it would be now, since in those days mourning was worn for quite distant relatives and most women had by them relics of the last funeral they had attended. The very poor looked to their patrons for discarded black garments, or failing these, home-dyed their own clothes or sewed on to them bows of black crêpe. Only the gipsies, of whom there were many living on the heaths around Heatherley, were seen wearing bright colours. They were indeed more colourful than usual in their dress, for they reaped a rich harvest in cast-offs of the sudden unfashionable red, blue, and green shades which the original possessors decided it was no good keeping, as the styles would be hopelessly out of date before their new black was discarded.

For the first three months after the death of the queen only the attire of the gipsies provided a splash of colour in the gloom; then, as the days lengthened and brightened, black and white mixtures and soft tones of mauve and grey began to appear. Finally, women's dress that year went purple. Wine, plum, pansy, heather, and lavender shades were in great demand. Traders sent their goods still in the piece and capable of taking such shades to the dye-vats, but a great stock of piece-goods as well as made-up garments acquired before the general mourning was left on their hands, and many of them went bankrupt. It was probably due to the representations of the traders, as well as to her own kind thoughtfulness, that, when King Edward died, Queen Alexandra issued a communication asking the women of the nation not to go to the unnecessary expense of buying new mourning. A black tie or a black sleeveband for men and a black hat or scarf for women would, she said, be a sufficient outward sign of the sincere grief which she knew the loyal, affectionate hearts of his subjects felt for the loss of their beloved king.

The general public deferred to her wish; the more readily because, by the end of the first decade of the century, private and family mourning had become greatly modified. It was becoming rarer every year to see in the streets a man whose all-black suit, deep crêpe hatband and black kid gloves proclaimed a recent bereavement, or a woman enveloped in crêpe, from the deep band of that fabric on the bottom of her black skirt to the crêpe bows and crêpe flowers on her headgear. Black-bordered pocket-handkerchiefs were less in demand than they had been, and although black-bordered stationery was still in use the black border had narrowed considerably. Laura could remember the time when some mourning envelopes were so heavily bordered with black that only a square of white about the size of a visiting card was left in the middle for the address. Jet ornaments for mourning had also disappeared. Relatives of those whose death (with address) had been announced in the newspapers no longer received by post, from too-enterprising vendors, little boxes containing jet brooches and buckles and lockets and chains with the request that they would kindly choose what they required and remit the cost, plus postage. The only survival from the old-time deep mourning was the widow's bonnet, a close-fitting affair with a soft white ruche to frame the face and long crêpe streamers behind; and that, some unkind people said, only remained in favour because it was extraordinarily becoming to most women.

293

When Queen Victoria died the war was still in progress, and when in 1902 peace was declared, great regret was expressed that she had not lived to see that day. 'It do seem hard she's not here to see the troops come home,' said one of her humbler subjects; "my troops" she used always to call 'em, always *my* troops, and she used to grieve over the casualty lists as if every one of the fallen had been her own child. Not that she was ever daunted, mind you; no, never, not even when things were not going too well. "I've got perfect confidence in my troops", she'd tell her ladies, and so she had, bless her! If she'd been young and a man she'd have been out there herself at the head of 'em. Ah, she was a fine-spirited one, was our dear old queen!'

Stories were told of Queen Victoria and simple people continued to revere her memory right up to the outbreak of the world war in 1914. Then, after that great upheaval had subsided, her figure became obscured in the miasma of so-called Victorianism. Recently she has become to many of the younger generation the Queen Victoria of the film with that title. A few months ago Laura went into a small second-hand furniture shop to purchase a copy she had seen in the window of Nicholson's drawing of the Queen, and found in the course of conversation with the young girl who attended to her that she had not recognized the subject of the picture. When told that it was Queen Victoria, she said, 'Oh, is it?' then, after examining critically the aged figure which, with no outer trappings of royalty, was yet unmistakably royal, she said, 'It's not a patch on what she was like in the film.'

When Queen Victoria died film entertainments in this country were in an experimental, tentative stage. No-one as yet dreamed that the cinematograph, as it was still called in full, would ever become overwhelmingly popular. There were so far no palatial buildings devoted entirely to film entertainments, one film was shown here and there, between music-hall turns or in the course of other entertainments. Laura saw her first film at Halstead, Essex, in 1898. It was billed as a 'Moving picture' and was entitled 'Night and Morning', or 'Morning and Night', the morning scene being of a wedding party coming out of church and the night scene was one of the bride performing a kind of a strip-tease act in a bedroom while the bridegroom peered round the edge of a screen, the whole moving in a flickering jig which dazzled the eyes of the beholders. During or immediately after the exhibition an elderly man stood up in the body of the hall to protest that the subject was not a seemly one 'with ladies present'. By the rest of the audience the film was accepted as a novelty, a freak turn. 'It's a bit of a puzzle how they make the figures move,' was the general comment upon it afterwards. No one then present dreamed that they had witnessed the first stumbling steps of a young art which was to become the most popular and the most remunerative of all arts in the twentieth century.

After the Boer War ended prosperity returned, and for a few years it seemed that the long-looked-for new era had begun. In society circles gaiety reigned. Accounts of opera nights, fancy-dress balls, dinners and garden parties, with lists of names of the distinguished persons present and a full description of the women's dresses and jewels, filled whole columns of the popular newspapers. About that time there were several divorce cases in high life and of these full unbowdlerized reports appeared in print, to the delight, if not the edification, of the average reader. For such news the appetite of the great public appeared to be insatiable in the days before fiction, as depicted on the films, made real life appear insipid. Picture postcards of society and stage beauties also helped to fill the void.

Before great houses in the West End when crimson carpets were laid from front door to curb and strains of dance music floated from brilliantly lighted interiors, a knot of women and girls would gather, like moths round a candle, to watch the arrival of the guests. 'O-ooh! isn't she lovely!' 'Isn't he handsome!' 'Did you see her pearls? and her white velvet cloak trimmed with swansdown?' 'What price that old dowager with the tiara?' 'How'd you fancy yourself in an ermine cape, Nell?' they would ask each other unenviously, tapping their feet on the pavement the while to the strains of *The Blue Danube*. The outdoor spectators would tire and go home. Most of them had to be up early to go to work the next morning. But the dance would go on until after sunrise, when the early milkman would thread with his barrow between departing carriages.

Dirt, squalor, crime, and disease lurked, as it were, just round the corner, for the London slums were very much worse than they are today. From homes only a street or two distant from some of those mansions children went barefoot, dirty, ragged, and hungry to school. Women in those terrible tenements sank into an aimless, effortless apathy, or made matters still worse than they would have been by taking to gin-drinking. Men were in and out of prison as a regular feature of their lives. The few individuals who stood firm and preserved their self-respect in such an environment did so by such an effort that they became aged and broken in health while they should still have been in their prime. Everyone knew that this was so. It was said daily that the slums were a blot on the civilization of the twentieth century. Some of those very dancers went in for what they called 'slumming', visiting the poor in their homes, organizing clubs for girls, raising money by bazaars and entertainments to send children for country holidays, and in other ways to alleviate suffering. The women of Laura's own class sewed garments for slum children, in turn with those intended to clothe the heathen. But with the exception of a few noble men and women who devoted their lives to the present betterment and the future abolition of such conditions, no one felt any personal responsibility.

Certainly no one that Laura knew, of her own class and condition, felt more than a vague pity for those living in slums. If pressed to state their opinion on the subject they would say that, sad as such things were, they were inevitable. There had always been rich and poor and there always would be. Some would go further and say that when people sank to that state it was due to some fault in their own characters. Rather, it appeared, like the poor old horse in *Childe Roland to the Dark Tower came* – 'He must be wicked to deserve such pain'. Even those few who felt such things more deeply had no idea that they themselves might do or say something to alter them, for the power of public opinion was as yet imperfectly understood and the conscience of the individual as a component of the nation was unawakened.

Of the two extremes of the social scale Laura had little personal knowledge. Rich and fashionable people sometimes came into the post office and she saw that as a general rule they were pleasant to look at, that they had charming manners and moved with an easy negligence and general air of being at home in a world they found thoroughly agreeable. She knew they were not free from their share of human suffering, that anxiety, illness and bereavement touched them as they touched others, and from her own inside knowledge she knew that, at such times and in such circumstances, they were humanly vulnerable. But of their everyday lives and their attitude to life as a whole she knew nothing. Neither had she any personal knowledge of the lives of those belonging to what was then known as the depressed, or submerged, class. She knew the farm workers and their families among whom she had been born and bred; but they were a race apart, a survival of the old English peasantry, still living by the stern old peasant standards of self-help, thrift, and unremitting labour. 'Living,' as they said themselves, 'where some might have starved', and in spite of poverty and hardship making a good job of that living. No one included them when speaking of the depressed classes. No one not directly concerned spoke or thought of them at all, except as an animate part of the country scenery.

Of the fashionable world and the underworld Laura knew little but what she had read. The great middling mass of the people, especially those slightly above the poverty line, she knew intimately as one of themselves. And for them, during the early years of the century, higher wages, though partly countered by higher prices, created an atmosphere of prosperity. It was exhilarating to handle and help circulate money, even if one were very little better off in reality. And there were new ways in which money could be spent – on machine-made, mass-produced furniture, on cheap, ready-made clothes of fashionable cut, and the bewildering array of new grocery products – peaches and pineapples in tins, brought from the ends of the earth to figure on the Sunday tea-table, egg-saving custard powders, tinned fish and tinned meat, sauces and coffee extracts in bottles.

In towns the new threepenny and sixpenny stores provided an inexpensive shopping centre. There, to the strains of gramophone music, the housewife could spend a whole afternoon, circling round and round the different counters with her friends and finishing up with a cup of tea and a cake which cost but a copper or two. Though they admitted that many useful things could be found there, some of the older house-wives said that a good deal of money was wasted; others that the blare of the music, the cheap, showy goods, and the surging of the crowds confused them. They liked a quiet life, they said, and preferred to do their shopping where the shop people knew them and would see they got what they wanted. 'But', would exclaim some friend or neighbour of the new school, 'how can you possibly know what you want before you see what's there?' – and in such remarks lay the clue to the old and the new attitudes to life. People who had formerly desired only such things as they needed were, under the influence of the new system of trading, learning to desire whatever was brought to their notice.

In country places new village halls were built where the villagers could meet for dances and whist drives, choral society practices, sewing parties and cookery lectures. Women were no longer cloistered in their homes. There were scholarships for village schoolchildren, and a little later, Old Age Pensions for the aged. The agricultural labourers' wages went up from ten to fifteen shillings a week.

On Sundays village churches were no longer as well filled as they had been. In some parishes the clergyman reinstated the old ways of worship and was supported by a small but ardent band of worshippers; but these, though enthusiastic, were but a small portion of the inhabitants. In other parishes the clergyman took a leading part in the secular social life of his village, sitting on Parish Councils, organizing clubs and sports and mutual-aid schemes, and good work was done in that way. But very few of the clergy preached to full churches or had much influence over their parish as a whole, for a common faith no longer knit old and young, rich and poor, into one family and the church was no longer the centre of village life. The new centre for the surrounding villages was the nearest town.

The motor-bus had not yet appeared, but there were horse buses, and there was the bicycle. People could reach in half an hour the goal which had previously called for an hour and a half of hard walking, and reach it not already tired out from the exertion of walking after their day's work, but fresh for the fun. The lighted shops, the jostling crowds, the sights, sounds, and smells of a town appeared to have a fascination for those of the younger generation of country people. A little cheap shopping, a street-corner meeting or a band playing were added attractions, but failing these, they appeared quite content to stroll up and down the High Street in twos and threes until it was time to catch the bus or to mount their bicycles and go home. To these the public houses had little appeal. Hard drinking was already out of date and by the middle of the first decade of the new century the sight of a drunken man in the streets was becoming rare. What the country people chiefly enjoyed on their trips to town were the lights and the noise; above all, the sensation of being one of a crowd.

The Heatherley people shared such benefits as came their way. For a year or two after the turn of the century more money came into the village; the villagers dressed better, had more amusements, wider ideas and a better time generally. Some building was done and many looked forward to seeing in their own lifetime their village develop into a kind of garden city.

But Heatherley was not destined to develop into a town, or even to increase in size and prestige as a village. The neighbouring settlement was more at the heart of the district, nearer the hotels and large houses set in the choicest part of the hilly scenery which had always been the chief attraction to visitors, and more than a mile nearer a railway station. It was there the development took place. More houses were built, more shops opened; and when the inhabitants petitioned for a post and telegraph office nearer their homes the petition was granted. The place then became self-sufficient and Heatherley was left on the outer edge of the favoured area from which for a few years it had drawn a temporary importance. Apart from considerations of distance, the few shops there could not compete with the newer and more luxurious ones in the sister settlement. With better and more plentiful accommodation nearer the centre of things, visitors to the Heatherley apartment houses and cottage rooms became few, and those few were not of the well-paying kind. The day after the new telegraph office was opened the number of telegrams sent and received at Heatherley went down 80 per cent. Laura's services were no longer needed; there was not sufficient work to keep her employed, and the postmaster's official remuneration in the new scheme of things barely allowed for Alma's smaller salary. So, as soon as arrangements could be made, Laura left Heatherley, as she then thought, for ever, transferring herself to another post office in a distant part of the county. A few months later she was married.

XI. *Post-war Pilgrimage*

When, twenty years after she had left Heatherley, Laura returned to live in that part of the country, the return was not of her own seeking but due to her husband's appointment as postmaster in the Heatherley district, an appointment which might have been to any other place of the same size in the south of England. But although she had had no choice in the matter, the prospect of visiting her old haunts was a pleasing one, and once there, she took the earliest opportunity of walking over the heaths and through the woods to Heatherley.

She found the village little changed in appearance. The two short streets looked much as they had done, a little dustier and shabbier as to paint, with new names over many of the shop fronts and the windows of what had been other shops, but were now private dwellings, covered with white lace curtains, but substantially the same. Madam Lillywhite's choice emporium had reverted to its old status; rolls of flannel and sheeting filled one of its windows, the other displayed saucepans, enamelled bowls, and built-up pyramids of rolls of toilet paper. No building had been done in the centre of the village. Where the short length of pavement which ran before the post office and shops ended, the broken bank, which Laura remembered as left broken by the builder of the last house in the terrace, still crumbled peatily. The heather, surging up from the heath, broke over the bank and filled the air with the old honey-scent. Where there had been groups of pines between the clusters of buildings there were still groups of pines, and at the foot of the red trunks there were still pine-needle houses, made and stuck about with shards of pottery by children, though not by the same children who had played there when the century was new.

Laura discovered afterwards that on the side of the village nearest the more progressive settlement new roads had been built with houses of a suburban type. The other building sites, which in her time had been staked out in plots in accordance with ambitious plans on paper, had reverted to heath. Sites which had been intended for rows of houses and shops and big corner hotels were blotted out by a vigorous new growth of heather and gorse; bracken had sprung up and buried the curbs of prematurely made roads and only the bees were busy where it had been hoped that money, not honey, would be gathered. Heatherley had not developed according to plan. The march of progress had taken another direction. What new building there was centred around the big hotel on the hill, and while the sister settlement had spread and prospered, Heatherley had been left, still a small village, on the outer edge of the favoured district.

That afternoon Laura walked among the old familiar scenes like a ghost of the past. Very few people were in the streets of the village and of those few none knew or recognized her. The only one of them all she herself recognized was a shopkeeper standing at his door and stifling a yawn. When she had last seen him he had been young, slender, and lively. During the interval he had become stout, bald, and apparently less lively. As he showed no sign of recognizing her she passed on.

Then, as she turned a corner, Laura saw, coming towards her, the reporter of a local newspaper and thought 'Ah, it's Tuesday!' for she remembered that Tuesday had been his day in the past for coming to Heatherley to collect such scraps of news as the place afforded. He was evidently then engaged in the same pursuit for he was walking, notebook in hand, in close converse with the village policeman.

That reporter had been one of the friends of Laura's youth and there had been a time when he would even have risked losing an item of news for the sake of a talk with her. They had once shared a rather gruesome experience. After sitting side by side on the top bar of a sluice at the lakes laughing and talking for an hour one summer evening they had learned the next day that, immediately after they left, the body of a drowned man had been taken from the water. They had shared happier experiences, a primrosing expedition on Good Friday, an August Bank Holiday tramp over the moors, with stewed whortleberries and cream for tea at a wayside inn, and it had been in his company, after a thunderstorm, that Laura, for the only time in her life, had seen rose and mauve mountain-tints on the hills. Since then, as she afterwards learned, he had served four years with the fighting forces in France and had married and had children. But these experiences had had little effect upon his outward appearance. He had still the same sturdy figure, bright inquisitive eyes and head bent a little forward as though perpetually in search of news for his paper. He was scribbling in his notebook and did not look up as Laura passed by, her footsteps muffled by the road-dust.

Laura herself had not changed greatly in looks. A few grey hairs lurking among the brown, a neck less white and plump, and a new faint vertical line between the eyebrows, discernible by herself but as yet unnoticed by others, were nature's first gentle warning of approaching middle-age; but meanwhile she shared with other women of her age at that time the extension, if not of youth, of apparent youngishness, due to the recent revolution in fashions. The long heavy skirts, the elaborately coiled hair, the fussy trimmings and loaded hats of pre-war days had disappeared and a simpler style had emerged. In a neat, scantily cut costume with the skirt reaching but a little below the knee and a small, plain hat worn over bobbed hair, many a woman of forty looked younger than she had done at thirty. This style of dress had, as they said, 'caught on' and was popular with women of all ages; but the ease, comfort, and freedom of movement it gave could only be fully appreciated by those of an age to remember walking in the rain with a long skirt grabbed up in one hand lest the hem should get muddied and the other hand supporting an open umbrella to protect the built-up edifice of wired ribbon and artificial flowers then known as a hat.

Seeing a remembered name over a shop which also displayed a notice of 'Teas' to be had within, Laura entered. The woman who attended to her needs was one of the old Heatherley shopkeepers. She did not recognize Laura, which was not to be wondered at, as to her she must have been but one of many who had come there and gone without leaving behind any special cause for remembrance. When reminded by Laura that she had been a customer of hers of old, she said she had some faint recollection of sending her lunch to the post office. Did she not once complain of too much soda in some rock cakes? The former critic of rock cakes did her best to wipe out the memory of past indiscretion by praising the cake she was then eating, and finding Mrs Apsley willing to let bygones be bygones, inquired about a few of the people she had known in the village. Some were married, some dead, others had gone away to live in other places. Alma had married about the same time as Laura and was living away from Heatherley. Except Mrs Parkhurst, whom she had already seen, no one seemed to be left there in whom she had felt any particular interest.

'And of course,' said Mrs Apsley, 'you heard of that awful affair at the post office?' Laura had heard, or rather had read in the newspaper, that a few months after she left Heatherley Mr Hertford had made a maniacal attack upon and killed his wife one morning as she was stooping over the bath in which was her newest baby. 'Murder, committed under an uncontrollable impulse' had been the verdict of a humane jury, and the sentence had been detention during His Majesty's pleasure. Laura had pictured the village as it must have been that morning. The screaming and rushing to and fro; the village constable suddenly called upon to face what was almost certainly, to him, an unprecedented situation; women running into their houses and locking their doors when they heard a madman was at large; other women forming a crowd outside the post office to watch the helpful few, called forth by any emergency, go in and out through the doorway; then the arrival of the closed carriage which was in use there, to take brides to their weddings and mourners to funerals, and the dazed culprit ushered into it, arm in arm with doctor and policeman, while all the time, but a few yards away, the sun shone on the heather, pine-tops swayed in the breeze, birds sang and bees gathered honey, as on any ordinary summer morning.

For some time Laura pictured that scene with horror during sleepless nights and days, haunted by misgivings as to whether there was anything she ought to have done, or anyone she should have told of the Hertfords' affairs, while she was living with them. Then, gradually, her horror and concern lessened, the sharpness and poignancy of the imagined scene softened and grew dim, and as the years flew by, bringing with them new responsibilities, new griefs and new experiences, the sorrow and tragedy of the Hertfords became to her but one of the sadder pages of memory.

By the time she revisited Heatherley 'the awful affair at the post office' had, even to the inhabitants of the place, become an old story, and Mrs Apsley did not dwell upon it. The conversation turned to Heatherley's palmy days, when trade was good in the shops, boarding-houses were full, and famous men were to be seen walking its two streets. The celebrities who had lived there in Laura's time had died or gone away. Mrs

Apsley said she thought two or three well-known people still lived on or near the hill, but you did not seem to hear as much about them as you would have done formerly; the war, she supposed, had altered ideas. Visitors still came to the hotels, though more of them to lunch or tea than for a longer stay, now that the motor-car had brought the place within easy reach of London. Since the war a new class of visitor had appeared, brought in crowds by the new motor-coaches for a day on the hill, and these, Mrs Apsley thought, had driven away what she called the better class of visitor. But she was quite tolerant of these new day visitors. When Laura said mildly that she supposed they enjoyed their outings, she said that she liked to see them enjoying themselves; they also brought a little money to the shops, and their money was as good as anybody else's; though she did wish they would not strew the place with orange-peel and paper bags. To show that she bore Laura no ill will for her long-ago criticism of her rock cakes, she not only brought a dish of water for her little dog, but also gave him a stale bun to eat, saying, 'You must bring your mistress to see me again one of these days.'

On her homeward way Laura came to the place on the heath where she had first seen heather in bloom. The hour was later than that in which she had first gazed on that scene and in place of rich golden sunshine a low, slanting light struck redly between the pine-trunks and cast long, searchlight rays on the heath; but, as then, the pale mauve of the heather misted hillock and dell and the bracken was turning from green to golden. The only apparent change was that a mountain ash which she had known as a slender sapling had grown stouter and taller and was hung with bright scarlet berries.

The little by-road appeared to be even less used than formerly. Before the day of the motor-bus it had been a short cut to the main road and the town and railway station, but now, when everyone had that useful vehicle to command, pedestrians were seldom seen on any of the country roads and such by-roads as this were especially deserted. A notice affixed to the signpost at the turning declared it 'Unsuitable for Motor Traffic', and it appeared to have been given over to rabbits and wagtails.

For a long time Laura stood in undisturbed contemplation. A grasshopper shrilled in a tuft at her feet and was answered by other shrillings among the gorse bushes; a solitary rook flapped heavily overhead, and a pair of goldfinches twittered among the thistledown; there was no other sound except the scarcely perceptible never-ceasing sighing of the wind in the pines and its rustling of acres of heath-bells.

When Laura had first looked upon that scene she had been young, with life, full of possibilities, stretching away before her; then, her heart had bounded and her nerves had thrilled with joy at the sight; she beheld it again as one whose youth had long ago fled and been followed by the better years of mature life, and the sight brought to her comfort and healing rather than joy. The intervening years had been crammed with the busy responsibilities, joys and anxieties, hopes and set-backs, inseparable from running a home and bringing up a family. Often, for months together, she had not been out of doors alone at a distance from home, as she was that evening. Now, standing apart, though but a short space apart in time or distance from her loved home ties, she was able, once again, to think of herself as an individual.

During the early years of her marriage, with her children small, her house to be kept as she liked it, and a very small income to be stretched to the utmost, she had had neither time nor inclination to think of herself apart; but of late, with her children growing up and less dependent upon her constant care, the old feeling had revived that in return for the precious opportunity known as life some further effort other than those involved in mere living was required of her. She had not entirely neglected to cultivate her one small gift of self-expression; short stories and articles of hers had been appearing occasionally for the past ten years in newspapers and women's weeklies. The remuneration for these had been a welcome addition to the family exchequer, but otherwise they amounted to little. It was not of writing small sugared love tales she had dreamed in her youth, and she had sometimes told herself with a somewhat wry smile, though not without enjoyment of the humour of the situation, that the pen she had taken for a sword had turned in her hands into a darning-needle.

She had heard or had read that every individual human life tends to move in cycles, that once and again we return to some previous starting point and are given a new opportunity. If that were so, she had that day completed one such cycle on the exact spot where her adult life had begun. What was to follow? A slackening and slowing down over the old course, or a new path, striking outward?